LINE RIDER

Reviews

"I felt like I was sitting along side of Joseph Pearce listening to his wonderful tales around a campfire in the late 1890s. A wonderful book narrated by a very interesting man. For you western history buffs, don't miss it." — C. Burke

"A pithy recollection of a law man in the Arizona territory. Without embellishments. It is a frank chronicle of his life as he looks back on it." — C. Perry

"A first person story of one man's attempt to rid the Arizona territory of outlaws and rustlers." — Chris Carver

"A great book written in the author's voice. The stories are exciting. If you like books about the old west, you'll like this book." — Rose B.

"Wonderful glimpse into the life and times of Joe Pearce. Simply spoken and a compelling tale." — Dale E. Enlow

Legal

LINE RIDER is copyrighted (2015) by LOST BOYS INK. It may not be reproduced in any way without express permission.

Contact

If you find an error in the text, notify the copyeditor at typos@jwashburn.com (and make sure to mention this book's title) — you'll go down in history as the hero of the second edition.

Contact the editor directly at me@jwashburn.com.

And check out jwashburn.com.

20 Oct 2015

LINE RIDER

by

Joe Pearce

LOST BOYS INK

Text copyright © 2013 by Lost Boys Ink.
All rights reserved.

LIST OF CHAPTERS

Map. vii

Editor's Note. ix

Milestones in the life of Joe Pearce xi

    I. Indian Country. 1

   II. House Guests 9

  III. The Hash Knife Outfit 21

  IV. Goodbye, Apaches. 29

   V. Flour-Brand Underwear 33

  VI. Calf Mooning 40

 VII. Forest Man 47

VIII. Judge and Jury. 54

  IX. Gun Acquaintance with Blackjack 59

   X. Climax Jim and the Britches 67

  XI. Arizona Ranger Training. 73

 XII. Into Mexico after Bad Yaquis 83

XIII. Tough Town—Clifton 90

XIV. Clifton Floods Bring Trouble 96

 XV. Trailing Horse Rustlers. 103

XVI. Breed of the Outlaw 114

XVII. Sleepered Calves 122

XVIII. Sheep on the Move 130

- XIX. Squaw Kidnapping 134
- XX. Cold Trailing a Kidnapper 142
- XXI. Skirts and Stampedes 147
- XXII. Wild Horses 152
- XXIII. Apache Quirks and Whimsies................158
- XXIV. Drink and the Devil 167
- XXV. Courtship, Marriage, Etc....................172
- XXVI. Cows...................................178
- XXVII. Trailing into Indian Country 183
- XXVIII. Throw Down............................190
- XXIX. I Make a Hand 198
- XXX. A Baby Intervenes 208

APPENDICES

- A Biographical Sketch of Joe Pearce 215
- My Lucky Number 13........................217
- Recap of White Mountain 221
- A Biographical Sketch of Minnie Lund.........228
- Minnie: Building the House 230
- Minnie: A Funny Story......................234
- Patriarchal Blessing........................235
- Last Will and Testament.....................237
- Last Words 240
- The Genuine Article 242

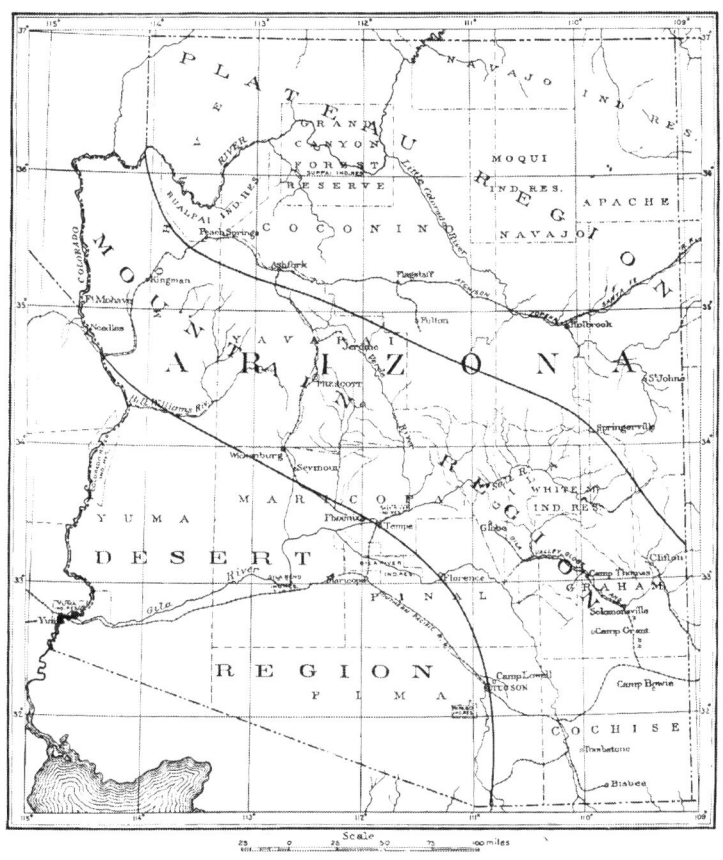

U.S. Geological Survey map of Arizona from about 1900, showing counties, railroads, principle towns, and Indian reservations.

EDITOR'S NOTE

Line Rider is the true story of the life of Joseph Harrison Pearce (1873-1958), written by his own hand.

During his lifetime, the "wild west" from the storybooks still lived and breathed in one of the last places to be modernized—Arizona.

Joe, as he calls himself, took various roles throughout his adventurous life, including sheep herder, cowman, courter, tracker, line rider, and, most famously, that venerated breed of law man know as the Arizona Ranger. His story leads him to encounters with cattle rustlers, gamblers, saloons, stampedes, horse thieves, Indian trackers, outlaws, and nearly every other subject that later made its way into western legend.

But this story is absolutely real, told in his own voice in vivid detail.

* * *

This is what you might call a reader's edition.

It has been polished and typeset with the aim of making it both easy to read and accessible to everyone.

For the most part, this edition is word-for-word the same as the one Grandpa Joe created. Still, it was clear he was in the middle of the revision process—that he was mid-stride to perfecting his book. In that spirit, a few minor editing liberties have been taken—mostly adding or removing commas. Rest assured, though, that his grammar has been left alone (e.g., "the horses *was*" was let to stand, as were the adjectives where adverbs should be, and the missing articles remain missing). As such, his dialect remains genuine.

Where Joe had written two different versions of the same paragraph, a little more creativity was required. When merging, care was taken to preserve as many details as possible (rather than trimming down, which is an editor's usual job).

It should also be noted that the photocopied version of the manuscript sometimes didn't transfer the ink from his edits. Other times his handwriting was illegible. In short, it is clear he wanted changes made, but it isn't clear what those changes were. In those cases, his first draft was given final-draft authority.

Another thing missing from this edition is the character a typewriter puts onto the page (along with, as mentioned, Grandpa Joe's own penmanship). If you're hankering after his original, unfinished draft, it can be found here: http://bit.ly/joepearce.

This edition was created by and for Joe Pearce's descendants. The lion's share of the transcription was done by Holly Ong and Dixie Grissom. Many thanks are owed to the two of them. Parley Pearce and Sonya Washburn donated the archived photos. Additional transcription, a final edit, and publication were done by J Washburn.

MILESTONES IN THE LIFE OF JOE PEARCE

1877-1888 Migrated with family from St. George Utah. A boy in the Pleasant Valley. Sheep and cattle warfare.

1899-1903 First forest ranger in Arizona and later head ranger in the Black Mesa Forest.

1903-1905 Arizona Ranger under Captain Rynning.

1905-1907 Line Rider and Special Policeman for Apache Indian Whiteriver Reservation.

1907-1913 Special County Ranger for Apache County, Arizona.

1913-1914 Livestock Detective for the State Livestock Sanitary Board.

CHAPTER I.

INDIAN COUNTRY

FATHER BROUGHT US DOWN FROM St. George, Utah, into the Indian country of northern Arizona Territory when I was about six years old, in 1877. Naturally I don't remember much of that trip except a few vivid flashes: Mother sitting there on the seat board in the rear wagon, holding the reins tight and wide, following Father's wagon into the bright-painted canyon country, and nursing the baby at the same time, with her knees humped up to hold it. Us kids crouched in the back of the wagon among a clutter of junk, bumping into the rusty iron stove with the jog of the wagon, the chickens in their crate making a racket. A bunch of Navajo Indians riding up to talk to Father and him giving them tobacco, us not knowing whether they were going to fight or be peaceful, and Mother holding a shotgun to be ready for them while Father talked.

That was the time of the Mormon migrations, when President Erastus Snow of the Mormon Church was pushing Mormon colonies into Arizona along the Little Colorado River. In those days the Indians were still hog-wild: the Utes, Piutes, Navajos, and mostly the Apaches still looked on the white as their enemies and prey for their thieving ways.

Sunset, Joe City, Brigham City, and Obed were the little Mormon villages, the first Mormon settlements in Arizona, getting along somehow under the United Order, a communistic system to make a go of their farms and cattle in the treeless grassy flats along the Little Colorado. They are all gone now. But it was in them that the Mormons got a foothold, and from them they spread out to settle in many other parts of Arizona. Each was a little walled town with a few families; they fought the Indians and the wilderness, but they were licked by the ugly temper of the Little Colorado that washed out their earth dams year after year during flood time.

Like one of the Elders prayed at the dedication of a dam: "O Lord, we pray that this dam may stand if it be thy will—if not, let Thy will be done." And the Lord's will was done over and over again.

Our destination was Brigham City, where the family stayed for awhile, but Father was too independent to take much to the communistic system. When the dam washed out, he got disgusted. He had an idea that southward, further up the Little Colorado which flows north, the floods might not be so bad. His Mormon friends advised him against the move. He was going straight into the Apache country, and, even including Piutes and Navajos, the Apaches were the worst Indians ever existed. They'd practically depopulated the whole Territory for the decade following the Civil War. But Father scoffed at his friends. He wasn't afraid of the red-bellies and knew how to handle them, he said.

James H. McClintock, in his history of Mormonism in Arizona, has this to say of my father: "The first settler of Taylor was James Pearce, a noted character in southwestern annals, son of the founder of Pearce's Ferry across the Colorado at the mouth of Grand Wash, at the lower end of the Grand Canyon. James Pearce was a pioneer missionary with Jacob Hamblin among the Paiutes of the Nevada Muddy region and the Hopi and Navajo of northeastern Arizona. He came January 23, 1878—in March joined by John H. Standiford."

Father followed down the Little Colorado, going upstream, until he reached what looked to him a likely place: cottonwood trees along the shallow stream, flat space that could be irrigated from the river for farming, in the distance low cedar ridges. Here he settled, built himself a house, and others came. The town of Taylor that he founded is still in existence, with a dozen Mormon families, and my Mother still living there on the old place, a very old woman now. Sunset, Obed, Joe City—the rest have all turned to dust.

South of our ranch at Taylor were the black, low humped elevations of the White Mountains and the Blue, heavy timber on the upper slopes, a great forest nobody knew much about then. North stretched the grassy rolling country that sloped off the mountains toward the painted-desert sheep country of the Navajo reservations, with its vertical, multi-colored buttes and its blue sky, the bluest in the world. Northwestward was the Hopi Reservation.

Father brought cotswool ewes from Utah down to Taylor to begin his sheep ranching. For summertime the grasses in the timbers was the best, and so, southwestward twenty miles from Taylor and near where Heber now is, Father built a second ranch house of logs, and a corral, as summer headquarters, and here in the high country among the pines we grazed the sheep. In winter we drove them back to the grazing ranges near Taylor—all open range, of course.

Though we were on the edge of Apache country, and though the ranch near Heber was on the road from Pleasant Valley and Tonto Basin (where the West's bloodiest sheep and cattle war was soon to be fought) to St. Johns (the county seat), Father settled himself down in this dangerous country with his two ranches and his sheep and a few cattle and horses, and tried to live at peace with his neighbors and his God.

This was the country I was to grow up in—with first Apaches and wild-eyed, heavy-bearded cattlemen and sheepmen as neighbors, and later on rustlers and outlaws: a raw, range-wild kid in a raw country, with toughs for my friends and toughs for my enemies and never sure which a man was. As the oldest kids in a family of nine, my brother Jim and me came in for our share of heavy work, a smattering of all kinds. Times we worked at Taylor helping with the farm, plowing, cultivating, milking, planting fruit trees and ash to make the place pretty, irrigating from the stored water behind the dam.

Other times we were at Heber, living in the little log house or following the slow grazing sheep, living in lonesome sheep camps on the Mogollon Rim, with our hearts bouncing around in our throats because of our fear of Indians. And when I mention a sheep camp, it was usually just a frayed old tent with sheepskins for bedding and chuck inside and a fire in front. At bigger sheep camps, there was sometimes a wagon too, and horses grazing nearby.

Jim and I learned to ride and rope and handle horses and cattle and sheep. And it wasn't long before we got acquainted with the friendly end of a six-gun. At fourteen I would have been rated top hand in most anybody's cow outfit.

I didn't know it then, but I was really serving an apprenticeship to be an outlaw or a law man, and in the West of my time, there often wasn't much more than a hairline difference between the two.

* * *

Before the railroads came to the territory (the Southern Pacific in the south and the Atlantic and Pacific in the north) the Apaches were perpetual trouble makers. I got well acquainted with them later in a friendly way when I was special policeman on the reservation and they were a little more civilized. Out in my boyhood they were in their wild state.

True, the government had assigned reservations to all the Indian tribes and endeavored to keep them there with forts and soldiers, but the Apaches, who had always been roamers, wouldn't stay put. In small bands they ranged up and down the entire eastern part of the Territory, little-known mountain and desert, far down and deep into Mexico as Chihuahua. Stealing and thieving was just a part of their natures, not from one another, but from their enemies. A solitary ranchman alone at his ranch, a sheep herder with his sheep, a miner off the beaten trails—these were often raided and sometimes killed and sometimes tortured before the killing, even as late as the eighties. Then the Indians would sneak back to the reservation and were hard to catch.

Before our first brush with them, there was an Apache murder in our part of the country. I was about twelve years old at the time, Jim fourteen. Often we were alone with the sheep, or sometimes there was a Mex herder with us, as Father had several, and always a dog. In times past, often we had seen the Apache bucks in bunches of two and three and four. They sometimes came to the ranch house and begged for things; they were the biggest beggars in the world and looked harmless, but we knew they weren't harmless. Once in awhile we missed a horse or a sheep. If they got what they wanted, they were peaceful enough, but if they were crossed some way, there was blood in their eyes.

The killing happened this way. Nathan Robinson came on a band of Apaches, fifteen or twenty, soon after a raid about six miles from Taylor. They had slaughtered a beef, quartered it, and were in the act of roasting one of the hind quarters over a campfire—little brown men squatting around the campfire on their hams and silent as Robinson rode up, making no hostile move, just squatting and looking at him with their expressionless black eyes like the Apaches will.

Robinson knew what was in the wind, that the beef and some of the horses they rode had been stolen. He was a brave man, but he did a damn fool thing: Without a word, he got down off his horse, turned over the wet hide, and looked at the brand.

The Indians stared at him and said nothing. They did not molest him as he cussed them and upped into his saddle, got on his horse, and rode away.

Contrary to what is usually thought of the Apaches, they will never shoot a man in the back except perhaps to save their own skins. And many a man has been lucky enough to save his life because his back was to the Indians. The Apaches say that only a coward will shoot a man in the back, and they are not cowards. It is only that their idea of bravery and ours is different.

When Robinson was about thirty or forty yards away, one of them hollered at him. The rancher wheeled his horse around to face them, and that was his mistake. The fifteen of them peppered at him with their rifles, and he pitched off his saddle face down. They did not scalp him. Instead they dragged him about two hundred yards down to Showlow Creek, shoved his body into a deep pool of water, and weighted it down with rocks. Then they took his horse and saddle and rifle and rode away, hoping to get onto the reservation before they were discovered.

When he was missed, a posse was organized in Taylor; Father rode with the posse. And in Showlow Creek they found the body and figured out pretty well what had happened, and then they took up the trail of the bucks to the edge of the reservation, where they had to turn back.

Years later Loco Jim, my valued scout on the reservation, told me these details (more about Loco Jim later; he was a mighty important Indian in my life). Of course we did not know them then. We boys knew only that Nathan Robinson's body had been found in Showlow Creek, murdered and left that way by Apaches.

Jim and I couldn't talk about much else besides this murder. It ate into our minds and worried us, for it was summer and we were alone with the sheep south of Heber. It might be our turn next. What was to keep the Apaches from killing us? Father never seemed to be afraid of the Indians, and we tried to imitate him, but we couldn't. We passed many sleepless nights, not wanting to tell one another how worried we were but lying awake and listening for the Indians to come.

Only a week after the murder of Robinson, they came. "Looky there, Joe. You see?"—Jim said it calm, as if like he'd expected them all along, which he had.

We were in timber country, but open country too, with pines fringed along thick down the slopes of the ridges. But the center of the grassy valley was almost free of tall trees. I looked where Jim pointed. They were a mile or more away, little specks against the green-grayness of the long valley. We saw them over the dirty gray backs of the moving sheep. We knew right away that they were Indians because they rode single file, while if they'd been white men they'd have ridden abreast.

"What'll we do?" I asked. I looked up to Jim, as any kid brother does.

Jim's laugh sounded funny because it wasn't really a laugh. And I didn't need to ask the question. As the Indians came closer, we saw that there were at least a dozen of them. Jim turned and took to his heels and I chased after him, panting, and overtook him and ran beyond him because I was the better runner. We didn't know where we were running; we just wanted to get away.

Our dog chased after us barking. I guess he thought that we were playing with him.

"The dog!" Jim shouted. "We got to get rid of him. He'll give us away."

We filled our hands with the red stones that are scattered everywhere in that country and rocked the dog back toward camp. He went whining and whimpering with his tail between his legs as Jim and I both clipped him with our pitches. We turned and ran again up the slope. Two hundred yards away the pines grew tall and close together.

It's next to impossible to climb the thick, straight trunk of a pine tree with no side branches for twenty feet above the ground, but we were lucky. We spotted ahead of us a tree that had been blasted by lightning and was lying over against another tree. This dead tree made an easy slope for us to scramble up and reach the lower branches of the standing tree. We shinned up several branches, and here each of us picked a limb and crawled out on it. Hidden in the green needles, we watched what went on below.

By and by the Apaches rode up to the fire and looked around. They circled the sheep a couple of times hunting for the herders, and satisfied that no one was near at hand, they got down from the bare backs of their ponies, and the dozen of them ate the breakfast we had been cooking. They squatted on the ground or slouched around for half an hour, in no hurry.

When they were ready to go, one of them shot a sheep with his rifle and threw it on the back of his pony; the others ransacked our camp, taking all the sheep skins we used for sleeping, a bag sack of flour, a slab of bacon. Then they rode away.

We didn't come down from that tree until we were mighty sure they were gone. Then we shinned down in a panic of fright, yet afraid even more to leave the sheep unprotected. With the help of dogs and rocks and shouts, we got the sheep into motion. Half a mile away we pushed them into a sheep corral, shut the gate and tied it with rawhide.

Now we started at a run for the home ranch five miles away. We would run for awhile, and then when we couldn't run anymore, we would walk until we got our breath and run again. That way we made good time through the timbered country. That lopsided little shack with its thatched roof looked like a palace to us. Here we picked up our rifles. But we didn't dare stay here with as large a band of Apaches as the one we had seen on the move, and the murder a week ago stinging fresh in our minds. Old man Rice's ranch was about three miles from ours, a little trading post and ranch combined, and there we decided to go for protection. Rice lived there with his Mexican wife and several Mexican vaqueros.

Again we started out on the run, feeling a little better because we carried our rifles, but still scared of the Indians. We didn't see a sign of them on the way, but every tree and bush might have hid an Indian—the shape our nerves were in.

Rice was glad to see us and made us feel at home and told us we'd done right in running away. That made us kids feel better, for what Father would say about our leaving the sheep bothered us a little. He put us up in his house and his Mexican woman fed us, and we slept easy that night. Rice told us he was grateful for the warning. "Never no telling what them devils is up to," he said. "Two to one they'll be here tomorrow beggin' a hand-out."

He was right. Next morning while we ate breakfast those same Indians—minus several, for there was only eight now—rode up to the trading post. Rice signalled to us boys and to his two Mex cowboys to stay where we were. He walked alone into his store, which was just a room built onto his house. Indians have a way of coming into a store that's different from any other people. Even today on the Hopi and Apache and Navajo reservations, it's the same. They wander in slow, like they're bashful, only they aren't; and they stand awhile, just stand without looking at anything. Gradually they begin to look around, letting their eyes go here and there, but not moving their bodies. Finally they begin to walk around, studying and fingering everything, but not saying a word.

Just like that now. Rice was in there alone with them, while in the kitchen with the door open we waited with our rifles cocked. After a long time the Apaches asked for breakfast. Their talk and Rice's was a mixture of Apache lingo and Spanish. Most Indians in those days couldn't talk any English, and only learned it when they younger ones was made to go to government schools.

"No," Rice told them. They couldn't have any breakfast.

Then they wanted some tobacco and coffee, and we heard Rice shoving the scoop into the bin to give them coffee, and making scraping noises as he got down a box of tobacco. But he didn't give them enough to satisfy them. They started to help themselves to whatever they wanted.

"Let it alone," Rice said.

The way the Apaches acted was threatening. They didn't stop their thieving. Rice stepped to the side door and motioned to us. "Come on, boys," he says.

The four of us—Jim and I and the two Mexicans—marched into the store with our rifles thrown down on the scattered bucks. We took them by surprise. They hadn't expected us; they'd thought Rice was alone in the store. But their faces didn't show any surprise. They kept looking at us, their black eyes staring, their stinking bodies grown motionless in whatever they were doing.

Rice stumped over to the door and flipped it open. "Yugushey—get out!" he told them. They took his word and knew that he meant it, and yugusheya, riding off at a gallop on the bare backs of their ponies, headed toward the reservation.

CHAPTER II.

HOUSE GUESTS

WE MIGHT HAVE HAD MORE trouble with the Indians if Father hadn't known from long experience how to handle them. He just seemed to savvy their natures and to be able to get along with them. Five times before our migration from St. George, he had come into Arizona Territory either as a Mormon missionary or as a scout for the government soldiers. Not that Father, even though a missionary, was a good Mormon in the strictest sense. He smoked habitually and sometimes drank when the notion struck him. I can still hear my Mother saying to him, "You know it's against the orders of the Church. You know you're a-killin' yourself to do it."

Both Father and Mother were children of the Mormon migration to Utah. Father did big things in his time. He was called on by the Church in the sixties to locate a road from Salt Lake City to San Bernardino, California, so that Mormon farm stuff could be marketed in California. And he did it. Afterwards he ran a freight outfit from San Bernardino to St. George and Salt Lake City—two six-mule teams and heavy wagons. Over this road he hauled many of the doors and windows that went into the new Mormon temple.

The Ute and Paiute Indians were pretty ugly in the seventies, but Father mixed with them and learned to speak Ute and became a Mormon interpreter to the tribes. And he did his part in missionary work. One of his favorite stories, I recollect, was his conversion of three hundred Paiute Indians to Mormonism. He led them from their village to St. George, and there they were baptized into the Church by some of the elders and given shirts and clothing and food and sent home. They liked those shirts mighty well. When Father revisited them some years later, they told him that the Lord hadn't given them any more shirts, and couldn't they go back to St. George and see the Lord again? When Father came to that part, he always tipped back his black Mormon hat, and his beard wagged with his laughter.

The Apaches made one important visit to the ranch at Heber in the timber country. Father was there, busy making breakfast, with his back to the door. Jim and I and one Mex herder were with him. I was about fourteen years old at the time, tall and gawky and too skinny, but feeling mighty growed up now that I was allowed to pack a six-gun of my own.

Father was mixing biscuit dough. The bacon sizzled as the fire roared under it, and the coffee churned hard in the big, chipped pot that was streaked by fire blackening. The Arizona Indians are the original peekers. They'd come up to a ranch house, and you'd not hear a sound of them. And unless you were looking square at them, you wouldn't see them with their noses flattened against the glass, if there happened to be glass, or lifting a crack into the sheepskin flap over the window so they could see what was inside.

First we knew of these Indians, they were coming through the door. They'd probably already looked inside and smelled the cooking. Jim saw them first and opened his mouth and clucked and got out a noise that made Father turn. The doorway seemed filled with armed bucks—even though there was only six of them—colored bands, mostly red, tied around their heads to hold their greasy black hair in place, loud calico shirts from the Government, but no trousers, only G-strings. They weren't painted.

Father glanced at them and without any change of expression went back to his cooking. But I noticed that with almost the same motion of shaking the bacon in the frying pan he reached up to the wall where his belt and forty-five hung, and lifted the gun out of its holster and poked it in his hip pocket. His coolness steadied Jim and me, though we were plenty scared. We had no guns on us.

The six Indians walked right into the house without being asked and without saying a word. That was their way. Several of them took seats on the boxes we used for chairs, and one of them sat on the floor. Father put the big coffee pot onto the table and slid some tin cups toward them. They filled the cups and drank our coffee, helped themselves to the bacon already in a tin plate on the table.

Meanwhile Father dropped his biscuit dough into hunks in a pan and shoved it into the oven, then went on to mix up another batch of dough. Out of the corner of his mouth he spoke to us in English, which the Apaches weren't likely to understand. "Get your guns," he said. "But do it easy like and keep the guns out of sight."

The Mex herders sat frozen. But we boys, trying to act indifferent the way Father did, slouched across the room to the head of the bed where we had hung our gun belts. We got hold of our guns and poked them inside our shirts. Father put the fresh cooked biscuits on the table and shoved another batch into the stove. The Indians ate the hot biscuits and still didn't do any talking.

"Keep your eyes open, boys," said Father. "This is a bad bunch. Be ready for anything."

When the Apaches finished breakfast, they smoked. Father had taken down his tobacco from a shelf—and in those days the tobacco came in medium-sized wooden boxes, the Bull Durham type. The Indians rolled cigarettes, lighted them with brands from the fire. Father rolled himself a cigarette and smoked with them. They all smoked slow and deliberate for awhile, and Father remained standing.

When they were all through, one of the Indians who seemed to be the leader stood up and spoke in Spanish, "You are good to Apaches."

"I don't want trouble with Apaches," Father said. "I am a Mormon—you see that. The same people that are on the Colorado River. A Mormon."

The Chief nodded. He was stocky built and very dark. "I know Mormon."

"We don't want trouble. We want peace."

Again the chief nodded. "The Mormon do not make trouble for my people. Not put cattle on Indian land. Not want to kill us. I am friend for you."

"Same here," said Father. Solemnly he shook hands with the chief. Then they smoked awhile longer.

"You know me?" said the Indian.

Father didn't know him.

"I am Geronimo."

Out of their talk, Jim and I caught that dreadful name—the most feared, the cruelest, the best known of all Apache chiefs. The man that had desolated the southern part of the Territory and had led government troops into unsuccessful chase after chase and was finally captured by Lieutenant Charles E. Gatewood deep in Mexico. When this man Geronimo was at last deported with his Chiricahua tribe to Florida some years later, the Apache troubles of the territory were ended. Here he stood talking to Father. I may have seen him before or since, but this is the only time I am positive of.

Father didn't turn an eyelash at the name. He said, "You are not Geronimo. He is a bad man. You talk like a good man to me. You are not a bad man."

"I am a good man," said Geronimo. "We are friends."

Once more they shook hands. After they had smoked awhile longer, the Indians got ready to leave. Father gave them a fresh box of tobacco and a bag of coffee and a little flour and the Apaches went off as quietly as they had come.

This visit of Geronimo and the friendship he made with my Father is probably the reason we were pretty much left alone by the Apaches, while other sheep and cattle men suffered.

The Apache Kid was a bad Indian of a different type from Geronimo, but in his way he is just as famous a character. Where Geronimo was a good leader, the Apache Kid worked alone, or sometimes with a few companions. He made many lone raids, committed many murders, got himself a name that was feared everywhere in the Territory. But where Geronimo was a hero to the Apache people, Apache Kid's name was mud. Government troops and Apache police both were after him.

The Apaches hated him because he kidnapped young Indian girls and took them along with him in his wanderings to keep him company. The fate of these many girls that Apache Kid used during his life was especially horrible because the Kid was syphilitic, and his taint was death. When he tired of a girl, he abandoned her and kidnapped another. Loco Jim told me in later years that the Kid had kidnapped at least fifteen Indian girls. The Kid knew just enough of white ways and had enough native Indian cunning so that he could have taught modern kidnappers a good deal about the business.

Soon after the visit of Geronimo, I was in a sheep camp with Jim and a Mex herder named Pedro. That afternoon Pedro killed and quartered a mutton, so we had plenty of meat, and the extra we hung high in a pine tree, not only to keep it away from wild animals and in the cool shade, but also to get it above the swarms of flies that always managed to find an open camp. Flies scarcely ever go above twenty feet from the ground, so thirty feet is safe to keep meat at.

While it was almost smudge dark, only a finger of twilight left, Pedro broiled the leg of mutton. Jim and I rolled on the ground, tired. Suddenly an Apache was sitting just at the edge of the firelight, and mounted on a low, shaggy pony. It gave me a start, the way it always did, when Apaches popped up out of thin air.

The Indian spoke some English. "I'm hungry," he said.

Jim kept his wits about him, saw that the Indian was armed. "Get down," Jim said. That was the invitation of the cow and sheep camps of our country to whatever hospitality there was.

The Indian turned and signaled behind him, and another horse came up, mounted by a young Indian girl. She looked young enough to be the buck's daughter, but bucks didn't go riding with their daughters and leave their squaws at home.

To me that girl looked mighty pretty. I spent so much of my life on the range I hardly ever saw a girl of any kind, and maybe that was the reason. But this girl was just particular pretty for the Indian. Her face was round, and she had very white teeth and sad eyes, which she kept mostly covered with her eyelids.

The buck said something to her in Apache, and she followed him a ways into the darkness, each of them leading their horses. After they'd got the horses hobbled, he sent her off to gather wood and tote water, while he returned to camp and began to eat our mutton.

After awhile, when she'd done the chores, she came and sat a little off from me and outside the circle around the fire. I was closest to her and far enough from the others, who were talking, that I could ask her some questions.

"Where you from?" I asked soft.

"Don't know," she said.

"He your father?" I nodded toward where the Apache buck was talking.

"Don't know," she answered again, and I judged that she couldn't understand any English. I tried her in Spanish, and it was the same. She said "No se, no se," to everything I asked. I was too young and too curious to be all satisfied, but I let it go for the time being.

That night after chuck, the four of us played high-five casino, and the girl sat off a ways and didn't open her mouth. There sat this smooth-face Indian, jabbering with us in English about stock and the range, but not really saying anything about himself and at that moment in the Revised Statutes of Arizona was a reward notice for his capture dead or alive of ten thousand dollars.

But if Jim or I or the sheep herder had known it was the Apache Kid, we wouldn't have had a try for that reward. We likely would have run the other direction. We certainly wouldn't have been sitting there calm as you please playing high-five casino with him.

Even not knowing who he was, we didn't sleep any too peaceful that night after he and his girl had walked off somewhere into the darkness to sleep hidden. Nothing happened, though, and he was up with us in the morning, helping with camp chores and cheerful as ever, but seeing to it that the girl stayed close to him.

They were ready to ride off, both mounted, and the Kid leaning down and talking to Pedro in Spanish, the girl holding her horse near me, and suddenly she leaned down. I could see terror in her eyes as she nudged her shoulder and whispered, "Him Apache Kid!" Maybe she hoped I'd try to shoot him then and there, or follow them and make him give her up. I don't know. I felt mighty sorry for her, but I for one was right glad to see them go and had no intention of following them.

The end of Apache Kid is still a mystery. History says he was killed by miners in southern Arizona soon after his visit to our sheep camp. I don't believe it because the story the two miners told is pretty vague and because the one I am going to tell is better substantiated. Around 1903, about the time I enlisted in the Arizona Rangers, at a place called Valley of the Caves in Sonora, the Apaches were raiding the cornfields of the Mormon settlement. Two Mormon farmers, Morton Harris and Johnny Allen, laid out for them one night, caught them at it, and opened fire. The body of one of the Indians killed was identified by several different Mexicans—who had known the Kid in life—as that of Apache Kid. An inglorious end to one of the West's worst bad men… killed stealing corn!

* * *

I think it's a good idea to tell about my first meeting with Loco Jim here, not because his name ranks with others, but because he was the finest Apache I ever knew, an excellent scout, soldier, trailer—called Loco Jim because he was so crazy brave in a fight. Loco Jim in later years taught me much of what I know about cold trailing, and was a loyal friend to me all his life long.

It seems he ran into trouble on a charge of stealing beef from a cattleman at Showlow. Joe Kay, storekeeper at Taylor, got the drop on Loco Jim and started with him as prisoner for St. Johns, the county seat, thirty-five miles away, Joe Kay keeping his shotgun ready to hand. After they had driven some of the way, Kay relaxed and got careless. He decided it was time for lunch and climbed down to hobble the team. Loco Jim saw his chance, dropped down on the other side of the wagon, picked up a rock weighing four or five pounds, and flung it at the storekeeper before Kay had a chance to throw down his shotgun. The rock caught Kay in the chest and knocked him to the ground, and Loco Jim took off at a dog trot over the flat grassy country.

Of course we didn't know anything about this until afterward. We were camped at Pearce Springs at Clerro Gordo, and Father was with us. Loco Jim trotted into our camp about Sundown, what little clothing he wore was in rags, legs bruised, feet bleeding and swollen, lips black. He panted that he wanted water and some supper.

Father, as I have shown, never turned down an Indian's request for food; we gave him water and then slabs of mutton and stale bread and he ate like it was his last meal. Afterwards we gave him a few sheep skins to sleep on and an old wagon cover to throw over him. The apache looked mighty grateful, almost like a starving dog that had been given a handout, but he was too tired to say much and dropped off to sleep.

Father shook his head worriedly, staring down at the Indian. "Looks like trouble somewheres," Father said. "A 'Pache don't look like that unless there's trouble. Don't know what to do with him. We could easy get the drop on him."

By and by Father answered himself, "We don't know nothing. Leave him be."

Next morning we gave the Indian breakfast. He gulped down the food and started off immediately at a dog-trot headed for the reservation. Not till years later did I hear the rest of the story. He made straight for his two wives, and they were full of joy to see him, for they had thought he was already rotting in the white man's jail.

For two years Loco Jim was a fugitive—both the Government and the Apache policemen after him and never caught him. He managed it this way. With the help of his two wives, when night came on, he went to Carrizo Gorge, a precipitous and desolate canyon with almost sheer walls, practically unknown to white men, yet Loco Jim knew it like a book, for he had been brought up in that part of the reservation.

For two miles the Apache and his women walked along the rocky edge of the canyon to hide their trail, until they came to a spot above a cave that only Loco Jim knew of. Here he tied several ropes together, putting knots into the stretch of rope. Fastening the end to a tree. Down he went, swaying over a thousand foot drop to the bed of the canyon. Hand over hand he lowered himself until he reached the cave. When he was safe, his wives used the rope to lower supplies to him: an olla of water, a sack of food, enough blankets to keep him warm.

There he stayed alone and patiently waited until the worst of the trouble blew over, while his wives continued to bring him food that the Government had rationed out to them. Though several times the women were followed by the Apache police, they always managed, one or the other, to give the police the slip, and not to reveal Jim's hiding place. Later on, when it was safe, Loco Jim hid out in the hills, while his wives continued to feed him with Government food.

After two long years of this kind of living, long after the Government thought him dead, Loco Jim tired of the game and decided to take his medicine. One morning early he strolled into the office of the Indian Agent at Whiteriver. Instead of the old Agent, a young lieutenant was there, seeking Apache good will and anxious to make friends with the Indians.

Loco Jim said to this young Agent, "I been a good man last two years. I want to be a good man now and make no more trouble. I am Loco Jim."

The Agent extended his hand. He knew all about Loco Jim. "We know your early record, how you were loyal at the Battle of Cibecue and what a good scout you've been. You go back to your Hogan and have a good sleep and forget that you ever had any trouble."

A little later on Loco Jim was appointed a scout and served under Lieutenant Gatewood in the capture of Geronimo in Mexico. After that campaign he was made a policeman and scout on the reservation, which post he occupied when next I saw him again.

EDITOR'S NOTES

Geronimo:

Geronimo was the son of a chief, and his Apache name was Goyaałé. He married a beautiful young woman when he was seventeen, and they soon had three children.

The war that had raged between Apaches and Mexicans for over a century was silenced by a time of peace. So one day he traveled south with a group of men to trade goods in a Mexican town. On his return, he was met by the few survivors of their camp, who said a Mexican army had murdered many women and children and stolen their food, ponies, and weapons. Goyaałé's wife and young children were among the dead.

The Apaches retreated, but Goyaałé soon returned, leading a band to take their bloody revenge. At one point in the ensuing battle, Goyaałé was seen facing a blaze of bullets with only a knife, and still striking fear into the hearts of his enemies. Though it's debated by historians, some believe the name Geronimo came from that battle as the terrified Mexicans cried out for St. Jeronimo to protect them from the relentless Indian.

Later Geronimo became chief, and he continued to lead many deadly raids on Mexican and eventually American towns. After living a life of infamy, he surrendered to U.S. authorities at the age of 63. As prisoner of war, he became a celebrity, admitting he sometimes regretted his choice to submit. He died at the age of 79 at Fort Sill, Oklahoma, far from his homeland.

The Apache Kid:

His Indian name was Haskay-bay-nay-ntayl. He was captured by Yuma Indians as a boy but was eventually freed by Al Sieber and a group of Army Scouts. The Apache Kid, with his father, then enlisted with the U.S. Cavalry as scouts, and he was quickly promoted to sergeant.

Once when Sieber was away, the Kid and a group of scouts were drinking, which led to an altercation in which his father was killed. The Kid's friends murdered the culprit, and the Kid killed the culprit's brother.

When Sieber returned, the Kid and his comrades submitted to arrest. But an unknown person in the onlooking crowd fired shots at the men, one of which hit Sieber in the ankle. In the confusion that followed, the Apache Kid and several others fled. The 4th Cavalry hunted them down, and they peacefully submitted to arrest once again.

The Kid and four others were convicted of mutiny and desertion and sentenced to death by firing squad. Thanks to their sympathetic superiors, their sentences were first reduced to life in prison and then to ten years. The five comrades spent months in Alcatraz till their convictions were overturned about a year later.

And yet they spent their freedom causing enough trouble among the Apaches that new warrants were issued for their arrests. They were captured a third time and sentenced to seven years, but they soon escaped Yuma Territorial Prison, killing a guard and badly wounding another (though the injured man said the Apache Kid had prevented the others from killing him after he was wounded). They fled the prison into an unusually fearsome snowstorm and were not pursued, which opened their futures to a life outside the law.

The Apache Kid's death was reported several times in different places, with enough uncertainty each time that his exploits became legendary. His legacy now includes the Apache Kid Wilderness in New Mexico, which bears his name.

CHAPTER III.

THE HASH KNIFE OUTFIT

The coming of the railroad to the northern part of the Territory was a big day for my world. Before it came, there was hard years for the Mormon villages on the Little Colorado, especially the years 1880 to 1882. There had been drouth, the dams washed out, crop failure. It looked like the Mormons would either starve or abandon Arizona entirely to the Indians. But the railroad saved the towns. It had to be built, and there were hundreds of Mormon farmers eager for work and food. After the crop failure of 1879, John W. Young (a son of Brigham Young) and Jesse N. Smith (a stake president) traded five miles of grading in the construction of the railroad for bread. Supplies were brought to the half-starved villages from as far away as Albuquerque, New Mexico, to keep them going.

The year following, Young secured a contract for one hundred and fifty miles of grading and fifty thousand ties. Men in the Mormon settlements went to work on the railroad, just as they had in the sixties helped to build the Union Pacific and the California Central. Some of them brought their wagons and hauled ties. Some brought only a pick and shovel. But most of them brought at least a team that could be hitched to a grader. My father did his share with the rest, not that the families in Taylor, the town he had founded, were as hard hit as the others, but a little loose change in the pocket always sounds good. While Father was away, Mother did the spring plowing.

By 1882 the railroad had been completed to about the point where the town of Holbrook now is. I recollect well that day of celebration—as well as anything in my boyhood—even though I was only nine or ten at the time. Then there was nothing of Holbrook except an eating house for the railroad workers and a small Indian trading post run by a man named Barado.

People gathered from a hundred miles around to see the first train in—folk from all the villages and ranches, gentile and Mormon, all there in holiday attire. And there was a scattering of quiet Navajo Indians in bright-colored headbands walking softly, cat-like among the crowd. Saddle ponies and cowponies and mustangs, and wagon horses hitched to buckboards and heavy mules hitched to covered wagons. Here I saw my first stage coach, Sol Barth's big Concord for running his mail contracts from Fort Wingate, New Mexico, to Fort Whipple (later Prescott), Arizona.

Banners were plastered on the eating house reading ARIZONA WELCOMES YOU. There must have been several hundred people at Barado Station whooping and hollering as the train puffed. My young eyes bulged when I saw the kind of critters that got down from that train—women in fat dresses with bustles and made of silk and rustling when they walked. Any time they came within a mile of me their perfume made my head roll. The men wore full suits of clothes: coat and vest and trousers. Duds like that were never worn in my country, and Boston bowler hats and moustaches without beards. I was afraid of those people and steered shy of them.

I heard one of them say, "Is this the end of the world?" and laugh. It was plain he thought my people a curiosity. But he was just as curious to me.

* * *

The Hash Knife outfit came in with the railroad and brought to hundreds of miles of country trouble and bloodshed and a sheep and cattle feud that was climaxed by the Pleasant Valley War but went on for years afterward.

Up to 1886, the Indian country had been settled by small ranchers, mostly sheep men, but some small cow outfits as well. These would take out homestead rights on a piece of land with water and fit for farming, and then range their sheep or cattle on government land, which was unfenced. Before the coming of the railroad, there wasn't any trouble between sheep and cattle men because there was altogether more land for everybody than they could possibly use. In the summer, sheep and cattle ranged in the timber lands, and during the winter went north toward Taylor and Showlow in lower country, or south of the Mogollon Rim along the Verdi River toward the desert mesas. For much of the land, the title was in dispute, but that didn't matter until after the railroad.

The Aztec Land and Cattle Company, which we called the Hash Knife Outfit, was an offshoot of the Atlantic and Pacific. The Government gave the railroad alternate sections of land, like it did for the other big railroads, and the Atlantic and Pacific wanted to get something from the lands, so leased them out to a Texas company. Many thousands of head of cattle were shipped in to graze the empty ranges south from the great Navajo reservation as far as the Tonto Basin. With the cattle came cowboys from Texas, forty of them first and gradually many others. Cowboys and cattle were spread out over the railroad land as far west as Flagstaff. This was fine rangeland with plenty of water, mountain streams, natural lakes, open springs; much of it was mountainous in forests or pine and cypress and blue spruce and white aspens, while much of it was flat country with tall grasses.

The Aztec Land and Cattle Company itself did not take part in the Pleasant Valley War and all the squabbles between sheep and cattle men, but its cowboys did. They were Texans. I remember seeing a batch of them getting off the train with their six-guns stuffed conspicuously in their belts; they came just aching for trouble. Some of them, of course, were good cowboys, good citizens, top hands, for Texas produces the best cowboys in the world. And these never wore a gun on the range and made good friends. One of them taught me how to throw down a six-gun.

But the majority of them were not of this breed. The Texas Rangers had been busy, and the big state was being cleaned up. What more natural than that the toughs and gunmen and outlaws and rustlers should hire themselves to a big outfit in another territory, where their names and reputations would not be known.

I asked one of the boys once, "What you boys wearing your six-shooters for? Why did you all leave Texas for?" Like any kid would, I tried to imitate their Texas lingo and Texas drawl.

This boy twinkled: "Reckon it was because folks back in Texas wanted us to build a church, an' we wouldn't build it."

Trouble started from scratch and lasted fifteen years.

Sheep and cattle don't range together very well because the sheep crop the grass too close, though many ranchers like my Father managed to be both sheep and cattle men. But that can only be true of small outfits. With the great herds of Texas cattle roaming the ranges and boundaries unmarked, there was bound to be trouble aplenty.

Even more than this cause of friction, it seems just plain natural for a Texas cowboy to hate sight and smell and sound of sheep as much as he hates rattlesnakes, and for him to look upon anyone that herds sheep lower than a sidewinder's belly.

The Tewksbury-Graham feud of 1887 was only the climax of the trouble. The Tewksburys represented the sheep men and the Grahams stood for the cattlemen. Texas cowboys for the Hash Knife Outfit flocked around the Grahams. The Tewksburys had friends and relatives all over the country. Cowboys and herders of each faction shot it out whenever they met; and some innocent people were killed. You couldn't go into Pleasant Valley and be neutral. You had to be one or the other. Altogether it's been figured that twenty-eight people lost their lives in the Pleasant Valley War of the Tonto Basin. Some put it as high as fifty, for there were a good many killings not known about; the bodies just vanished. The three Graham brothers were killed to the last man, which was the idea Zane Gray used for his book *To The Last Man;* and only one of the Tewksburys survived.

But like most wars, this feud didn't settle anything. Friction went on between Hash Knife cowboys and sheep men until range boundaries were either clearly marked or fenced and the cause of the war vanished.

While it was going on, the Tonto Basin and the Mogollon rim and even Heber wasn't a very healthy place—Heber in the high timber and on the edge of the trouble. Some folk moved out of the region entirely. But Father and a good many others stuck their ground.

Before the war we knew the Grahams and the Tewksburys some. The

Grahams, who were the cattlemen, once visited our home in Taylor on their way to St. Johns to testify at a trial for horse stealing. They stopped overnight and awed Jim and me with their paraphernalia. The Grahams boys then were in their late teens or early twenties, and each lugged a .45 strapped to his hip and packed a .45-.60 Winchester in a saddle holster. Their belts carried one full round of pistol and rifle cartridges. Each wore stogie boots and clanked heavy spurs.

I was even more impressed by the Tewksburys that sometimes stopped by our ranch at Heber looking for horses. We studied those younger Tewksburys that were later to die. They had Indian blood in them it was said: their skins were smooth, their eyes black and glittery, and their noses hooked. They were slow moving, slow talking; they took soft panther steps.

Their outfits popped our eyes out: *chaparajos* chaps made of cowhide with the hair out, shoes, not boots, with long work socks pulled up high and their pants tucked into the socks. Their hats carried leather chin straps that fitted almost to the point of the chin, the hat sitting straight on their heads and not tipped back.

Jim and I hung around them listening to their talk of range and sheep and the brewing of trouble in the basin. We were bashful and half afraid of them, but we couldn't take our eyes off them. They paid no attention to us kids. After palavering awhile, they described to Father the brands of the lost horses and then rode off.

I got Jim aside. "I want to be like that when I get growed," I told Jim.

"Me too," said Jim. "Did you see them rawhide cow ropes and rawhide hobbles? That's something."

If we could have seen then the kind of death some of the Tewksburys were to die, their flesh eaten by javelinas (wild hogs) after they'd been shot and before the flesh was yet cold, and their families not able to come out and bury them because of the fusillade of lead the besieging Grahams faction kept up around their house, we wouldn't have been so anxious.

* * *

Because Father ran both sheep and cattle, we managed to stay about as neutral in the war as anyone could, but that wasn't entirely out of it. I got into a peck of trouble with some of the Hash Knife cowboys. Charley Wagner and John Payne and Red Holcomb were just as tough gents as any who racked out of Texas looking for a new spread.

I had run the sheep to the Pinedale dipping vat for their creosote bath. Around here was unsurveyed land at the time, so we felt we had as much right there as the Hash Knife outfit did, and I was directing the dipping with two Mex herders under me. This happened after the killing off of most of the Grahams and Tewksburys in 1887.

We had run sheep in this section of timber country long before the Aztec Land and Cattle Company come in, and there was priority on my side if nothing else. But the three Hash Knife boys—Wagner, Payne, and Holcomb—didn't see it that way. They came riding towards where we were holding the sheep, quirting their horses, opening fire on the sheep to drive them off, cussing me and the sheep and God himself. They swarmed in amongst the sheep trying to ride them down and shooting at the ground to get them moving.

I didn't just stand there watching them. When I saw what they were up to, I stepped behind a pine tree. I was a little older now and better able to take care of myself. And I was well armed with weapons I'd learned how to put to good use—a .45 and a new octagon barrel .44 Winchester, a fine rifle but scarce.

The three cowboys hadn't seen me because I was standing off from the sheep to supervise the dipping. They'd spotted only the Mex herders. Now I stepped from behind the tree and pulled down on them full-cock that octagon Winchester. "Lay off!" I shouted.

They spun their horses around, and I stayed where I was just long enough for them to see I had the drop on them. Then I returned to the full protection of that pine tree. They could see I had all the best of it, with them in the open and me behind the tree and ready to let rip. I kept my gun on them while we talked.

"You've gone about far enough!" I shouted. "You leave them sheep alone. Vayete."

"Like hell we will," Red Holcomb bellowed back. "This is our range an' we damn well mean to keep you sheep herders off."

"Get out," I answered back.

Red Holcomb said to the others, "I reckon the kid means it by God. We better be a movin'."

The others studied awhile. They looked at the sheep and then at the steady octagon barrel. "Guess so," said Charley Wagner. And the three of them rode off.

But they kept laying for me. They had the notion that young Pearce ought to get his, and they aimed to see that he did. And it wasn't more than a couple of weeks before young Pearce did get his. That second time I might really have been trespassing on the Hash Knife lands. As I've explained, it was hard to tell with nothing to mark boundaries. Just to give them the benefit of the doubt, I'll say that I likely was trespassing.

I was alone doing the herding, and had the sheep west of Taylor at Four Mile watering place giving them a drink. My guns were in camp, and I was afoot and unarmed. There was only two of them this time, for Red Holcomb was elsewhere. They spotted me out in the clear and saw that I was alone and unarmed, and with a whoop and a holler they rode down on me.

I saw them coming and started on a run back toward my camp, which was more than a mile away, but of course it was impossible to reach camp racing against cow ponies, even though I was a good runner. They galloped their horses on each side of me and took licks across my back with a double rope, and licks over my head, and a few hefty swipes on my rump. The whipping they gave me cut and stung. One of the swipes circled around my neck and caught my lip and swelled it and started it to bleeding.

They whaled me until I stumbled and fell, and then they sat easy and laughing while I pulled myself to my feet.

"That ought to learn you," said Johnny Payne.

I was mad clean through, and hurting where they'd lamed me. "That's all right, you damn sonsofbitches!" I hollered at them. "Some day I'm coming back to this country, and then I'm going to cool you boys off plenty, and don't forget it. I'm going to clean out the whole damned Hash Knife outfit!"

They gave me the horse laugh and rode away, yet the time was to come when I'd return as I said and do some cleaning up. But how was

I to know that I'd come back to my country wearing the star of an Arizona Ranger?

And my chance for cooling off those particular cowboys just never happened. John Payne was one killed a short time afterwards in the sheep-cattle trouble. And to Red Holcomb the Pleasant Valley Vigilance Committee served notice that if he ever came back into the timber country of the rim they'd hang him to the nearest pine that was handy.

Red Holcomb's reply is famous in the region. "You jus' tell 'em from me that if they ever hang me from a pine tree they got to move the pine tree down to the flats of Holbrook to do it."

EDITOR'S NOTE

Aztec Land & Cattle Company:

The Aztec Land & Cattle Company operated in northern Arizona Territory between 1884 and 1902. The company was often called the Hash Knife Outfit because its brand resembled the shape of a hashknife (a tool you'd find at the chuck wagon; the handle fit in the fist, while a metal shaft protruded between the fingers and attached to a wide, curved blade). At its peak, the Aztec Company was the third-largest cattle company in the United States, with a range spanning over 2-million acres, from the border of New Mexico west to an area south of Flagstaff.

CHAPTER IV.

GOODBYE, APACHES

News spreads as news will in a sparsely inhabited country, with sometimes many ranch houses a dozen or two miles apart, that the Chiricahua Apaches were to be shipped on the railroad from Holbrook to Florida. How such news gets around I don't know. At any rate we heard about it at Taylor, and the line of march was through Taylor!

Another change brought about by the coming of the Atlantic and Pacific! The government had finally lost patience with the Apaches. Grawager had placed them on reservations—Chiricahua, Fort Apache, Whiteriver—and had fed them and cared for them. Yet the massacre of whites continued. Bands of murderers would leave the reservation whenever they got into the mood and go on thieving forages over the desert.

Not all the Apaches, mind you, for there are many tribes and branches of them. But certain smaller units, and especially the Chiricahuas under Geronimo. The government had finally pacified the Navajos and the Utes, but some of the Apaches were still the bad boys among the Indians.

So, when the government cavalry (under Lieutenant Gatewood) at last ran down Geronimo and his followers in Mexico, it was decided to end Apache troubles for all time by deporting the rambunctious ones to Florida. All known recalcitrants and many that were only vaguely suspected—their wives and children and the widows of bucks that had been fighting the whites—were included. And the railroad was at hand to take them away. When you get right down to it, the railroad was responsible directly or indirectly for all the changes going on in my country.

Jim and I were young enough to be wild about the coming of the Indians through Taylor. We looked forward to it the same way kids look forward to a circus, and as we hoed down weeds in the fields, we kept looking south along the road every five minutes or so to see if the troops were coming. It became a game which one of us would spot them first.

I was the first to see them, a small clot of dust that grew larger until we could make out the van of the cavalry in their dust-covered blue uniforms and broad hats. We ran down the road to meet them. Mother had told us there was nothing to be afraid of now that the Indians were all captured and in the charge of the soldiers.

In the long column, the cavalry was in the lead, hats set jaunty, sabers clanking. Their uniforms and their horses and their fine equipment dazzled Jim and me. Next came a string of pack mules and wagons loaded with chuck and bedding, wagons loaded down with Indian mothers and children, wagons drawn by two and four mule teams and urged on by cussing muleskinners, wagons lumbering and jolting and raising clouds of dust.

The women were dressing in their full skirts with yards of cloth to them, and short blouses, just the way they dress today, and their straight black hair messy. Some of them held their faces in their hands. I noticed some just sitting, some nursing babies, the children sitting quiet too. The Indian women and children squatting there in the wagons stared at us with black eyes, and Jim and me stared back at them.

The bucks didn't ride in the wagons. Some of them rode scrawny ponies; some of them went afoot. The wagons were for the women and children. There was no soldier guard surrounding the wagons. All the soldiers rode in front, for in that flat open country there was no danger of any of the Indians escaping. I noticed there were far fewer grown men than women, and judged that the others had been killed off in fighting and many of the women were widows.

A few of the Indians Jim and I recognized. They had visited us at the ranch house near Heber and had been friendly. They didn't look like bad Indians to us. We tried to spot Geronimo himself, but couldn't find him. We were told later that he was not with his tribe, but was being sent on later. However, Lieutenant Gatewood was there, and so were the famous scouts Tom Horn and Al Sieber that we had heard a good deal about.

Wood and water were plentiful along the river near our ranch, and there the cavalcade stopped for the night, a hundred soldiers perhaps and three or four hundred Indians. They threw some of their stock into our pasture and some of it into the pastures of our neighbors, and the wagons were unloaded, tents scattered everywhere over the ground in no time at all. Fires began to crackle here and there among the tents of the soldiers and among the Apache tents that were a little distance removed.

Jim and I stayed as long as we dared, circulating about the tents, staring at the soldiers and then wandering over to stare at the Indians. When it was nearly dark, we raced home for supper and gulped it down.

I said between mouthfuls, "When I get growed, I want to be a soldier."

Father stared at me very seriously. "Now how'd you come to take that notion, boy?"

I was put out by the way he spoke and just shrugged my shoulders. "Look at them," I said.

"Put it out of your head right now," my Father told me. "A soldier lives lazy. When a man don't want to work, he joins the army." All the time my Father said this, Mother nodded agreement. The way Father said it impressed me so that I never forgot it. And it was true. Those at least were my observations at Fort Apache when I was on intimate poker terms with the garrison. Men that will not work enlist in the army.

Such a weeping and a wailing as went up that night from the Apache camp! It was the women. I hope I never hear that kind of racket again. I didn't know what it was all about, but it bothered me. After supper Jim and I sneaked over and watched them, and the women were all gathered in little groups of five or six and crying together, and of course the children were crying too, the way children will, not knowing what it's all about but crying because their mothers are crying. The women ran their fingers through their long black hair and around their ears and under their chins and howled.

Only later I understood how real their grief was. They were leaving their home and the home that had been their ancestors for many generations, shipped off to a country they didn't know anything about where some of them were to die and the rest to be so unhappy that the Government relented a little and shipped them back as far as Oklahoma.

We didn't stay long in the Apache camp. Instead we returned to the army camp where a group of soldiers had gathered around Al Sieber and Tom Horn, who talked about their brushes with the Indians, spun yarn after yarn of fighting and killing. Jim and I squirmed through the crowd until we were close enough to hear and see everything going on, and our heads were full of those stories for a long time to come.

Around the quieting camp a dozen sentries paced. Every hour we'd hear them sing out, "Nine o'clock and all's well."

What took my fancy most was the way Tom Horn and Al Sieber could throw a rope and tie a diamond hitch in less than a minute. The following morning Jim and I were there ten minutes after the bugle had blown, and an army cook fed us some chuck, and we hung around to watch the camp break up. Tents came down, the wagons loaded quickly with the equipment, the Indians herded to their places.

Down a row of forty mules went Al Sieber and Tom Horn, one on one side and one on the other, and the ropes seemed to come to life in their hands and jump about amazingly as they lashed the packs tight, forty mules in forty minutes. I've never seen anything like it.

Big Tom Horn noticed us standing there gawking and asked, "You wish you could throw a rope like that, kids?"

"I sure do, Tom," I said.

We watched them go northward and vanish into a cloud of dust along the straight road; then we walked slow back to the house, not feeling like work after all the excitement.

Later I said to Father, "Guess I've changed my mind. I'd ruther be a scout than a soldier."

Father studied me awhile. "Now that's something worth aiming for," he told me.

And the desire to be a scout and throw a diamond hitch like Tom Horn and Al Sieber never left me.

CHAPTER V.

FLOUR-BRAND UNDERWEAR

When the cowboys of the old Hash Knife outfit used to ride through the small Mormon villages, they'd say, "Well, I see where the girls have their underwear wash hung out on the lines. What brand of flour are you goin' to dance with tonight, Joe?"

It was true. Conditions of the old frontier were not the same as today. Every scrap of box or packing case, every piece of burlap, every flour sack found some use. Nothing was thrown away.

There was the ladies' underwear flapping in the breeze, with the name PRIDE OF DENVER in big red letters on it. And at the next ranch there would be PRIDE OF COLORADO on the seat. And sometimes there was PRIDE OF DENVER, and a large patch right over it and running in opposite direction, PRIDE OF COLORADO, where the PRIDE OF DENVER had worn out. Mixed brands, that.

Later on there came in such fancy brands on the underwear as BUTTERFLY and SEA FOAM FANCY FLOUR. But less than twenty years ago when a bunch of five of us were riding down through Sulpher Springs Valley and across to the Mormon town of St. David, we noticed that some of the underwear was still branded DIAMOND M, an old standby of pioneer ranchers and nesters.

I tell this mostly to show the kind of life that folks led on the frontier of the Arizona Territory. There weren't any luxuries of any kind the way there is today. Many's the time I've eaten barley bread when the corn and wheat ran out. I can remember Mother grinding up the barley in the coffee grinder and cooking the bread in the big iron stove that we'd brought down from St. George. Soda was suppose to make it rise, but it stayed unleavened and soggy usually, and before we ate it we had to pick out the beards of the barley or they stuck in our throats.

There weren't any doctors available, and a Mormon mother wouldn't think of having a doctor anyhow to help her with having a baby. That's true even today in the Mormon towns, where the Mormon midwives still do the trick and do it well. Sometimes Father couldn't bring a midwife in time, and then he himself helped women make the delivery of the baby.

And there weren't any doctors when we kids were sick, mostly with colds that didn't amount to much. I hated Mother's mustard plasters that use to burn me and her onion poultices that use to stink rotten, but I guess they did what they were intended for. When we had a fever she dipped a sheet in cold water, wrung it out, and wrapped us naked in it. She gave us sienna tea and rhubarb tea for laxatives, and she dosed us up with quinine for almost everything, and when there wasn't anything the matter with us, she gave us quinine any way.

Most of the things she did for us probably wouldn't be approved of by modern medical practice, but she had nine children and all nine of them lived to grow up, and proof of the pudding is in the eating. (Mother was a nurse and midwife. Bringing more than a hundred children in the world and never lost a single case.) That first winter at Taylor must have been a rip-snorter, with the house not finished and with freezing weather, and the baby not yet weaned. But we all lived.

* * *

Our lives weren't all made up of excitement and trouble and bloodshed, Indian scares, and ructions with the Hash Knife punchers. There were plenty of long peaceful times, with monotonous drudgery of farm work and lonely days in the sheep camps, seeing no one for a week at a stretch.

There was schooling too. I never was much for school and hated it. Yet I know now that the little schooling I had was a great help to me in living out my life. I was never the temperament for school, always nervous and itchy to be out on the open range instead of penned up with other kids. I could never satisfy myself to get down to solid work.

But my Father believed in school, all that his boys could get, which wasn't much in my younger days. Father sent me on horseback, me and Jim, to a pay school conducted by a cultured woman three months every year. I went to this school for three years and got some of the rudiments of learning pounded into my skull. That school, though, didn't much prepare me for attendance at the Arizona Normal School (now the

Tempe State Teacher's College). I was given a special scholarship to go because there was no one from Apache County in attendance at the time, and Jessie N. Smith, member of the Territorial Legislature from Navajo County, selected me.

The college was very new then (in 1896)—just about the same level of scholarship as any good high school now, with about the same subjects taught. For a year I was in college right from the saddle and off the open range. It was a funny thing that of all my subjects I disliked military drill the most, and was out of step in more ways than one and always the awkwardest in the awkward squad and hating soldiers and their fussy drill.

The school paper took some notice of me when I came down from a corner of the Territory little known. It said, "We have all the various tribes of Indians of Arizona represented in this school except for the Apaches. And now since Joe Pearce has blowed in, we have that savage tribe well represented."

My year up at Tempe, Father sent me for awhile to Brigham Young University at Provo, Utah, which had in those days four or five hundred students. About as soon as I arrived I contracted measles, diphtheria, and flu. That was the end of my schooling.

* * *

Before the days of movies, radios, and cars, the Saturday night get togethers and dances were the chief amusement. Word got around through the scattered villages and settlements that there would be a dance at so and such a place, and then preparations began and lasted intermittently through the week. People came long distances to be there, driving in their buggies and rigs, two and four seaters, or if they had no buggies, they came in their heavy wagons. Some rode horseback—the cowboys, of course, came horseback.

Usually the dance was held in the district school house, with a violin and sometimes a foot pedal organ to furnish the music. But these dances were not like what a modern young one would think of as a dance; they were more of a social meeting for everybody, those that danced and those that just watched. Everybody was there, mothers and fathers and children of all ages, even babies asleep in their mother's arms. Those that didn't dance lined rough wooden benches along the walls, and kids scampered about playing on the edge of the dancing. Only the old square dances were allowed because the Mormons did not approve of young folks putting their arms around one another.

Gentiles were welcome to come, and many gentile ranching families took advantage of the opportunity. Those were orderly parties in spite of some of the roughest characters in Arizona being present. No drinking or petting or spooning, no shagging or jitterbugging, not even smoking allowed inside the building. If you wanted to smoke, you had to step out of doors and stay there till you were through.

For each dance a floor manager was appointed to keep order, and lynx-eyed mothers aided him aplenty. You would have to be pretty clever to swing your partner by the belt instead of by the hands as some of us more daring fellows often tried to do and sometimes got away with. But there was always the risk that the mother of the miss would spot you and report you, and then you would be ruled off the floor by the floor manager. I have been ruled off the floor more than once, and have not always been able to wheedle the floor manager into letting me back on again before the end of the evening.

The buildings were of adobe or logs and very rough inside and out; the floor was of rough pine boards that got warped or were laid uneven so that sometimes you caught your toe on an edge of them. The music wasn't the best in the world. And yet everyone seemed to have a good time and no complaints.

"Lively there. All men left. Swing your partners. Women left. Swing your partners." So the dances were called. The music squeaked, the fiddler all sweaty red as he pumped up and down on his bow, the organist pedaling like mad, and the two not always in time. But the dancers thumped and stamped and swung about, their clean rosy faces from much unusual washing that day silvered with sweat.

Between the dances the sexes separated. The girls, in their flannel skirts and alpaca shirt waists, their hair twisted up in tea pot style upon the tops of their heads, stood in little bunches at the end of the hall talking of the things that girls talk about—what Maude or Sis or

Patricia is wearing, and, "Doesn't Ellen look pretty tonight?"—mighty jealous and not meaning a word of the compliment.

The boys were strung out at the other end and pretended to do a lot of talk, but mostly they looked slantwise at the girls, picking out the pretty ones and hoping to get them for partners.

Cowboys no matter what creed were welcome at the dance if they came sober. And there was a fluttering amongst the girls when a cowboy came in natty outfitted with high boots polished and smelling of grease, and trousers stuffed into them. It was generally true that the cowboys left their guns outside hid under a bush or rock, and then they'd mark the rock somehow to remember where they'd put the gun. Or they might stuff their guns in their shirts to keep them out of sight.

At the small town dances, cowboys were generally sober because Holbrook was the nearest place where they could buy whiskey, and it was a long ride to Holbrook from most of the settlements—seventy, eighty, ninety miles.

Sometimes, though, the boys would go on a tear and shoot up the most peaceful dances. Not out of meanness but out of plain high spirits when they were drunk. If pay day happened to coincide with the dance, then that was bad, for somehow the cowboys would get hold of the stuff; and then there might be trouble.

In a lifetime of handling bad men, I've noticed that a young fellow will do things when liquor is in his belly that he wouldn't think of doing if he was cold sober. Ninety percent of the Western shootings wouldn't have happened if the fighters hadn't been hog wild drunk. And the first rustling that a young fellow does is usually with enough tarantula juice in his belly to make him feel just twice as big and important as he is.

I'm not preaching, and haven't led a sinless life by any means, and wasn't regarded as straight enough to be chosen as a Mormon missionary like my father was. I've had my drinks—perhaps too many of them in my younger day—and even now I'm not averse sometimes to sneaking a small one against my conscience. I couldn't have entirely avoided drinking in my youth, mixing like I did with the harder elements of humankind. The hardest drinkers in the world, when they can get it, are cowboys and Mexicans. And setting up a drink for them has often meant the difference between friendship or not. One drink might make a cowboy brand ten of my calves on the range with the proper brand for friendships sake, or give me a tip on a man hunt that would keep me going, or help in a deal on two year olds for market when I was a cattle buyer.

But just the same a man sober can shoot steadier and straighter and is not so ructious. Drinks often led to trouble, like the time one of the Slaughter boys started to shoot up Crazy Murry's hall at a dance in Springerville. Nothing really bad about the Slaughter boys, working for their dad's outfit on Black River. They were just lively boys, and this was Christmas time, and they'd been drinking heavy when they came in. They wore their hair long and packed guns and liked to think of themselves as bad men when they really weren't. *[EDITOR'S NOTE: Ructious is a rare word from a fading dialect. It changes the noun* ruction *into an adjective. If a person is ructious, he causes ruction, i.e., disturbances, quarrels, contentions, or general unpleasantness.]*

The oldest boy was full to the tonsils with spirits when he told old Kirt, the fiddler, to play "The Old Gray Mare." Kirt had a way of obliging. If he saw that a fellow was getting a kick out of a tune, he knew how to bear down on it.

The way Kirt played it, the Slaughter boy got to feeling so good he kicked his legs around and clacked off a few steps and bellowed, "Whoopie-wow-yow." Next thing he'd grabbed out his six-gun and went to shooting up the ceiling. Crazy Murry got up and sauntered over, not packing a six-shooter, took young Slaughter by the collar, flopped him onto the floor, twisted the gun from his hand.

Then Crazy Murry shoved the gun against the kid's head and cocked back the hammer and squeezed the trigger. That should have been the end for young Slaughter, and would have been except for his long hair. Some of it caught in the gun cushioned the blow of the firing pin. Before Crazy Murry could yank the trigger again, the crowd pulled him off.

Sometimes the cowboys came in large bunches to the Mormon dances, usually Hash Knife punchers, and then the dance committee got worried, knowing there might be a rumpus, for when they came in a crowd they were usually liquored up and anxious to dance with the pretty Mormon girls. The committee had several ways of handling them. Sometimes they were all barred if their condition seemed to warrant; or the committee might rule that they could take turns, a few dancing at a time.

The rest would stand on the sidelines in their range clothes and stumping on high-heeled boots with long shanked spurs, breeches in their boots and still wearing their hats, and make loud comments about the dancers, or call out to the girls to tease them, "Hey, pretty, how about dancin' with me?" The girl addressed would flick her head and pretend not to notice them, but often enough she blushed and was pleased at their attentions.

There was still another way of handling fights that the Mormons had and I've never seen it tried elsewhere, at least not at a dance. If trouble got started and looked bad, the floor manager would give a signal. Then everybody would go get their hats and wraps and file out silently, leaving the hall empty except for the troublemakers. The dance was over. And there wasn't any fight without an audience.

Once, I remember, a big bunch of the cowboys got mad that they were barred from a dance, and they poured out of the hall, peppering away with their six-guns to make a racket. They mounted and rode out of town shooting and whooping in real western style. Everybody at the dance dived under the benches at the first shooting, and one fat woman got stuck and had to be pulled out later. The cowboys stopped on the edge of town beyond the jurisdiction of the J. P. and sent word back by one of the punchers that if an officer came to arrest them they would tell him to go to hell, but if the folks really wanted them arrested, they should send some of the pretty girls to get them and they'd come.

No officer and no pretty girls went after them.

CHAPTER VI.

CALF MOONING

In those days I had girls aplenty like any young buckaroo with his eye to the misses. I was bashful too at the time when most boys are bashful. I used to think a lot of a girl in Joe City, Emma Richards, whose daddy was a pioneer from Utah. She was pretty, and coy, and had a way about her I liked.

But I was a bit backwards about telling this girl what I thought of her. When my time came—four of us buggy riding—I got a bit strangled and queer feeling at the idea of kissing her or putting my arm around her, but I did hold her hand and I thought this was going some, and was right proud of myself until I learned afterward that "Joe Pearce was the biggest coward on Silver Creek."

Somehow I didn't go with her much after that.

Then there was Sis Hartnett—that was more serious—and I had a good deal more competition, for Sis was from Holbrook and had a fine skin, and all the boys liked to dance with her.

Doug Perry of the Hash Knife outfit was courting her too, and Doug didn't leave much room for anybody else. He was a lady's man, no question, with very black hair and black eyes and a dash to him that young misses can't resist. Sis Hartnett favored him some, but she didn't altogether leave me out of the picture, and I mooned about her times between seeing her.

At this time I was working for the M&O Cattle Company, for my father had sold out his range stock and was grazing only sheep that a Mex herder could handle as well as a cowboy. Six of us boys from the M&O blew into Heber and talked up a dance that night. We couldn't get ahold of a fiddler, but this needn't prevent the dance because two of us boys could play the harmonica and I could lay down a few chords on a piano. A harmonica is a handy instrument for the range; it can be carried in the hip pocket and there's a whole orchestra for you after you shake out the wheat (tobacco) and the lint from your pocket that's collected along the mouthpiece.

Sis Hartnett was visiting some of her folks in Heber. When I heard that, I had chills first and then fever and then chills again, especially after I heard that Doug Perry was coming too, and some other Hash Knife boys.

That dance was a disappointment because I had to spend most of my time playing the piano or the harmonica, and there wasn't much time left for dancing; and when I did get the dance, Sis was most of the time well occupied. Once or twice I saw her glancing at me in a certain way, likely just to show me she knew I was there, but these glances were little satisfaction.

Every time I looked her way, she was dancing with Doug. I got mad and jealous and wanted to do something, but couldn't figure out what to do, for Doug had some reputation as a gunman, and I didn't want to tangle with him that way.

I waited, and my chance came. Toward the middle of the evening, Doug got a notion to do a jig dance. He was a fancy stepper, and no doubt he figured that a good jig dance would improve his chances with Sis Hartnett. He held up his hand for everything to stop and strutted out to the middle of the floor. He said to me, "Joe, can you play 'Swanee River' in jig time?"

I studied awhile and said, "I don't know, Doug, but I'll try it."

I reeled off a few bars, and he did a few practice steps. "*Bueno*," he said. "Let her go, Joe, and mind how you play."

I pulled down into it, and he went at it most lively, hopping into the air and clicking his heels, clacking away on the pine board floor, pushing back his black hair with his hand as he danced. I could see Sis watching him, and if I read what I read in her eyes correct, Doug was making a fancy impression and Joe Pearce might as well have died yesterday.

Now it just happened that I got mixed up with my tunes somehow, and right in the middle of 'Swanee River' I found myself playing 'Old Black Joe' in very slow time.

Doug Perry quit dancing. He humped over to me, with hair all raised up on the back of his neck, his fists opening and closing. He was mad. "God damn you, Pearce," he snarled. "You done that a purpose."

"Why, Doug," I says, "I didn't know how it could've happened. Honest I didn't do it a purpose. You know how easy it is to get off a tune."

"I oughta kill you, damn you."

"I'm right sorry," I said meek enough.

"No apologies go with me on that," he said. "I know you done it a purpose."

While Doug talked, the hall began to empty. Soon Doug and me were the only ones in the room. Doug looked around, and even Sis Hartnett was gone with one of the other fellows. "I'll get even," Doug promised and walked out himself.

He didn't let it go at that. Next morning he came riding over to our outfit, just as we were getting ready to move the herd. He told Gentry, our foreman, "I'm looking for Pearce."

Gentry was a nervy little devil. "You needn't go hunting Pearce," he said. "You got any grudge, you can talk to me."

"I got something to settle with him."

"No. I know Pearce didn't do that a purpose. If yo're hunting anybody, yo're hunting me."

They sat there awhile and eyed each other, and then Perry jerked his horse's mouth around and rode off cussing. That was the last I ever heard of him; he must have left the country, and left Sis Hartnett to me. I guess he had too much pride to stay and was a footloose puncher anyway.

But if I thought Sis Hartnett was my girl now, I was mistaken. She never spoke to me again.

* * *

Schoolteachers were regarded as extra special young ladies among us, both because they were more educated than the average run and because they were imported; that is, they came down from Utah to teach in the country Mormon schools. I never got really serious with the misses until I fell in love with a schoolteacher. I'd passed the coltish stage and was a forest ranger in the Black Mesa Forest.

Maude Nobles was a home girl that had studied at Provo, Utah, and come back to teach school at Nutrioso, a little village near my headquarters. Her family lived at Alpine, a few miles away. I was in the marrying mood, then, with a steady job, and there wasn't too much competition because Nutrioso and Alpine were so isolated from the other settlements.

But Maude's daddy furnished me the stiffest competition of anybody. Someone had told him that young Pearce was a pretty tough *hombre*, not the right sort for his daughter to marry. He must have believed it, and maybe he was right in doing so. Quien sabe. I was a range horse and not a buggy horse, no question.

Everything I seemed to do with that girl was wrong. Whenever I came around to the log cabin where she lived, her father set the dog after me. You can't make a good impression on a miss when she looks out of the window and sees you tearing around and around her house with a dog yapping after you, and you hollering to her father to open the gate. Especially you can't if you are running in high-heeled cowboy boots. A ballet dancer would look like a plow horse if she had to wear stogie boots.

Then there was the Christmas celebration in the schoolhouse, mothers and fathers bringing their children to the Christmas tree for prayers and singing and exchange of gifts. I'd spent a month's wages on a watch and chain to give to Maude that evening, and I thought if things were ripe I'd have a try at asking her to marry me.

It was a fine evening for Christmas. Nutrioso is high in the pines and a cold country. Outside there was two feet of snow on the ground that gave a real Santa Claus atmosphere. Time came after the singing for exchanging gifts, and Maude seemed mighty pleased with the watch and patted my hand and smiled sidewise at me. Everything was going fine. She had made me a small quilted piece which like a cowboy I stuffed into my hip pocket.

The prayers began, and after awhile Maude said to me, "You pray, Joe."

I didn't know I was getting to my feet. "Sure," I said so low she probably didn't hear me. I didn't know any prayers, and I was too flustered to make any up. My Mother had given us good religious training, but it was a long time ago. By lamplight she had read to us out of *The Book of Mormon*, and there had been always a blessing before each meal and a nightly prayer. All I could remember was the blessing because each of us kids had had to take turns saying it against our plates, and I'd said it often enough so that I'd never forget it.

I said it now. "Our Father in Heaven, bless this food, that it may nourish and strengthen our body, that it may do us good, and that we may have strength to carry out the required work of the day."

About the middle of the prayer, I knew folks were staring at me looking queer, and I began to feel mighty hot as though someone had stirred up the fire and thrown on a couple of extra logs. Sweat began to leak down my face, and right in the middle of the blessing I reached into my hip pocket, pulled out my bandana, and mopped my face, and then I finished the prayer still holding that bandana and wondering why the children had began to giggle and even the older folks to cough and choke.

I sat down, still holding my bandana, but it wasn't the bandana at all. It was the quilted piece Maude had given me.

Later Maude whispered to me, "Don't you mind, Joe."

"I don't mind," I told her.

"You ride home with us." (They passed right by my place on their way to Alpine.)

"Your father—"

"You sneak in back," she suggested. "He'll never notice you."

About the time the party began to break up and the people to go outside and unhitch their teams and buggy horses from the hitching rail, I went and stood in the shadow of the school building near Mr. Nobles' team of pretty grays. Soon Maude came out, holding to the arm of her daddy.

Her father didn't see me. "Hurry up," the old man said. "It's late. Thank God we're rid of that damn scallywag, Joe Pearce. Maybe we can get away without his seeing us." He hustled her into the buggy.

As soon as they started off, I chased after the buggy and got my hands onto the end of it, all ready to jump inside. Just then the old man happened to look behind and saw me. "That you again!" he hollered. He laid on with the buggy whip.

The right horse of the team stumbled on the ice and went down to her knees, but she was up again right away and with such a jerk, and me half in the middle of my jump, that I spun off into the air and landed rolling in a snow bank. Last I heard was the old man's laughter as the wagon bumped off into the darkness. I walked home that night.

Somehow the children at Maude's school found out about the watch I had given her even though it had been privately that night. I don't know how such things get around children, but it happens. And nothing will interfere with a match quite as much as kids.

In February, I was on my way through Nutrioso towards headquarters and stopped at the schoolhouse to ask Maude to go with me to a dance at Springerville. Maude frowned in the middle of something she was saying; the children all turned and stared at me, thirty faces turned to me, and some of them began to laugh. I got out of there quick and waited until recess.

Maude didn't like my being there. "I wish you hadn't come in, Joe."

"The kids—"

"They found out about the watch and opened it up and wrote something inside."

"I wanted to ask you—I reckoned—"

She was cold to me. "Don't ask me—"

"What's the matter?" I managed to get out.

"Father knows about the watch too. Here it is. You'd better take it."

I took the watch. "The kids—" I mumbled. I couldn't get my thinking straight. Like a horse kicking me in the belly, it had knocked the wind out of me. I walked out of that building and across the schoolyard toward my horse.

The kids all spotted me and set to hollering and laughing. "Teacher's fellow! Teacher's fellow!" one of them began, and the rest took it up.

A little girl that looked about eleven years old, with long hair flying, came running after me, and walked behind me imitating the way I walked. "Teacher's fellow! Teacher's fellow!" she yelled.

It made me mad. I turned around and looked at her sniffly nose and freckled face and the red tongue that she wagged at me. I aimed a big kick at her that almost took me off my feet, and I was that mad I meant it to land, but she dodged out of the way and kept yelling at me, "Teacher's fellow! Teacher's fellow!"

That was the end of things between me and Maude Nobles. I've heard talk that parents disapproving will make young people go into each other's arms, but I don't believe it. At least it didn't with Maude and me. I gave the watch to another girl who kept it. The name I've forgotten.

Maude Nobles finished out that year and another of teaching at Nutrioso, and then she moved out of the country and back to Utah, where I understand she married a man that was fifty years old. He probably made her a much better husband than I would have made her because I needed to get gun matter and such out of my system.

The little girl with the sniffly nose that chased me across the schoolyard? Why, that was Minnie Lund whom I married eight years later.

CHAPTER VII.

FOREST MAN

My most important duty as the first forest ranger in Arizona, then the same as now, was fighting fires. But in 1899, when I was appointed, the chief cause of fires wasn't the stub of a cigarette or a careless campfire, but the intent and purpose of the Apache Indians, whose reservation bordered on the Black Mesa Forest. They set the fires deliberate for the smoke. They had a sincere belief or superstition that smoke would bring rain. And in the driest seasons, when the forest was all ready to burn like tinder, up would pop a big fire near the boundary of the reservation. And you couldn't catch the sly beggars at it.

Before Teddy Roosevelt took a hand in his conservation program, and had dams built, and set aside national forest, the Black Mesa forest had no attention at all. The only folks interested in checking fires were the cowmen and sheepmen of the region, and they got interested only if their ranges were threatened.

That was a great stretch of timber I patrolled, alone at first, and then with several Rangers under me and a title as chief ranger. It was the largest section of untouched virgin timber in the United States, and so it was reported to President Roosevelt by Guifford Pinchot of Pennsylvania, who was also chief United States Forrester under the original Roosevelt and who inspected the forest with me while I was ranger. My territory included land from Flagstaff east to the New Mexico line, and from Springerville south to Clifton, a stretch larger than a couple of those New England states.

* * *

The Black Mesa forest reservation included the White and Blue Mountains, country almost unknown to the white man, range on range and ridge on ridge of thick close-standing pine and blue spruce and wide groves of white aspen, interrupted by clearings in the valleys where no trees grew. There were very few trails. Some of the timber was thicker than a jungle to get through.

The forest was alive with game. Stock ranged free in the lower stretches. Some of the stock escaped, and bands of wild horses grazed through the forest. The streams ran full of trout, with not enough fishermen to keep them caught out. When I was a boy, the turkey came down within a mile of our ranch at Taylor, and we could hear them gobbling in the spring. But as the country settled up, they moved back into the mountains. The forest was thick with deer of every kind—blacktail, mule, whitetail. And I couldn't ride a day in the forest without seeing a flock of antelope streak over the hills and into the canyons, their white rumps bouncing. Mountain lions had their hideouts deep in the forest, and from their caves they sneaked out and into civilized country to prey on sheep and newborn calves. Sometimes I spotted mountain sheep high on the ridges.

This was the kind of forest that was to be my home for three years, and I liked it. I liked my job. I knew much of the country from boyhood except the deep parts of the forest. And I was able to take care of myself in the toughest spots—handy with an ax, handy with a horse, and even handier with a gun. My wages was sixty a month, and I had to mount myself with horse and packhorse, and feed the stock myself on my wages. Later as chief ranger I was paid more money.

The toughest fire I had to fight was the one at Pinedale, and how I handled it makes an interesting story, I think. A cowboy came racking along at top speed to my headquarters at Nutrioso to tell me that a fire was blazing away at Baker's Butte and Long Valley, and the cattlemen were unable to check it. That was in the spring of '99.

My horse and packhorse were grain fed and in fine condition, and I had them packed and saddled and ready to go in fifteen minutes. In two and a half days, I was in Long Valley, almost two-hundred miles away, and much of the trip over mountain trails. I pushed those horses. When I arrived I summoned more help, cattlemen and sheepmen anywhere I could get hold of them, putting them on government pay. It took three days for forty men to get the fire under control. Smoke-blackened and tired, but satisfied, those Stockman returned to their ranches, with an order for two dollars a day wages from the government in their pockets.

On my return along the Tonto rim, I bumped into the pinedale fire mentioned above. It had no doubt been started by the Apaches, for it had nothing to do with the Long Valley fire. It was boiling along south of Pinedale, a settlement of twenty families in log houses. A south wind fed it and whipped it, and Pinedale was direct in the path of the fire. What made it worse, the folks of Pinedale having need of logs for one thing and another, had cut down a great many of the trees surrounding the settlement and had left the dead branches scattered everywhere on the ground. If the fire got to those dead branches, nothing could stop it. I didn't have much hope of saving the town.

But I rousted out every available man, promising them two dollars a day from the Government. I arranged for supplies at the Pinedale store, corralled axes and shovels and picks from everywhere, hired a cook to keep the men fed and have hot coffee available every minute.

Mounted and on foot we rushed south three miles through the pines to the fighting line. There was a fire! The smoke had piled up into a thick gray black mist that made the sun of the color of blood. With smoke stinging our eyes, we could see the red flames crawl up a hundred foot pine tree in a half a minute, and then like as not the pine tree would go down with a shivering crash. We saw the fire leap twenty, thirty, forty yards from one tree to the next. The fire was so hot we could only face it a minute or two and then had to turn our backs or move away.

I set the men to beating out the flames with green pine branches where the fire ate through the dry grass. This had been successful with other fires but now did no good at all. When we had the grass smudging and the fire almost out on the ground, the wind would make it jump clear over us into a pine tree behind us, and there it would crackle and snap through the green branches.

Stronger remedies had to be used. I ordered the men back some distance, and here we began to cut down a fire barrier two rods wide, chopping down the trees, cutting them up, and rolling them out of the way, slashing out the bushes or pulling them out by the roots, raking dead pine needles and brush to one side. When the barrier was ready, we tried a back fire along the distance I thought we could control.

For a while it looked like we had licked the fire. The back fire slowed it down, and we had great hopes it would burn itself out behind the barrier. But then the southwest wind blew out stronger, and one place or another it began to jump over our barrier.

The men were tired, back-weary, some of them slightly burned and most of them singed in their beards and hair, faces black from smoke. They shrugged when the fire leaped over, spat on their hands, chawed a little harder on their tobacco. They was willing, but they couldn't do it. I needed more men. We had to build new barriers, fight harder. They couldn't do it. Yet I had called out every available man I could find. More than ever it looked like Pinedale would burn up.

I was about ready to butt my head against a tree trying to think where I could get more men. Then I had it. Why not? I grinned at the idea. It was worth a try, anyhow, I decided, and leaving instructions to the men how to continue fighting the fire, I saddled up and rode to the Cooley Ranch, some twenty miles away and 20 miles north of Fort Apache. At Cooley Ranch was the nearest telegram, and from there I sent the following message:

Commanding Officer, Fort Apache:

Forest fire, originating inside reservation, burning north to top of mountain, now moving fast towards Pinedale. Unable to check it. Send all available scouts and Indian police to Pinedale with three days' rations.

Joe Pearce, U. S. F. R.

That was my idea. The Apaches had likely started the fire. Why shouldn't they help to stop it?

Thirty mounted Apaches, riding plumb wore out ponies, reached Pinedale at dusk of that same day and went immediately south to the fire line, where I put them to work extending the fire barrier, cutting a new barrier where the fire had crossed beyond control on the other side. Some I kept busy beating out with green pine branches to spots where the fire crossed but could be controlled. I had some sixty or seventy men in all now, and worked them in relays. From behind the line, drinking water was brought up on mule back, and in camp the cook kept steaming-hot coffee ready all the time.

We held back that fire until the direction of the wind changed, and the fire died out of its own accord. The Apaches had saved Pinedale. I sent back the following note by the scout Skippinjoe to the commanding officer at Fort Apache:

Your scouts and police saved the day. Pinedale was saved from going up in smoke. Good firefighters and not afraid to fight. Many thanks.

Joe Pearce, U. S. F. R.

The tame animals in the Black Mesa Forest—the stock—caused me more trouble than the wild ones did. Just one example or two of dozens will show what I mean. It was part of my work to estimate the number of sheep and cattle using the forest and collect the government fee for grazing privileges. But the hard-bitten sheep and cattle men couldn't get this new idea into their heads and regarded the land as theirs. They weren't even willing to secure the proper permit for grazing privileges.

Many times I've come on close-packed flocks using forest lands and have ordered them off, and more often than not they refused to go, the owners claiming the land had been theirs for 40 years and they'd be damned if they'd give it up now, government or no government. When this happened it was my duty to report them to my head, W. H. Buntain, Forest Superintendent at Santa Fe, New Mexico, and secure warrants for their arrest. A few arrests and trials, with stiff fines, began to make the Stockman change their minds.

There was a bearded old timer, a sheepman and a nester, in a little shack on government lands. I went up to his shack peaceable enough for the third time.

"Come in," he says to my knock. He was cooking breakfast when I went in, looked me over scowling, went back to his cooking. "It's you again! What's on your mind this time young feller?"

I told him, "Just wanted to make a little correction for the government on your sheep. I'll need to make a little round up to count 'em."

He turned around then, eyes on fire, and braced heavy on the flats of his feet. "You see the door there?"

"Sure I see it."

"Know what it's for?"

"Reckon so."

"Listen here, young feller. I pay the territory and the county taxes on my sheep and goats. I like to see the color of a man's hair that'll make me pay my taxes twice in Arizona. You see the door?"

"I seen it already," I said. "I judge you want me to use it." I walked outside and he followed me and stood in the doorway. "I'm coming back," I told him, "and when I come there'll be ten Rangers with me, and we'll round you up."

"Like hell you will!" He slammed the door shut.

But I returned, like I said, with two other Rangers and a warrant for his arrest, and in the end he paid the fee—about eighty cents a year per sheep—and in addition a stiff fine. There wasn't any more trouble collecting it from him after that.

The wild horses in the Black Mesa Forest and other reservations caused trouble, but this didn't come until after my time as a Ranger. I'm glad of that because I've always been a lover of horses, and I'd have hated to carry out the government order to clean out the mavericks.

There was reason enough for such an order. Wild horses were a bother and a nuisance because they used forage that might just as well been used by sheep and cattle that were of some use to man. The order specified in addition that any branded as stock should be killed also, after the owner had been duly notified and had failed to remove his property from the forest land. A little sense in carrying out this order would have saved a massive trouble.

But the Rangers went to killing cowponies as well as mavericks, fine saddle stock worth a hundred dollars and up per head. One ranger named Fears shot several head belonging to a rancher named Trammel, and Trammel filed a criminal complaint against Fears, charging him with wantonly and maliciously destroying his animals. A Stockman jury convicted him, but on appeal his case was thrown out of court on the grounds that he was merely carrying out orders.

In another case the stockman warned a ranger who had been killing saddle horses that this was a very unhealthy climate for a man to shoot down horses on an open range. The ranger replied that he represented the U.S. government and intended to keep on carrying out his orders just the way he had been doing.

A few days later he vanished, and no trace of him was ever found.

CHAPTER VIII.

JUDGE AND JURY

Two weeks ago I read in the Springerville paper that Bailey Leverton was dead. "The quartets sang by young people at the sawmill at Vernon were beautiful. Norman Whiting sang 'Empty Saddle' and 'The End of the Trail,' accompanied with the guitar, and brought many tears to the eyes of the congregation."

This piece in the paper reminded me of one of my strangest duties as forest ranger, the time I acted as judge and jury, with Bailey Leverton as one of the litigants. It was an important case because it had a bearing on many quarrels, and I was involved because it was partly forest land.

It seems that the sheep of the Morris Brothers had trespassed on the Leverton land which they held by permit from the government, and the sheep trampled down some cornfields. This fellow Leverton was a hot blooded Texan who did not even allow mutton to be brought under his roof, let alone his cornfield. He and his daughter Mrs. Benson had filed a damage suit charging criminal trespass and demanding $250.00 damages.

The justice of the peace of the Vernon precinct where the case was to be tried had been disqualified, and Mr. O.M. Bigelow, J.P. of the Springerville precinct, had been called in. At that time attorneys in Apache County were as scarce as hen's teeth, and as I knew a little about law, Mr. Bigelow thought I might come in handy some way, and as well as being interested because it was forest land. On the day set, Bigelow and I rode the nearly fifty miles to Vernon. When we arrived, a crowd had already gathered around the old log schoolhouse to hear the trial. Horses and buggies and wagons, and pack outfits and camp outfits, sheepherders and cowboys, and one attorney at law—a Mr. Larsen from Holbrook who had been retained to represent the Morris Brothers.

Witnesses for both sides was in an ugly temper, talking loud, waving their hands, arguing, and ready at a moment to pounce on each other and decide the case then and there. It looked like peace proposals was in order if there was to be any trial at all. The J.P. and I walked up to the crowd of wrangling people.

I shouted at them: "Folks, the J.P. is present. Please respect the court enough to pull down your voices." I was acquainted with most of the people there.

When they got kind of quiet, I told them a story about a sheepherder, the Mexican that had been arrested and charged with shooting holes in the tent he was using because he was ready to quit and didn't like his boss. They began to laugh and got into a better mood. Then I told them about a Mexican puncher that had been tried before Judge Bigelow on a charge of stealing sheep, found guilty, and sentenced to six years hard labor in the territorial prison at Yuma.

"That's the kind of law in Arizona now," I said.

I was bashful talking, but I made a hit with the crowd. They began to holler. "Let Joe Pearce decide. Give it to Joe Pearce."

And Judge Bigelow told the crowd that he would be only too glad to let me decide if both parties in the dispute were willing. But he made one condition, that whatever I decided would be final and that there was to be no appeal. Both Leverton and the attorney for the Morris Brothers agreed as long as I was a disinterested party, with friendship for both.

Out there in the open I took the litigants aside, first the older Morris brother. And I listened to what he had to say. It seems that his herder had no intention of trespassing on the Leverton range and farm, but with no fence or markings he didn't know the land wasn't free for grazing, and his sheep had got into the cornfield before he could head them off.

Next I talked to Bailey Leverton and his daughter. "Now listen here, you know Charlie Morris' sheep ain't done $250 damage to your place." They agreed the sheep hadn't.

Leverton said, "I just wanted to make it so expensive for him, Joe, that he'd not be runnin' sheep on my land again."

I pondered my decision for a time and decided the following to wit:

1. That inasmuch as J.P., Mr. Bigelow and self, had ridden fifty miles to hold court, that the Morris brothers should pay court cost of ten dollars, which the judge and I would split.

2. That it seemed to me about twenty-five dollars damage had been

done to the Leverton corn, and this amount should be paid as damage by the Morris brothers.

3. That as long as the Morris camp outfit was there at the trial, they should serve dinner of coffee and mutton to the crowd, including Bailey Leverton and daughter.

Court was adjourned with much cheering immediately afterward, with everybody satisfied, drinking coffee out of the same pot and eating Morris mutton, and the Levertons were out there with the rest *eating mutton*.

* * *

Besides fighting fires and collecting range fees and helping settle disputes, I had other jobs as a forest ranger, everyday jobs. Blazing trails, posting fire notices, marking timber to be cut.

After Pinchot's report about the value of the timber in the Black Mesa Forest, the McNary Lumber Company was organized in the East and got a contract from the government to cut standing timber. In the national forests, though, the government doesn't permit a company to go through a section cutting down all timber. Where timber is thickest, I had to mark trees for cutting, while a good healthy pine standing alone I left as seed pine.

Each tree to be cut had to have two notches, one above the cut and one that would remain on the stump. In the mill each log had to have a U.S cut into it, and I had to estimate the number of board feet in each log and make a report of how many board feet had been cut. For this I used a Scribner and Doyle snap rule, getting the diameter of the smaller end of a log and then doing a little figuring.

I trail-blazed on horseback, scalping the bark of the tree about six feet above the ground, which was safe above the snow line, usually about four feet. I made trails to possible fire areas, and trails that could be used crossing the mountain, and trails to springs that stock and humans might use. I cleaned out and deepened the springs.

Generally in trail blazing over rough country, I would follow the backbone of a ridge, as this was usually the safest and best way down off a high place. One could stay away from the ups and downs of gorges and canyons.

I got well acquainted with those mountains, living there for three years alone and during fire season on the move all the time. I've often been lost in a storm. There are two kinds of lost: being turned around and being stranded. For being turned around there's one way to safety that I've never known to fail. A good horse—not a bronc, mind you—but a good saddle horse will always remember the last place where he has had feed and water, and he will know the way there: give him his head. In a storm, if I've thought the horse could make it and I could stand the severe cold, and my *cabeza* was twisted about where I was, I'd just say, "Come on, Bob. Let's go home." A man never needs to be lost riding a gentle horse.

Storm-stranded is another matter. I've been in snow so thick with whirlwinds in those mountains I couldn't see ten feet in front of my nose, and blizzards howling for three days without let-up. In a storm like that, there's no use trying to go on; you have to make some kind of shelter for yourself. A hatchet was always part of my equipment.

I'd unload my packhorse and unsaddle my horse and leave the stock to shift for themselves. Then I'd stretch my rope from one pine to another, cut branches from the small pines and lean them slantwise on each side of the rope. When I was done, there was a cozy shelter. Next I'd collect dry wood –and a forest man can always find it –and pile the wood inside, build me a fire. There I'd lie snug with my fire and wait for the storm to run itself down.

When Pinchot came for his inspection of the Black Mesa Forest, I took him along a trail I'd blazed some time before beyond Alpine southward toward Clifton. We came to the place the Blue Range breaks off almost sheer, and down below the mountains roll away toward Clifton.

Pinchot said "Guess we'll have to turn around and go back. We can't get down off this mountain, Joe."

Then I told him I'd blazed the trail down there so that a rider could get through to Clifton. To prove it, we went down, leading the horses.

That evening in camp I asked him, "Do you think there'll ever be a wagon road there, down the Blue Range to the flats?"

He got a laugh out of that. "There'll never even be a good horse trail," he said. "The only way a man'll ever get down there easily is to grow wings and fly down."

That was forty years ago. And now every day automobiles go along through there and roll down the slopes of the Blue Range following almost exact the trail I blazed in 1899, now the Coronado Trail.

CHAPTER IX.

GUN ACQUAINTANCE WITH BLACKJACK

Of all the wild animals in the Black Mesa Forest, the human wild animal was the worst. Probably the safest place in the Territory for rustlers and outlaws to hide in was the White Mountains and the Blue Range. Ranchers and sheepmen were only thin on the edges and anxious to stay on good terms with the bad men so their stock wouldn't be rustled. And the forest was in striking distance of the Mexican border on the south, and north through the Navajo Indian reservation it was safe to take stolen stock to Utah and Colorado. Or the stock might be disposed of to the Indians themselves. West of the forest was the big Apache Reservation, miles and miles of it uninhabited and little known. East was the most uninhabited stretch of New Mexico.

The Black Mesa Forest continued to be a nest for outlaws long after the rest of Arizona was cleaned up, until just a few years ago.

As a forest ranger it wasn't any of my business to meddle with the outlaws. So far as they were concerned, I was only interested in looking after myself. Many's the night I've ridden into an outlaw camp, eating chuck with the young fellows lounging about, just noticed their stolen stock and the blotched brands without comment, slept with them, and ridden off in the morning.

For my protection I packed for awhile a .30-.30 Winchester and steel jacketed bullets. But I found that this gun wasn't powerful enough to put a bullet through the trunk of a pine tree, so I got rid of it in favor of a Spanish Mauser that would shoot through an ordinary tree.

I had heard of Blackjack before I ran into him and his gang. He had a reputation for being one of the itchiest fingered and quick shooting outlaws in the Territory, one of the kind that would shoot first and ask his questions afterward. There was a flock of killings to his credit, and what he did later bore out his reputation.

At this time I was patrolling the forest along the Continental Divide between Nutrioso and Alpine, tacking notices to trees warning against forest fires. Behind me I heard the sound of horses coming. Not exactly heard them either. Hoof beats on soft earth can't always be heard, but make a kind of vibration to a forest man that hits his nerve centers. I turned in my saddle, looked back, and saw them coming—one man in the lead, behind him five pack horses, and following the pack horses four other mounted men.

I didn't pay any more attention until they caught up with me. About thirty yards away the man in the lead pulled up. I turned again and saw that he had thrown up his hand for the others to stop. He was riding on alone toward me.

"Howdy," he said sourly, looking me over and looking my horse over, and studying my boots and overalls and sheepskin jacket and the broad hat I wore slouched.

I recognized Tom Ketchum, alias Blackjack; I had met him at the Hash Knife Outfit at Holbrook.

I nodded to him.

"What's your business?" he asked.

"Yours?" I asked back.

He spat into his hands and rubbed them like he was warming them for future service. Now he stood up in his stirrups and finally I figured out what was worrying him. It was my forest badge.

"Just a forest badge," I told him. "I'm a ranger—Government ranger."

"You're damn sure of that?"

I said, "I'm not sure of anything else."

He jabbed his horse closer with his heels and read what was stamped on the badge: Department of Interior, U.S. He was a dark, tall fellow, with a hat too big for his thin face. "If you're a forest ranger, you're all right, but you better be damn sure you are. Where you from?"

"Nutrioso."

"You live there?"

"Yeah."

"You ridin' our way now?"

I told him I was and pointed to the warning I'd just tacked up. He read it and spat and nodded and seemed convinced that I was what I said. After that his tune changed. He didn't want to get rid of me anymore. "You can ride along of us, young feller, you want to," he said.

That was how I rode with Blackjack's gang for a piece, and I soon learned what it was he wanted. He began to fire questions about the road north from St. Johns to the Santa Fe Railroad, which had been the Atlantic and Pacific. "Any place to get water along there?" he asked. I told him of the location of a spring about halfway, but he'd have to turn off near a half mile to a ranch house to find it.

He nodded.

"You heading that way?" I asked.

"Maybe," he said.

Like I said, at that time I did know they was Blackjack and his gang, but I'd had enough speaking acquaintance with bad men already to know the breed blindfolded. So far I hadn't had the chance to see what the four riding behind looked like because it was near sunset and the forest almost dark under the tall trees. Just in case I ever needed to remember what they looked like—and I needed to later—I wanted to look at those four men.

"Hell," I said to Blackjack, "my cinch come loose."

That happened plenty often, so he didn't suspicion me as I pulled down while the bunch rode past and pretended to tighten my rear cinch (we all rode with double cinch saddles), and then I upped into the saddle and rode after them. When I'd caught up, I slowed down and rode alongside the men in the rear passing the time of day and incidentally getting a good look at them.

One was a tall, slender kid, another dumpy and older and with black teeth. The third was a hunched up little fellow, the oldest, and the only one that didn't open his mouth. The last was a Mexican. All of them packed six-guns and Winchesters in saddle holsters, and there wasn't much joking.

I rode with them six miles maybe and then turned off, and that was the last I saw of any of them until the hearing at St. Johns six months later.

On their way down to St. Johns, they slaughtered a beef belonging to Henry Barnett, who found the remains of the carcass and swore out a John Doe warrant for their arrest, but by this time the men had ridden on down below St. Johns and were headed north toward the railroad.

Sheriff Beeler and a posse of five men took up the trail from the remains of the dead steer. I'm not sure that Beeler was over-anxious to catch those men, and no blame to him. At any rate one of the outlaws dropped behind the rest to refill a canteen, and the posse came in sight of him half a mile away. The men dismounted and pulled out their saddle guns. Seeing what the posse was up to, the outlaw opened fire with a high powered rifle, scattering slugs all around them. They fixed their long distance sights, taking account of the wind, and tried to give him slug for slug, but their bullets only popped up dirt way in front of him, while his rifle carried the slugs so close that they scattered for shelter.

He rode off while Sheriff Beeler sent a man back to St. Johns for reinforcements.

Two boys, hardly reached twenty yet, La Sweer La Seuer and Bill Gibbons, was among those that left St. Johns to join the posse. They trailed it by the hoof marks, but somehow they got switched off from it, and while the sheriff waited for other men, they hugged the trail of the outlaws, following them fifteen miles.

A trick of the outlaws when they reach a black rocky ridge or a cedar ridge, is to take the horses ahead a ways and leave their horses, coming back on foot where they can lie hidden on the ridge and knock a posse off. An experience trailer, when he hits country like this, will leave his men stationed a ways back and pass around the ridge one side or the other to be sure the outlaws have gone on.

But of course La Seuer and Gibbons didn't know they was trailing outlaws instead of catching up with Sheriff Beeler. They were on foot and in rough country, leading their horses, when they ran into the ambush and the outlaws opened fire. They ran on foot for cover after they were hit, but the outlaws followed them, pumping lead into them, and after they were dropped, the outlaws knocked their heads to pieces with slugs.

Safe out of Arizona, Blackjack's gang killed a sheriff and two deputies in Bluff, Utah, then swung back towards Mexico through the Indian country. But before they reached the border, several of the supposed gang were captured in Silver City, New Mexico.

That brought me into the picture again. I was asked to go to St. John to try to identify two of them held there. From a store window, with a deputy, I watched people going past, cowboys mounted and some on foot, Indians and Mexican and whites. By and by three men walked by, and one of them was the tall, slender kid with the narrow shoulders. "That's him," I said and pointed him out to the deputy. Later in court I repeated the identification, and they were held for trial.

But before the trial had ever begun, extradition papers came from Bluff, Utah, and the two men were sent there with a guard. On the trip north, both escaped.

Yet that wasn't the end of my acquaintance with Blackjack and his gang. While I was still forest ranger, he returned to Arizona and held up the Winfield Brother's Store at Camp Verdi. He was alone in that hold-up, slouching into the store and throwing down a six-gun on Winfield, Clawson, McDermott, and a clerk and bookkeeper, who were all in the store at the time. In the midst of the robbery he heard some noise outside that worried him. In cold blood he shot down Winfield, Clawson, and McDermott, killing all of them without giving them a chance. Then he escaped.

The first I knew of this last inhuman killing by Blackjack, Sheriff John Mund of Prescott and Billie Winfield, brother of the slain Winfield, rode into my camp in the White Mountains down toward evening.

"Seen anybody suspicious?" Mund asked me.

I told him I hadn't.

"But you once seen this Blackjack feller?"

"I think it was him."

They told me what had happened. And while I whistled, Mund asked me, "You want to go along?"

"Sure," I said. "I'll go along. Maybe I can be of some assistance."

"We trailed him this far. But you know this country, Joe. You might help us with the trailing." Already I had had quite some experience trailing and had gained some reputation. This time my reputation bounced back on me. I was still young and thought I knew a good deal more than I did. "Sure I can trail him," I said. "I know this country better'n a book. I got a map of it all spread out in my head."

"Billie here'd like to get first crack at him, we find him," the sheriff suggested.

I shrugged. "That's *bueno*," I said. I knew how Billie must feel with his brother dead and on the trail of the killer.

We picked up Blackjack's trail, still fresh and easy to follow, the trail of a single horse. And there were three of us. We pushed the trail hard with all its warm signs, riding toward Luna, New Mexico. Next day that trail led straight to a small adobe ranch house with a curl of blue smoke going up from its chimney.

I pointed to the shack. "Blackjack's in there," I said. "But you'd better be careful. He'll cut us down if we give him the chance."

Mund knew that as well as I did. "You sure he's in there?"

I told him I was quite sure.

He had us crawl up to that house from three sides, crawling on our bellies, so that we had the little adobe surrounded. There we lay until a shade the other side of twilight, which is a good time to bust into a house. Mund signaled us and we closed in on the shack. When we were near enough, the sheriff eased up to the door and hollered, with his rifle thrown down when the door flashed light.

"Throw up your hands," he said from the shadows.

"Dios mio!" said a Mexican voice in Spanish. "What is the matter?"

We searched the house, but the only one there was the Mexican rancher. I'd of sworn it was Blackjack's trail led up to the house. I still think it was. He was a right clever outlaw, and I still think that he'd slipped through us somehow in the twilight, covered his trail, and got away.

But this was the dead end. I couldn't pick up any trail from here. And the old Mexican swore that he had seen no one until we came. He was probably afraid for his skin.

I am glad to recount that Blackjack was later captured in Santa Fe, New Mexico, and hanged by the neck until he was dead.

EDITOR'S NOTE

Blackjack:

His real name was Thomas E. Ketchum (1863-1901). His gang was known for robbing trains, and Blackjack himself was alleged to have killed several men.

His brother Sam and several other outlaws were hunted down and killed in a gunfight after one train robbery—an event from which Tom was absent. Five weeks later, Tom singlehandedly attempted to rob the same train at the same place and in the same way. Before the robbery got fully underway, he was sighted by the train conductor, who knocked Tom off his horse with the blast of a shotgun. The next day a posse found the wounded outlaw lying alone next to the tracks and brought him back for medical attention and a trial. His mangled arm was amputated, and he was found guilty of attempted train robbery and sentenced to be hanged.

Above is an actual photo of Blackjack on the gallows. His final words were as follows: "Goodbye. Please dig my grave very deep. Alright, hurry up."

CHAPTER X.

CLIMAX JIM AND THE BRITCHES

He got the name Climax Jim because he chewed so much Climax Plug, and he was one slippery *hombre*, the slipperiest *hombre* I bumped into while I was a forest ranger, though not the same type as Blackjack, who was just a vicious gunman. And of all the outlaws I've had to do with in my life, he turned my face the reddest. I'll never forget how the Rangers laughed at me when Climax sidled up, trying to keep straight that one-sided smile, and handed me a ragged pair of pants. That was down in Clifton, with the Arizona Rangers gathered for labor trouble, ten or eleven of them standing around, and Climax blinking his blue eyes. He was a humorous fellow all right.

"What the hell!" I says.

Climax put out his big paw and rannied my hand up and down. "Thanks, Pearce," he says. "Thanks for the loan of them pants. You'll never know how much I appreciated the way you was so willing to give them to me when you had to go bare bottomed."

But this is the end of the story. The beginning was in Springerville, with Climax under guard of two men, charged with steer rustling, and to be taken to St. Johns next day for hearing. "Why, I thought I was doing Henry Barret a charitable act when I driv them old Mex steers to the butcher at Morenci," Climax told me later, explaining his lapse from law and order. "Them steers was so skinny, time I got to Morenci, the butcher'd had only plumb wuthless hides and meat fit only for Mex tamales."

Climax always talked circulating his wad of plug from one cheek to the other and swallowing the juice the way some fellows can do. High cheekbones like an Indian, eyes way deep in his head, smile that was one sided, but he had a look you was bound to like.

Barret and a Mexican vaquero had him prisoner in a little room in Springerville, and aimed to set up with him all night. But Climax wasn't worried, not by a jugful. He'd been mixed with the law before between peaceful times of straight cowboy work.

"Usually a woman's skirt will make a man open his eyes," says Climax telling me about it, "but this time it was different."

The two men had marched him in there, careful about everything, for he already had a reputation for breaking jail, for being able to crawl through a rat hole and get away. "None of your tricks," Barret warned.

Climax yawned. "Nothing in my head, gents," he says. "I'm too sleepy." He began to take off his clothes, pulling off a boot and tossing it into a corner. Then he pulled off the other boot and threw it straight at Nacio Gonzales, who ducked and swore and fingered the trigger of his Winchester. And Climax rolled back on the bed and laughed.

"None of that," Barret said.

Climax tossed his pants in the middle of the floor, pulled off his shirt and stuffed it under the pillow to raise the pillow a little, put his head down and stretched out. After awhile he raised up. "Reckon I'll have a smoke before sleepin'," he said.

He slouched to the door where he'd thrown his trousers. There near the door and hanging on a wooden peg was a heavy woolen skirt. Climax didn't usually smoke, but now he got the makings out of his hip pocket, patted some tobacco into a brown paper, twirled the cigarette into shape. He reached as if to get a match, but instead his hand went to that woman's skirt; and he whirled around, swinging the skirt. The skirt smacked Barret in the eyes and blinded him and made him yowl. Another swat went to Nacio Gonzales, who had laid down his Winchester seeing Climax undressed and all ready for bed.

After those two hefty swats, Climax, with only underwear on him, was through the door and up the road like a rabbit. Barret and Gonzales, time they had wiped the tears out of their eyes and could see, couldn't see anything of Climax.

About the time all this was happening, I was patrolling the forest thirty-five miles south of Springerville, on the lookout for summer fires in the dry season before the heavy summer rains. One evening about sundown I rode into a sheep camp, figuring on a few bites of chuck and a place to throw my roll down with some human companionship.

A Mexican will serve that yearning for a human face and human voice if a white man isn't handy.

In this camp, the Mexican owners was away, but there was a white man, the like of which I hardly expected to see. A man in nothing but underwear. You might expect that beside a bathtub or elsewhere, but not in the middle of the Blue Mountain forest. Here was this white man dancing around on one bare foot and trying to pull something out of the other, and he was cussing high and natural. I thought he must be crazy as I rode up and looked him over.

He said straight enough, "Get down and lay up here," while he pulled a bur out of his foot.

"Sure," I said. I wasn't accustomed to asking embarrassing questions of anybody. I stepped off my saddle horse, throwing the pack on the ground. He watched me close and solemn, not saying anything until I went to my saddle to uncinch it.

"I've got to ride down to Pete Slaughter's ranch on the Black tonight," he said slow and matter of fact. "I was jest wondering, stranger, could you make me the loan of your horse? I'm afoot and I want to ride your horse down."

Nothing yet to show me the kind of fellow he was, but I didn't loan my horse to anybody. "No," I said. "It ain't possible."

Next I knew he took a long jump toward the horse, yanking the bridle out of my hand, and was half mounted and ready to go. But I was uncinching the saddle on the side that held my saddle holster and my Winchester. I pulled out the gun, stepped back, and threw it down on him from my hip. "Get down," I says.

He laughed and got down. Keeping my eye on him and the Winchester crotched in my elbow, I finished the unsaddling, put rope hobbles on my horses, and turned them loose.

"You won't give a man a chance!" he pleaded. "When I get out of this, I'll help you some way. Jest leave me the loan of your horse..."

"No," I said, keeping the rifle ready for him, because I'd had one sample of how slippery he was, and I was suspicious now that he was an outlaw hiding out in the forest.

After dark the two Mexican herders came into their camp, and I told them in Spanish to look out for Climax, that he was a bad *hombre*.

"May have to tie him up tonight," I said. "You boys make some supper, and I'll watch him."

Climax, as sober as an owl, understood every word of Spanish I was saying just as well as the Mexicans. The herders fixed supper while Climax and I watched them. With coffee and frijoles and boiled mutton in our bellies, we all warmed up a bit. Climax was the kind that couldn't keep still for long, and soon began to talk. He told us how he'd broken away at Springerville to account for him being in underwear, and now he could get clean away if I'd loan him the horse. He said he'd take good care of the animal and leave it for me at Slaughter's ranch.

"I don't loan my horse to anybody," I told him.

"All you're trying to do is get two and a half out of me." That was the reward for him—two hundred and fifty dollars.

I said, "I don't want a penny of that reward. But I'm going to protect my horses and see that you don't ride either of 'em away."

"You wouldn't shoot a man just because he broke jail."

"I'd shoot a man that tried to take my horses. I don't want anything to do with you," I said, "except to get shut of you."

Seeing that it was hopeless, Climax began to complain to the Mexicans about his feet, which were badly swollen and banged up. They were good boys and gave him several pieces of frayed sheep skin, and these he tied around his feet and over his ankles, wool side inward, with rawhide.

That Climax was a humorous fellow and a good talker. He began to string yarns, and most of them funny, and we listened, not thinking about the time, and me not quite decided whether to tie him up or not. But I kept my Winchester handy, not trusting him a mite.

"The sky-pilot used to come around from Solomonsville to the outfit I worked for last spring about every two weeks to do a little praying over us," he says. "One time he asked me if there wasn't something he could do for me. Not for me, I told him. I thought I was doing all right. But he might offer up a few words for our cook."

Talk like that, and we laughed and laughed at him until deep in the evening. We weren't any closer to bed, and it didn't look like we'd get there. Late we heard the tinkling of several bells near camp. I jerked my head in the direction of the bell and said to the herders, "You better take the bells off those animals, *amigos*, or you're likely to be missing a mule or saddle horse by morning. This *hombre* can find them easy in the dark."

Climax looked sly when I said it, but the herders only shrugged their shoulders Mexican-like and said, "*No lease.* (It doesn't matter.)" They'd already got to trusting Climax by his talk. I wasn't convinced, even though he seemed friendly.

"It's late," I said. "It's about time we tie you up."

"I'm not sleepy," he argued, "not a mite." And he went on talking fast with his jokes. I began to yawn a few times. Twice I caught myself half asleep, propped against a pine tree, and I came out of it with a jerk, grabbing for my Winchester. Finally one of the Mexicans dropped off to sleep.

Climax planned this long talk, and I wasn't savvy enough to see it, even after his telling how he'd broken away at Springerville. The last time my head nodded, he jumped to his feet. Another jump took him behind a pine tree. Then he started to run zig-zag out of the arc of the firelight. I was up like the snap of a spring, wide awake; I hollered at him to stop. When he didn't, I fired three shots over his head to try to scare him into stopping but not wanting to kill him. Branches of quaking aspen rained down on his head as he ran. And then he was out of sight.

"You better go down and look after your mules," I warned the Mexicans.

"He don't do nothing," one of the Mexicans said.

"Well, anyhow," I said, "now we can go to sleep, but first I'm tending to my own stock." I went out into the darkness and found my animals and led them quite a piece from camp. There in the heavy timber, I re-hobbled them. Returning, I unrolled my bed near the fire, and naturally after all the excitement I wanted to sort of air out my britches, so I hung them on a bush just above my head.

I guess I had dropped off to sleep. But I came awake suddenly. Just enough light from the near dead fire to see Climax standing above me, still in his underwear, and snitching my britches from the limb. I could see him grinning. He was a humorous fellow all right.

"Now, damn you, Pearce," he said, "you try it awhile." Britches and Climax went before I could even turn to get my Winchester, and I was pantless. Like I suspected, he stole one of the herder's mules, using the bell strap for a halter and a hobble for a nose piece. He rode as he had planned to Slaughter's ranch.

That was why my face was red when he returned those old britches that day at Clifton in front of a dozen Arizona Rangers.

CHAPTER XI.

ARIZONA RANGER TRAINING

I WAS RIDING THE BORDERLINE between the centuries, and I was riding changes. What I did not know about was I was living through a time and not knowing what was going on; I couldn't see beyond my nose. Troubles with the Apache Indians had gone forever. Sheep and cattle trouble still menaced my country, but the Tonto Basin War was over. The Spanish-American War had been fought. The forest and grazing privileges had come into government control. Things were already greatly changed since I was a boy. I'd had a part in these changes without realizing how important these changes were. When you get old and look back, you see things you couldn't see at the time.

The Territory of Arizona was the last stamping ground of the outlaw roughs and the range bad boys and the old time gamblers with quick fingers. And because my country was the most isolated part of the Territory, I figured I had the privilege of living on the last real frontier of the old West before it changed to modern. I was chasing old-time outlaws and rustlers through the Indian country long after southern Arizona had settled down to being civilized.

With the new century coming in, Arizona was still the roughest part of the United States. There was a good many reasons for this. Part was in just the name Arizona. From the days of the Apache and the lawless days of Tombstone it had always had a reputation for being what it was. Texas and California and some of the territories had been cleaning up, sweeping out the refuse of the past fifty years into Arizona. Then there was the copper camps and towns—Douglas, Morenci, Clifton, Globe, filled with the rougher elements of mankind and law enforcement tied up with local politics so that there wasn't any, until the formation of the Rangers.

The Arizona Rangers carried law into mesquite. At no one time were there any more than twenty-five of them, yet they did what hundreds of sheriffs and deputies hadn't been able to do. In March, 1901, the

Arizona Territorial Legislature passed a bill giving the governor authority to form a body of men to bring law to Arizona. But not until 1902 when Captain Rynning took charge did things begin to hum. Between 1902 and 1907 the Arizona Rangers pretty well cleaned up Arizona. Any kind of law enforcing was their job, from catching a lone rustler to confiscating the guns in a dance hall so that there'd be no trouble. And because local officers resented their authority, they not only had the bad men to contend with but sheriffs and deputies as well, at times.

Often their duty took them beyond the boundaries of Arizona, deep into Mexico, or north into Colorado and Utah, east into New Mexico. They settled labor troubles and the future of gunmen; they almost started a Mexican revolution.

In his book *Gun Notches*, Captain Rynning has told their story so well that there's no use my repeating it. Some of the things he tells I was intimately acquainted with, one way or another, but I won't repeat them here because they are already told. Instead I'll give a Pearce-eye view of the Rangers, and tell of the things I took part in that Captain Rynning left out of his book.

* * *

After three years of ranger work in the Black Mesa Forest I was hankering after a change, and I heard of the Arizona Rangers. It sounded like four aces to me. Though I was getting close to thirty, I couldn't get gun matter out of my *cabeza*.

And the chance came. The sheriffs of Navajo and Apache counties were advised by Captain Rynning and Governor Alexander O. Brodie that there would be one Ranger appointed from these counties. Because I had some reputation already in the counties and wanted the job bad, my name was sent in.

A letter came from Captain Rynning. With a bellow I packed my outfit and started for Douglas. I printed the letter below because it gives a good idea of the qualifications for a Ranger:

HEADQUARTERS ARIZONA RANGERS
October, 1902
Mr. Joe Pearce
Springerville, Arizona

Dear Sir:

In reference to the matter of your application and correspondence with our first sergeant W. B. Ellison, wherein you apply for the appointment of Arizona Ranger, I wish to ask you whether you have the qualifications. Have you been in the cattle business, and continuously for the last eight years, and have you a working knowledge of the Spanish language? Let me know whether you have such knowledge.

We have made it a practice to enlist only single men, as we have found from our experience that they render the best service, as the men of the service have to abandon their homes and their families and are liable for service in any part of the Territory and thus may be called from their families for as much as six months or a year at a time.

Each man to enlist must provide himself with a horse, saddle, and complete pack outfit, a Colt .45 six shooter (no less) and a carbine .30-.40 (no less). Can you secure such an outfit? Let me hear from you whether or not you're single, can speak Spanish, are a practical cowman, and can furnish this complete outfit. If so, we can arrange for you to come to some point and be inspected and enlist you.

Very respectfully,
Thomas H. Rynning
Captain Arizona Rangers.

I had been a bust as a Romeo with that Nutrioso school teacher, so I was still single. I had been raised with the other qualifications all my life. And as to the outfit, it was the same I had in the forest service. I rode down through the White and Blue Mountains, where the Coronado Trail now is, and through the Sulpher Springs Valley to Douglas.

Douglas had been made the headquarters of the Rangers because, next to Clifton, it was the toughest town in the Territory, the one most in need of cleaning up. Two things was against it: It was on the border and got all the riff-raff from below the line, and it was a mining town. Gunmen paraded the streets. Every train that came in, sheriffs and deputies hung around the station with their six-guns showing on their hips as big as trench mortars. And the saloons was run by as rough an element as ever got together. Killings weren't unusual.

But I'd been in towns like that before; Douglas didn't scare me any. I rode down the dusty street toward evening, into a racket of honky-tonks and gambling joints running full blast, and even a circus going for the entertainment of the populace—a Mexican circus from across the line. After my long ride I wasn't in any hurry and felt the need of some entertainment and human companionship, so dropped twenty dollars at a roulette table before I'd figured out it wasn't on the square and walked out of the place.

I was feeling low about that twenty dollars, with my shoulders hunched, as I walked along and came opposite where the circus was playing with Punch and Judy show and clowns and various kinds of concessions. I saw a big crowd gathered in front of an adobe wall and heard shooting, and slouched over toward the noise.

A Mexican and his wife was conducting a shooting gallery. A Mexican silver dollar with a hole in it was tied with a string against an adobe wall, and the idea was at twenty-five feet to cut the string and drop the peso to the ground. You could use your own six-shooter if you preferred, or they furnished one, and the cost per shot was twenty *centavos*, while if you cut the string you got a Mexican dollar.

"Sombrero Blanco!" the man hollered. *"Usted trata, no?"* He was talking about my big white hat, trying to get me to try while the crowd hung back waiting for another goat. "Sure," I said. "I'll try."

In my life I'd had considerable gun training—from my father, from some of the Hash Knife boys, from practice. So I bought two dollars and fifty, Mexican money, of shots, which was about the same as a real dollar. I got my six-shooter steady and cut the string first shot and the crowd hollered. I tried again, and cut it again. The Mexican looked funny as he handed me two silver pesos. Third shot I missed. But I kept pecking away at that string, while folks left and others came. I didn't cut down the peso every shot, but often enough so I was soon winning back the twenty dollars I'd dropped at the roulette table. My pockets began to fill with Mex silver dollars, and when you get a quantity of them, they get mighty heavy.

I noticed a big man standing near me in the crowd, tall and thick through. "How's that?" I says to him, pleased with myself.

"Pretty good."

"Pretty good. Hell," I said, "it's damn good."

"I know men can shoot better and faster. They got to know a lot of other things besides."

"Who are you?" I asked him.

"I'm Captain Rynning, Arizona Rangers. And you're Joe Pearce," he said grinning as he shook my hand. "Let's have a drink and talk things over."

Territory of Arizona.

County of GRAHAM,
City or Town of SAFFORD.

I, JOSEPH H. PEARCE

the State of IOWA Utah aged 30 years and 2 months, and by occupation a COW MAN DO HEREBY ACKNOWLEDGE to have voluntarily enlisted this 23 day of NOVEMBER 190 3 as a soldier in the ARIZONA RANGERS OF ARIZONA, for the period of ONE YEAR, unless sooner discharged by proper authority. And I do solemnly swear that I will bear true faith and allegiance to the Territory of Arizona, and will support the laws thereof, and the Constitution of the United States; and I will faithfully observe and obey all laws and regulations for the government of the Arizona Rangers of Arizona, and the lawful orders of all officers elected or appointed over me, so help me God.

Subscribed and sworn to before me this 23 day of NOVEMBER 190 .

CAPTAIN ARIZONA RANGERS.
Recruiting Officer.

* * *

The headquarters of the Arizona Rangers was located out on 15 Street, two small adobe rooms. The front room was used as an office, the other as Ranger quarters, when they were in Douglas, usually not more than four or five at a time. Here we kept our beds, shooting irons, even our saddles, for it was not safe to leave the saddles in the board corral a few yards south of the quarters because of the thieving propensities of the Douglas population.

Stock was kept in an open corral rather than a barn, with manger and feed boxes, because it would take too long to get a horse out of a barn and sometimes a Ranger must leave in a hurry. At least one horse was kept saddled night and day, while A. A. Hopkins, the secretary, or Captain Rynning himself was always in the front office to get "phone calls or telegrams."

Just to show the kind of men that were enlisted in the Arizona Rangers, I tell the following story. Some of us boys were listening in when Johnny Brooks called at the office to try to enlist and talked to Captain Rynning.

"Well, Cap, I'd like to enlist in your outfit," Johnny said.

"Yes? Where you from?"

"Down around El Paso," Johnny said vaguely.

The Captain stood there and studied him awhile, frowning. "What's your name?"

"Brooks. Johnny Brooks."

"Where was you back in the eighties? It seems to me—"

"I was smuggling cows and horses across the Rio Grande, back and forth. There was money both ways."

A broad grin spread over the Captain's face. "I thought I knew you. I was right there myself. Hopkins, enlist this man and I will swear him in."

Most of the Rangers were men that had seen the dark side of life and had actually been through rustling and border fights; and often they'd left places in the dark of the moon, as we used to say. That was the kind Rynning wanted: men who spoke the language of the rustler and outlaws, ate the same kind of chuck, drank out of the same coffee pot, and knew the rustler's next move even before the rustler himself thought of it. Rynning believed that it took a thief to catch a thief, but he wanted reformed thieves and could get them. Not a single Arizona Ranger ever broke his oath to support the Constitution of Arizona and the laws of the Territory, and to do his best always to uphold the law.

And Rynning wanted men who weren't too itchy fingered who didn't get nervous in a tight place and get his gun hot when he didn't need to. In Rynning's opinion one live outlaw was worth ten dead ones, and even more than that to the reputation of the Rangers. He didn't want killers.

We had a good deal of gun training to that end, even though most of us had lived with guns all our lives. Hours that we weren't chasing bad men, we spent in practice, and Rynning was a fine leader. To my notion, as fine a one as ever lived. We had to learn to measure distances with our eye and know how to shoot without trusting to the adjustable sights of our Winchesters because in a pinch there wasn't time to use them. We'd ride outside Douglas a ways, and suddenly Rynning would point to a stump or bush on the hill and give orders to dismount. We'd drop off our horses and lie on our bellies and lam away, while Rynning would tell us whether we was overshooting or undershooting.

We had practice too at firing six-shooters from horseback. A rifle isn't much good for a mounted man because of the motion of his horse. A six-shooter because it is shorter can be used up to fifty yards with fair accuracy, but a man should always dismount to use his longer barreled rifle. And we were taught dismounting not to use the stirrups, but to slide down backward over the rump of our horses, leaning down and withdrawing our Winchesters from saddle holsters while we were sliding. That way we could get off much quicker and had the immediate protection of the horse between us and what we were shooting at.

One thing Rynning taught us which always came in handy and is probably the chief reason I'm alive today is how to throw down on a man. If an arresting officer comes up face to face with an outlaw and tires to throw down his gun, he runs the risk of the outlaw beating him to the draw or his having to shoot, and in addition his shot isn't going to be so accurate. Rynning taught us to walk past the outlaw indifferent, getting a good look at his face to be sure he was the man wanted, and then walk a few paces beyond him, turn sidewise, jerk out your gun, and be all ready to throw down his back, then call on him to put up his hands. I've used this method many times. It may seem cowardly, but it is an officer's job to arrest a man and not to kill him.

I've mentioned throwing down a number of times, and throwing down means just what it says. Drawing a gun in a tight pinch, there's seldom times to do any aiming. The gun is drawn and raised and then thrown forward, just like you were throwing a rock, with the finger out along the gun and pointing to whatever you're shooting at. I spoke above about "ready to throw down" and I meant with the hand and gun pointing upward and ready to come down. If you kept the gun pointed at the outlaw, you couldn't shoot near as quick or accurate.

Many men I've known could handle a rifle or shotgun almost as quick as a six-gun, throwing down and shooting from the hip. The great Commodore Owens, Sheriff of Apache County for many years and with more killings to his credit that he could keep count of, was very successful with this kind of shooting. He was one also that carried his six-shooter on his left hip with the butt forward, and we usually looked on that kind of man as a bluffer, a show-off, without the guts to go through with a fight. And we thought the same about men who wore their hair long below their shoulders. Sheriff Owens did both, but he was neither a bluff nor a show-off. However he was the exception.

There was considerable discussion among the Rangers about the best way to pack a six-gun, and there's still a lot of misunderstanding about it. Ordinarily the old Hash Knife cowboys didn't carry holsters at all, but kept his gun loose in his belt. When he went to town or to a dance he would put his shirt over his gun, and if he saw trouble he would tuck the shirt loose from over the handle.

Some men carried their guns low on the right leg with the bottom of the scabbard tied near the knee with rawhide, and some carried their guns in the middle of the front of them and tied down, maintaining this way made the quickest draw. I'm of the honest opinion that a gun packed on the left hip with the butt forward is the quickest draw. But I didn't carry mine that way, nor did most of the Rangers, though there was exceptions that carried their guns all the different ways mentioned above.

Most of the Rangers carried their guns on the right hip with the butt pointing backward, sometimes loose, sometimes with an outside scabbard, sometimes with an inside scabbard fitting inside the belt. The strongest reason was that the gun sat more comfortable that way and could be covered by a coat. Guns in other positions, especially when a man mounted, were always getting in the way. But a gun on the right side could be pushed back so it rested over the buttocks, and he'd hardly know it was there.

Most of us bought our guns from a gun store in Tombstone, which was the best in the Territory, and we bought new guns rather than second-hand because we were sure we could trust them. Even though most of us carried Winchesters, we figured the best rifle on the market in those days was the Spanish Mauser, which was being circulated around after the Spanish war, but was scarce. We regarded it as even better than the Cragg-Jorgenson. Some of the Rangers had them. For a six-shooter, the German Luger used in Spain had the best reputation. It was larger and heavier than our Colt .45 and a better shooter.

With the above training and the above guns, the Arizona Rangers set out to bring law into the mesquite country.

CHAPTER XII.

INTO MEXICO AFTER BAD YAQUIS

Captain Rynning was on friendly terms with Colonel Kosterlitzky of the Mexican *Rurales* of Sonora, so that when our business took us south of the border we weren't hampered any by legal and political technicalities. The Colonel, a Russian by birth and a Mexican by marriage, was a very strict old soldier, but he thought a lot of us boys and our abilities, and even in those early days ideas of law were pretty much the same north or south of the border. If we saved his *Rurales* a tough assignment, so much the better for him.

The Arizona Rangers were disliked or liked pretty much by how a party regarded the law. Many of the county sheriffs and deputies would rather see a rattler any day than a Ranger, and so regarded them. The larger cowmen were always glad to see us and made us feel at home and sometimes loaned us fresh horses when we were on the trail. But the small man who was building up his herds at the expense of the big outfits' calves would give us a cool reception. Or he might, on the other hand, wine us and dine us so freely that he would tip his hand that he was currying some sort of favor from us. We got so we could tell when a fellow was overdoing it, and looked upon him with suspicion.

This particular occasion when we entered Mexico, a telephone call came in at the front from Cooke and Orme, railroad contractors, that several of their best mules had disappeared. Cooke and Orme were doing a stretch of repair work to the grading on the El Paso and Southwestern, now merged with the Southern Pacific, nine miles west of Bisbee.

About five Rangers were at headquarters. Captain Rynning called us in. "I gather," the Captain says to us, "that this rustling was done by Mexicans or Yaquis. You boys don't look at the border when you cross it. It's not there."

"At least it ain't visible," said one of the boys, laughing.

We rode to the mining camp of Bisbee, which was sprawling wooden buildings almost falling down on the top of one another, the sides of the canyon are so steep. And beyond Bisbee we came to the grading camp down in a wide valley with blue mountains far away, looking hazy south where they were in Mexico. We gathered the information that in addition to the disappearance of the mules, two Yaqui mule skinners' had vanished without waiting for their pay. Mules and Yaquis fitted together like two and two. And the mules was worth about four-hundred pesos apiece, which was considerably more than the Yaquis were worth.

The Yaquis had always been, and still are to some extent, a thorn in the side of the Mexican government. They've caused Mexico more trouble than any three other Indian tribes and have licked the Mexican regulars in battle on more than one occasion. They live in a far corner of the Republic, northwest Sonora beyond the Yaqui River. They're very independent cusses, and being Indians, they're not always easy to trail.

But we picked up the trail without much trouble. It led in a south-westerly direction toward the old town of Fronteras, which was some sixty kilometers south of the border. From various indications we judged that besides the dozen mules there was at least a half-dozen fifteen rustlers—mule and horse tracks aren't the same. And we guessed that the two muleskinners had made all arrangements in the grading camp and then had sent word to confederates.

Following the tracks slowed us down, and it took us a full day to reach Fronteras, where the tracks veered off without going into town. But we entered the town for refreshments and sleep, knowing the tracks would still be there in the morning because there was no sign of rain. We obtained corn for our horses and jerky for ourselves to carry, along with so much Mex food on the table that we filled up like buzzards in a drouth.

Fronteras was like dozens of other small Sonora towns that date back a century or two—very dark reddish brown adobe buildings, some with iron gratings in the windows, built next to one another with no space between and close to the street, which was always filled with brown dust. The buildings looked very old and crumbly. So did the big church. There's always a plaza, and on one side of the plaza is the church that is a little out of plumb from age, and plastered (while none of the other buildings are) but with some of the plaster falling off. And sometimes part of the church is burned brick and part is adobe, with no special reason for the mixture. Always on the other side of the plaza is the presidio, and jail, which is newer and in much better condition.

Here in Fronteras we ran into a bunch of Kosterlitzky's *Rurales*. At that time he had charge of four hundred of them in Sonora. Their job, like the Rangers, was to keep order, and they kept order. When they heard what we were after, they wanted to go with us, all twenty-five of them. Now the addition of twenty-five men to us five to capture fifteen Yaquis and twenty five mules under ordinary circumstances would have gladdened our hearts.

But we knew the nature of the Mexican *Rurales*. They were made up of the very hardest men that Mexico had produced. Usually they had been convicted of murder, treason, or other high crimes either to be executed or to enlist in the *Rurales*. Of course the choice was easily made.

For Mexicans, they were well equipped. They were booted with spurs—silver-mounted spurs. They wore a greenish-colored pair of britches and shirt, and a very wide straw *sombrero*, often with silver braids. Their horses were small Mexican range ponies, wiry and full of endurance; their saddles were light but well made, not army style but on the order of cowboy range saddle, with bit and headstall, silver mounted. For their arms they carried the American-made .44 Winchester and the Colt .45 if they could obtain them, which some of them did from the Arizona Rangers. For after the monthly confiscations of guns in the tough joints of the tough American towns, the Rangers were not averse to making a not too dishonest dollar, even though of Mexican coinage.

The *Rurales* lived on jerky, *chile* beans, and coffee; this was the extent of their chuck that I ever knew of their having, with of course *mescal* as a washer—a brand of firewater that is more fire than water. It kept them tuned up to high pitch all the time, and maybe contributed to their reputation for not having a coward among them, just as it likely helped their propensity to letting a man go that had the *dinero* to buy them off. And finally, it was always easier to shoot a rustler or horse thief than to run him back to law and justice, with no one the wiser out there in the wilds of Sonora. Who was to say he didn't try to escape? Because they were so lazy, they'd sometimes have the sport of watching him dig his own grave first, though graves weren't especial necessary in a country cloudy with buzzards.

Knowing this last propensity, we didn't want twenty-five *Rurales* with us on the trail of the Yaqui rustlers. Out of humaneness we didn't want to kill any of the Indians. We just wanted the mules. But even worse, what kind of international scandal would there be with the Arizona Rangers tied up in killing Mexican Yaqui Indians?

I said, "What will you do with them when you take them?"

That was a good joke, or seemed to be. All the brown faces surrounding us laughed like it would be a joke anyway, and some of them winked. We talked with each other in English and Spanish. Twenty-five was too many, we told them. We weren't cowards to need a whole army. But we would take five of them with us. And that would even things up.

We trailed all the next day, the tracks growing fresher all the time. And the five *Rurales* were getting pretty excited, so we watched them as well as the tracks. In the minds of all of us was some of the last words of Captain Rynning. "You boys go down there and follow them and do just what they did. They stole the mules. You slip down there quiet an' steal them back and don't stir up a mess. No telling where it might end. And don't get into a killing."

By and by I began to talk to them as I knew Spanish better than the other boys and them Mexicans couldn't talk English. I told them I thought it was a coward would stand a man up and shoot him when all he'd done was rustle some mules. And the poor Indians didn't know any better than to steal somehow. I knew they were all brave men that wouldn't do such a thing because a brave man wouldn't do it. Why not just get the mules and let the Indians go?

They looked sullen. They wanted a fight, and then they wanted the horses and guns of the Indians to keep or sell off. My talk didn't make sense to them.

"It looks like we have to fight Yaquis and then maybe *Rurales*," I said to the boys.

Parsons tapped his Winchester. "Long range," he hinted, and we all got the idea, knowing what notorious bad shots the Mexicans are at any great distance.

"Maybe," I said. "Worth a try anyhow."

In the afternoon the trail got so fresh we knew it wouldn't be long, and we went slower to keep watch for ambush of some kind. About four we came to the top of a rise, and stretching below us was a cottonwood draw leading south, a stream of water meandering down the middle of it, mesquite and brush and cottonwood trees heavy along the bottom and sides of the draw. We rode up the rise to the top of a hill and from here spotted the Yaqui rustlers. They was camped in a small glade beside the big trunk of a cottonwood, near which was built a fire. Horses were tied to the brush a few rods back from the fire, while we could see the stolen mules grazing in some rolling open hills on the opposite side.

All the Yaquis were squatted or standing around the fire. They had slaughtered a beef and were roasting red strips of the meat over the open fire, fastened to the ends of green willow sticks. The distance was about three-hundred yards and downhill.

We five Rangers dismounted and went on our bellies, drawing bead with our Winchesters, which rested in the palms of our hands, our elbows on the ground. The *Rurales* didn't dismount. They began to talk fast in Spanish. They wanted to ride whooping down the hill in a regular charge.

"Get down," I said in English. They understood that all right. Even though he sometimes thinks he hates Americans and always talks like he is their equal, a Mexican doesn't quite really believe it. He respects the American.

There was some ticklish seconds. Then the *Rurales* dismounted and lay down beside us. "Shoot for the fire," Parsons said, in English.

We opened up. So did the *Rurales*—in deadly earnest. But just as we counted on, our shots smacked into the middle of the fire, scattering hot coals and ashes for many feet, piling up a cloud of smoke. Shots of the *Rurales* were miles short at that distance; they were undershooting. We could see them pop up dust fifty yards in front of the Yaqui camp.

The Indians hopped away from the fire and scattered like quail in every direction. They were in such a haste that they didn't take time to untie their bridles and halter ropes. They jerked out their knives and slashed through leather and rope, swung onto their horses, and were off into rough country through the vegetation.

When we rode down, their camp was a mess—ashes and meat were scattered everywhere, pieces of frayed rope and leather still tied to bushes and trees. One saddle horse had been deserted; evidently the rider could not rein his horse through trees and brush and so concluded to take it on foot. The *Rurales* jumped down and made a dash for the horse, pulling up the fallen saddle and cinching it. While they did that, I slid off the bridle. It was the only souvenir we took back of our scouting into Sonora: a finely finished bridle bit laden with silver conchas, the headstall covered with silver buttons.

Back toward Fronteras we went, driving the mules and the saddle horse, and we parted on good terms with the *Rurales*. I don't think they ever guessed the trick we played on them, or even suspected it.

We returned to Arizona by way of Naco, a border town about eight miles south of Bisbee, and went first to the construction camp, where we returned the mules, thence to Douglas. Cook and Orme mules ate hay and grain in their camps unmolested from then on.

* * *

But we Rangers weren't always so successful. Once we got whipped pretty badly, just after our foray into Mexico, when we were feeling hilarious, even though tired. A big circus had blowed into Douglas, and we wanted some fun with it, so we five bought fifteen cent masks and rubbed flour on our hands, and joined the parade through Douglas, packing all our artillery and gun paraphernalia with us.

The band struck up. We galloped our horses along the wagons and their teams till we reached the front, ahead of the big wagon with musicians and clowns on top. The parade hadn't reached the main streets as yet, and the circus was in a hurry. What more natural than we should slow our horses down till they was barely moving, holding up the whole parade like a bunch of kids? The clowns cussed us, and the musicians cussed us. The band wagon wanted to gallop to make up time. We hollered at them and we laughed at them. Five Rangers on the loose with nothing on their minds and a little rat poison in their bellies.

Two of the clowns stepped off the wagon and went into a store. We noticed them but didn't pay much attention when they came out with two paper bags. We thought they went after something to eat.

At last the parade reached the main street, and we turned in through the crowds leading the parade! Down half a block the clowns opened up on us, and they could throw about as straight as we could shoot. Squash! Squish! Plop!

Eggs! Dozens of them hitting us square and dripping their gooey mess down our necks, from our hats, over our pants, over saddle gear and our horses' backs. The crowd roared, thinking it was all part of the show. Smeared from head to foot with eggs, we threw spurs and quirts and moved on, with clowns and crowd hollering and laughing behind us.

That little episode brought a full house that night, but we did not share in the gate receipts.

CHAPTER XIII.

TOUGH TOWN—CLIFTON

When I was with the Rangers, the mining town of Clifton was the toughest town in the Territory, no question. Douglas and Globe and Tombstone ran along pretty close behind, but in some ways Clifton had it over them for just plain ornery toughness. The time I was sent to Clifton—with several other Rangers and Timberline Sparks—as a kind of sergeant, I ran right into a race riot first thing. And then I nearly drowned four Chinamen soon afterward, but it was unintentional. Orders from Captain Rynning was to bring Ranger law and order to Clifton—to see that Clifton stayed a part of the United States.

Clifton was wide open. Something like twenty-five or thirty saloons and gambling halls running day and night, and in each was three to ten girls singing and dancing. Now one thing I learned here and I learned sure: that these fine looking young misses used more paint than baking powder. And they were so heavy on jewelry that they were too cluttered up for dishwashing.

Well I remember Sheriff Parks saying to Timberline and me, "I'm going to clean up Clifton and bring it back into the Union."

And Timberline says, "You clean out the fast women in Clifton and there won't be no women left."

As a boy I'd been often to the mining town of Globe, but the custom of playing the platform wasn't in vogue in the saloons then.

However, it was common practice now in the mining towns. The platform was located in the corner of the room, raised a foot and a half above the floor. Here the real sports, the money spenders, disported themselves—the gamblers, cowboys, miners, sometimes hold-up men and rustlers... and the girl entertainers.

The gamblers and the girls would sit here waiting for the fish to bite. Whenever a guest sauntered in and took his seat on the platform rather than somewhere else, it meant that he was going to spend some money. If he called for drinks around, he included only those on the platform and not in the rest of the house. The same applied when drinks were on the house. Men sitting elsewhere than the platform either didn't have much money to spend or none at all or didn't intend to spend what they had.

If things went slow on the platform, the house would slip some money to men in their employ, and they would hop on the platform and start things going, tossing money around, treating right and left, but treating to water in whiskey glasses and not firewater. The newcomers would win for several hands, and reluctant bystanders would see that things looked dead easy and would invest in a stack of chips, and soon they were crowding up on the platform so thick, you couldn't get a table and would have to ask someone else to put money on a card for you.

It wasn't often, except early in the evening, that business was dead on the platform. In those days money was wild. Wages were good in the copper business, and the miners mostly unmarried young European immigrants far away from home. Easy come, easy go.

The sporting misses and dance hall girls made a good thing of their jobs. Many of them got rich, and as I have said spent their money on jewelry, which was a way of saving it in those days. They loaded themselves with diamond rings and gold bracelets and pearl earrings and diamond brooches, the best that Tiffany afforded. They had several ways to make money. Drinks was fifteen cents, two for a quarter. Each of the girls had a small pocketbook, and when a guest bought drinks and the change was coming back to him on the wet tray, these ladies would scoop up the change and put it in their purses as percentage for playing the platform. When the little purses were filled, they tightened up their garters just below the knee and drop the nickels and dimes and quarters inside the tops of their stockings, a safe compartment, while they filled their pocketbooks again.

Sporting ballrooms were separate from the saloons, usually one story adobe buildings. Here a girl would go with her partner to dance to the music of a bass violin and a violin, a piano and a guitar. The smaller joints had only a violin and a piano.

For their dancing, the girls received a percentage on their drinks, and believe me they earned it dancing with those drunk and stinking cowboys and miners and rustlers. The girls was many different nationalities—a few Americans, mostly Mexicans, that had drifted in from Chihuahua, a scattering of French and Chinese and Japanese misses that had come up the same way, many of them smuggled over the border.

Men were not the only tough element. Many of those sporting ladies were just as good hold-up men as Clifton afforded at the time. They did not hesitate when a man folded up with too much snake juice to increase their bank rolls by rolling him (robbing him). Once a man was in their clutches, him and a month's wages often separated company.

But with all that, gambling was the quickest way to lose money. Most of the gamblers were professionals that had drifted up from San Antonio and Houston and El Paso, looking for a cooler climate, and some of them hightailed it out of the dying mining camps of California, blowing into the mining towns of Arizona with all their sporting style—diamond ring or diamond stick pin or both showing conspicuous, soft black hats with brims always turned up. When they played they always wore these hats tipped onto the backs of their heads and their shirts open at the neck, whether they had a tie or not.

The usual gambling games were played: roulette, faro, Mexican monte, and poker. The gamblers knew how to cheat whenever they could safely get away with it, and sometimes they misjudged and a shooting followed. Drunker the players got, the more the gambler cheated. Faro wasn't an easy game to cheat with because the gambler couldn't get his slippery fingers onto the deck of cards. The cards were played from a metal box the size of the deck. In both Mexican monty and faro, bets were made on sequence of the cards, whether an ace would come ahead of a king or a deuce before a trey.

Mexican monte cards were always of Mexican make, contained only from aces to tens, and the deck was in the hands of the gambler, who found it easy from long training to palm cards when necessary. Of course monte was the favorite Mexican game, while faro found favor with the Chinese, who were experts at it.

Each house had at least one roulette wheel, sometimes two and three. The percentage of take for the house was sometimes increased by using a metal ball painted white, attaching a dry-cell battery underneath the wheel to a spring manipulated by the gamblers foot. The dry cell shot current into a magnet underneath the table when the gambler pressed down his foot, and the magnet pulled the metal ball into the right compartment.

I liked roulette and have played the wheel considerable, and at times have even run a game for a house in Globe just because I enjoyed it. I think the reason is that roulette is a straight piece of luck, not requiring any brains. Poker is my second choice, a game I play good enough to lose my money to the sharks and hold my own with the ordinary cowboy or miner or soldier.

Clifton had many foreign miners, mostly from the lower classes—Mexicans, Greeks, Italians, Russians, with Mexicans in the greatest number; most of the cowboys were from Texas ranges. And there were railroad men of all nationalities. It was the railroad men furnished the cowboys the stiffest competition for the favors of the ladies. Cowboys and railroad men sometimes mixed it in hefty fights, but only as individuals. With all this mixture of the foreign element, the only real racial hatred seemed to be that of the cowboy for the Mexican.

A cowboy is just natural born to hate a Mexican—the way he hates sheep—if that Mexican don't keep his place. And his place isn't on the dance floor with a cowboy.

Timberline Sparks and the three of us came to Clifton from Douglas by train, and the very first night I ran into trouble between cowboys and Mexes. Timberline and I was scouting around among the various saloons and places of pleasure, just looking around, and we lounged into Jeff Dennigan's Saloon. Jeff was a former cowboy himself, and the cowboys came to his place, and this was cowboy pay-day.

Tonight it seemed the cowboys had not yet much arrived, and a flock of Mexican girls was playing the platform, with a gang of Mexican miners—spending their money freely on these girls. Things went along peaceful enough until a bunch of a half dozen cowboys blew in, all of them drunk. Now I've seen many a cowboy drunk, but seldom down and out with his liquor and not knowing what he was doing, while I've seen many Mexicans and other nationalities lying in the streets of Clifton and Globe and Douglas, rolling around in the dust and puking and groaning, or lying flopped under a table like they were dead.

This bunch of cowboys came into Jeff Dennigan's place like they owned it, thumping with their high-heeled boots, bandana handkerchiefs around their necks, very broad-brimmed J. B. Stetsons tipped back a little bit on their heads. You could see the bulges of forty-fives under their shirts.

These boys humped up to the platform where all the Mexican miners and Mex girls were, and one big fellow shouted, *"Vayate!"* which is the same in modern language as *scram*. The cowboys wanted to play the platform or dance with the Mexican girls, and didn't want any interference from Mexican miners.

What may be contrary to popular opinion, most Mexicans are brave men and very prideful. There were more of them than the cowboys, and they didn't take very well to such orders. They stayed. The cowboys began to rough them, bump into them and shove them, as if half by accident, and the brown-skinned miners cussed a beautiful mixture of Spanish and English.

The big cowboy suddenly whipped down, took a little fellow by the waist, lifted him with legs kicking. The cowboy roared with laughter and fight and drunkenness as he tossed the little fellow clean off the platform, where he landed on his seat.

That started the fight. And while it lasted, it was a good fight. Six cowboys against fifteen Mexicans, with Timberline and me not interfering. This kind of law enforcement wasn't our job. As there wasn't any policeman in Clifton, it belonged to the sheriff and his deputies, and none of them was there at the moment.

Mexicans and cowboys went to it with their fists, whamming away, with that familiar sound of bare fist whacking flesh and bone. That fight I didn't see any knives or guns, just bodies of cowboys and Mexicans mixing it, with two or three Mexicans to a cowboy, trying to get him down some way to jump on his belly or kick him in the ribs or face.

The cowboys began to get the worst of it. There were a couple of pool tables handy, with their racks of billiard cues. One cowboy and then another got hold of those billiard cues and lamed into them Mexes with them. You should have seen the miners scatter when the cowboys laid on with those billiard cues. The door wasn't quick enough. Those that wasn't lying on the floor went out through the windows, some of them head first.

The screaming of the girls on the platform stopped as sudden as it had started. The cowboys took possession of the platform, and there wasn't any racial hatred between the cowboys and the Mexican misses, who usually showed preference for Americans. By and by, a deputy came around and hollered in, "You boys come around tomorrow morning and see what the J. P. has to say about all this."

"Sure," says the big cowboy. "Sure we'll be there."

No doubt the J.P. would fine them five dollars apiece and let them go. And that was my first introduction to Clifton.

CHAPTER XIV.

CLIFTON FLOODS BRING TROUBLE

Even though restrictions against Chinese entrance to this country were in force in 1903, the Chinese got in. A good many of them came through Mexico and paid confidence men about a hundred dollars to smuggle them through the brush across at Nogales or Douglas or Naco—a hundred dollars that might be all the savings they had. Soon as they reached this country, they got jobs as cooks or launderers or working in the mines.

Nowadays the Border Patrol and customs takes care of smuggling and illegal entry, but then it was one of the many duties of the Arizona Rangers.

Soon after our arrival in Clifton, we heard of four Chinese working as cooks and launderers at the Longfellow Mine in Metcalf, a few miles away. Roundtree and I started out to arrest them, going on foot because the distance was short, and the road rough through the canyon. The way we heard the story, these Chinese had been tipping the officers most of their wages for the privilege of not being deported.

We arrived at the mine cook house and arrested the four Chinaman, little Orientals scared to death of the law and turning a queer green color when they saw us and our badges.

"You got papers?" Roundtree demanded.

"Paper, paper, paper," they jabbered to each other like they didn't know what we were talking about, but they knew well enough.

"Get your stuff and come along," I said. They ran around getting their things together, and jerky moving, and looking at us all the time like we might suddenly take a notion to shoot them. I guess the guns we packed did look kind of frightening.

We herded them away to the town of Metcalf and put them in jail pending a hearing. To keep them in good humor, we let them keep all their clothing and bedding and plunder, and even their long opium pipes and jars of opium to pass the time away.

Metcalf was just a small edition of Clifton. Both towns sit in the bottom of a steep canyon of red rock, the walls almost sheer, a little widening of the canyon where the towns themselves are. Clifton lies about the junction of Chase Creek and San Francisco River, and Metcalf is up Chase Creek a ways.

Both towns had jails that had been blasted out of the solid wall of a cliff, with the entrance a small opening with a barred metal gate across it, and the inside widening out into separate cells where the prisoners was kept. That seemed to be a handy way of making jails in the mountain towns. Nogales had one too.

On our way home it began to rain. The clouds piled up black and heavy, shoved along by a stiff breeze, and the Arizona sun that is almost always shining was blotted out. Fat rain drops came down widely scattered, and some of them plopped against our faces.

Roundtree looked up the steep walls at the sliver of sky. "We better hustle," he said.

How could he or I know this was the beginning of one of the worst floods Clifton ever had?

"Hustle is right," I says, and we began to dog trot.

We didn't get to the hotel too soon. It had begun to pour. I've never seen it rain harder. We stood out on the porch of the hotel and listened to it swooshing down, the blanket of rain so thick we couldn't even see a tree a few feet away. But we thought we'd done a good job arresting those Chinese, and we enjoyed the rain, feeling quite comfortable indoors. We enjoyed our supper too. "Let her rain," I said to Roundtree. "What do we care?"

I'd forgotten all about the Orientals in that jail, and nobody knowing about them there but us and Dutch Kepplar, a deputy who had the key, and he wouldn't think about them.

I woke up toward morning with the recollection of those Chinese hammering away inside my *cabeza*. I woke Roundtree up. He was too sleepy for my words to make much sense. "Those Chinese... that jail... you notice how low it was along Chase Creek. I bet you it's flooded full. I got a hunch those Chinese are only corpses now."

"Go to sleep," says Roundtree.

"I can't."

"Well, we can't do anything about it till mornin' anyhow."

He was right. I lay there awake until first signs of daylight showed in the room. The rain had stopped. I roused him up, and we dressed and set out once more for Metcalf. Chase Creek, where we went careful high along the bank and sometimes had to climb along the steep walls of the canyon to get out of its way, was a boiling flood of muddy brown water. Big cottonwood and pine trees was bobbing around in it, knocking against one another, washed out by the roots and carried down from the high places. We could hear big rocks and boulders rumbling and rolling at the bottom of the flood as they racked along.

Both of us shook our heads pretty dubious about those poor Chinese and ran when we could.

Sure enough the water in front of the jail looked deep and dangerous. When we ploughed into it, it came almost up to our shoulders, and we knew the floor of the jail was hollowed out deeper than the rock floor outside. "*Adios*, China boys," Roundtree growled as we splashed along.

But it wasn't to be so. When we reached the barred door, we heard them hollering in a jabber of Oriental, the like of which I'll never hear again. They waved their hands at us, and their eyes in their yellow faces looked ready to pop from fear. But they weren't dead yet. Short as they were, with nothing else to stand on, they'd had the sense to pile all their belongings—maybe even the opium pipes—into the highest place in their room and stand on that.

We hustled away to get Dutch Kepplar, and he waded in, and we pulled them out with ropes. Another hour of that flood and their heads would have been covered.

"Well," I says to Roundtree, when we were safe on dry ground and the Orientals shivering with fear and cold and looking like drowned chickens, "as far as I'm concerned these here Orientals died in jail. So far as I know they don't any longer exist, so we don't have jurisdiction to hold dead men for hearing and trial."

Roundtree studied a minute, glanced at the Chinese. "They look that way to me too," he says. "I don't know of any live Chinese around here without papers."

We walked off arm in arm down the canyon, leaving the four Chinese free men, at least so far as we was concerned.

* * *

When we managed to get back to Clifton, the town was a mess. I have already described it situated in the bottom of a deep canyon. The heavy rains in the mountains had brought down a wall of water, and now the town was mostly river. Already many of the smaller buildings had been floated away, and the water reached way back to the business district on the south side.

Looters were at work in the flood. The business men could not watch the flood water and their goods at the same time; so looters plied their hand and plied it well. At first they were only interested in kegs of whiskey, not wishing to see them washed away and wasted. Great crowds of shouting men gathered here and there in clots in the street, wading in the water.

They'd spy a forty-gallon barrel of whiskey and with a shout go after it, rolling it to some high piece of ground. There they'd drive a nail in the head of the keg, tip the barrel on one side, and take turns putting their mouths to the hole and sucking out the whiskey. Sometimes as high as forty or fifty miners were around a barrel. By and by somebody would come up with a cup, the hole would be made larger, and they'd gulp down that free whiskey by the cup. You can imagine, drinking whiskey that way, it wasn't long before those tough miners was all drunk.

At first they had been interested in just the barrels of whiskey going to waste. But now, with them all drunk, they began to loot the stores in earnest. The stores were mostly covered on the floor with a foot of water, and these miners would slosh in and take whatever they wanted that their eye took a fancy to.

Nobody seemed around there to stop them.

"Looks like we got work to do," said Roundtree. "Come on, let's get Timberline."

We ran to the hotel, which was high enough to be on dry ground, and rousted out Timberline and Blank and told them what was going on. The four of us returned and began making arrests. We didn't run into any real trouble even though the drunk miners was pretty rambunctious, some of them. But the four of us would walk up to the man that seemed to be a ringleader, or we'd lay hands on a man in the act of running off with stolen goods, and lead him back to the Clifton jail, which was like the one at Metcalf that I've described, only larger, and on high enough ground so the flood wasn't reaching it.

One after the other, we took those looters and locked them up until the jail was pretty near full. There they stayed until the flood went down and things got orderly again and the mines resumed operations.

The sheriffs of Arizona just didn't love the Rangers, and Sheriff Jim Parks of Clifton wasn't any exception. There was several reasons for this antipathy between county law officers and Territory law officers. Every arrest a Ranger made was a black eye to the sheriff of that locality because he hadn't made the arrest first. Then there was the matter of fees. When a Ranger made an arrest of a hard character, he robbed the sheriff's office of a nice fee. Finally, in the case of Jim Parks, the county seat of Greenlee County was Solomonsville, but Clifton and Morenci had the population to keep voting Sheriff Parks into office, which they did term after term, and Parks knew how to stay on the good side of the leaders among the miners to get their votes.

Some of those that could swing votes were among the men we arrested for looting after Clifton floods.

When things had quieted, County Attorney Rollins and County Sheriff Parks conferred together and decided that past was past and the flood an unusual happenstance, and the looters didn't mean no harm nohow, and that they ought to be freed without prosecution. Most of the looters was loosed pronto and went hightailing it for Metcalf and Morenci where they stowed away in hiding until they were sure it was safe to be public citizens again.

This didn't sit so well with Timberline nor the rest of us Rangers. Timberline jutted out his jaw, spat disgustedly, looked very grim. "Rynning tol' us to clean up this place, an' make it fit so decent people could live in it," he says. "An' that ain't no way to do it. Let those bastards go? Why some of 'em was even holding up people with guns! They orter be executed, not let loose." Timberline was a character. Podgy—set and dogged, when he made up his mind to a thing—he got hold of it like a Gila Monster. That was how he got his name, when he was working for an outfit that had trouble with another outfit and there was a killing; he took to the high timber. When the law tried to arrest him, he said like hell he'd lie up in that Solomonville jail all summer that was so hot you could fry eggs on the floor. He aimed to be cool in the tall timber and if they wanted him they'd have to get him. He hid out in the tall timber all summer, and when fall came he went down and gave himself up, and he and his outfit got acquitted.

We agreed with him, and the four of us went up to Morenci and then to Metcalf and re-arrested as many looters we could find and locked them up again. Timberline went to see Jim Parks and Rollins and demanded that some of the culprits be brought to trial. They agreed except that some of the men, the worst of them, should be let loose. Timberline refused. There the law stood divided, neither willing to budge.

Timberline went straight to the telegraph office and wired Captain Rynning in Douglas: "Send more Rangers here immediately. Place needs cleaning up." In reply to his telegram, Rangers came by rail from all over the Territory—Rangers from Naco, Bisbee, Tombstone, Globe, Douglas. Altogether Timberline had a dozen Rangers to back him at a showdown.

The showdown came in Judge Neff's court a few days later. The Rangers had their rifles stacked in a little adobe room near the court, with one of the boys left to guard them. Led by Timberline, they filed into the courtroom, packing only their six-guns, and sat on the benches around the room. I sat next to Timberline.

After the Rangers got seated, Sheriff Jim Parks led in his deputies, some of them appointed only that morning. As I remember, there was about fifteen deputies on hand, each packing a six-gun. It was mighty quiet after they were seated, and the J.P., Neff, looked over his court suspiciously and not very comfortable.

Timberline stood up. He humped over to the door, turned the key in the lock, and pocketed the key.

"Timberline, what're you doing that for?" Parks hollered.

Timberline says, jutting out his jaw and looking ugly, "I'm doing that so if you bastards start anything you can't get out." Timberline turned and faced the judge. "Now, judge," he says, "I think you better make some disposition of our prisoners that we demand to be handled."

The J.P. cleared his throat, glanced at Sheriff Parks. "It seems there's some other cases to come first." It was a trick of the County Attorney, to hold off prosecuting our prisoners and finally let them go.

Timberline continued to look ugly. "We demand of the court our prisoners be tried."

Another long hush in that court room, with the judge studying, and us Rangers not saying a word and sitting there ready for hell to break loose, and the deputies shifting around itchy and restless, all standing in a group together.

There must have been some kind of nod of agreement between Parks and the County Attorney and the Judge.

Neff nodded to Timberline. "Go ahead," he says. "We'll hear the cases."

"Al Robinson," Timberline called for his prisoner. He turned to us, "All right, boys," he says. "You're dismissed. Go back to your quarters."

That was how the looting troubles of Clifton was settled, and later on, when four hundred miners got ructious, Sheriff Jim Parks was to be mighty grateful to Captain Rynning and the Rangers for saving his hide. As I remember the case, eight of the prominent looters and robbers were convicted, given heavy fines, and imprisoned in the county jail.

CHAPTER XV.

TRAILING HORSE RUSTLERS

NOT A LITTLE PART OF the work of the Rangers was trailing cattle and horse rustlers. Gangs of outlaws drove cattle north and south of the border, conducting quite a profitable business. Up north in the nearly vacant Indian country, there was often trouble. Rangers Lonnie McDonald, Bud Bassett, and Jess Rollins trailed rustlers of a hundred horses near Flagstaff, up through the Indian country, and into the winter snows of Colorado. They came back six months later with the rustled horses and some extras. That's the kind of work the Rangers did, and they put a mighty crimp into rustling of every kind, though of course they couldn't entirely stamp out the rustling of calves in thousands of square miles of open range. Calf rustling is usually harder to detect than any other kind.

One time Rynning called several of us into his office—Oscar Roundtree, Jeff Kidder, and me. "Now, boys," he says, "I got word down here from Fort Apache that rustlers are busy on the Reservation driving off Indian horses. Joe, you know that country well. These boys are slippery devils, but I think you three can catch 'em. And if you find those rustlers, you talk peace right now; you bring 'em back. I don't want any of you going up there to build your reputation as gunmen. I'd rather put one bad man behind bars as an example, than kill a dozen. You know my sentiments." Most of this last was directed at Jeff Kidder, who was a gunman as well as a law man, and in a pinch would shoot first and ask the questions later on, if there was anybody left to answer them.

We three got our pack outfits, saddled up, and headed for the White Mountains into one of the toughest assignments ever given us. Our outfits were light, consisted of bedding and chuck. We had butter and coffee and flour and soda and jerky, plenty of chuck, so we could fry our bacon in a frying pan and cook our hot cakes. That chuck seemed like a luxury before we got back.

It was the middle of February and cold even down in the valleys; we knew how it would be in the mountains. We dressed warm, though, with a heavy woolen jumper under our coats. The Rangers never wore a regular uniform and were known by their badge and reputations—usually wore pants rather than overalls, and stuffed pants into their high-heeled boots, just an ordinary coat, and a Stetson white hat with about a four-inch brim, nothing conspicuous, for you could see men dressed like that all over Arizona.

Our horses were grain fed and in fine condition, and that was good because we were in a mighty hurry to pick up the trail of the rustlers. We rode across the Sulpher Springs Valley, over to the small town of Wilcox, and from there to the Mormon town of Solomnsville, the county seat. Beyond Solomnsville we made for Clifton, where we went straight up the Frisco and the Blue Rivers into the mountains.

It was bitter cold when we reached the mountains, with flurries of snow cutting along behind a hard wind, and the horses' tails sticking out with the wind. The horses braced hard against snow and wind as we pushed them along the trail. We had ridden night and day, only snatching a few hours of sleep for ourselves and mounts. Night riding with no moon and a hard wind biting at you is nobody's circus. You have to know the country and the trail you're following in order to ride it at night, and even then you're liable to get lost off the trail. But we were in a hurry. In only three days we covered two hundred miles of country, some of it through the mountains, in the dead of winter—one of the fastest jaunts ever made by the Rangers.

In the upper stretches of the Blue, we began to stop at the little out-of-the-way ranches to inquire about the rustlers. Most of the ranchers had lost saddle horses lately, but had never seen the outlaws. As it was hard to take a trail out of that mountain country, they figured that the stock had been driven east into New Mexico, but that didn't bother us as we had orders never to bother to look for a territory line when we were trailing a criminal.

We didn't get any real clues until we stopped overnight with Toles Cosper, owner of one of the largest outfits on the Blue. "Boys," he says, "you're welcome visitors." And he hollered at the cook to fix extra portions of supper for us.

While we ate we asked him if he'd been missing any stock. You bet he had. And he told us, "One of my punchers spotted three mean looking *hombres* driving what looked like might be Indian horses. Going east."

"How long ago might that be?" I asked.

He thought a minute. "Two days." Then he adds, "I'll see your horses are took care of. Tomorrow I'll mount you on new horses, the very best I have in the brand. You go after those critters and bring them back."

We thanked him, and I proceeded to ask, "Did this puncher have a notion of what the rustlers looked like?"

"Sure," he said. "There was one tall slim fellow, kind of good looking, brown hair and brown eyes. Dressed expensive. Other two fellers was short and skinny and flat headed and thick lipped, wore their hair long. They looked mean."

Toles Cosper did like he said and loaned us fresh horses that was in A-1 condition. We struck right out across the mountainous country, east toward the New Mexico line, hoping to pick up the trail. It was bad weather, raining and snowing and raining again, and it was bad going through rough-country, criss-crossed by canyons and hills, where often we'd have to turn back to find a better way through. The rustlers had the advantage of us because they knew the trail and must have kept in better ground. The rough places we went they couldn't have driven a bunch of stolen stock.

Near the Arizona-New Mexico line, we struck their sign. We came on an old abandoned pasture which had evidently been used in the last day or two, judging by the freshness of the droppings of the horses. And we found their camp, where they had slaughtered a yearling steer, carcass and entrails remaining, but in addition we spotted where they'd hung up the leftover meat with bailing wire. They had used a quarter and left the other three-quarters hanging. Only gents in a big hurry leave stolen and butchered beef that way.

We were on the trail, and the trail was hot. There's a difference between a hot and a cold trail: A cold trail is much more difficult to follow and is easy lost in various ways, but a good trailer will seldom lose a hot trail unless it goes into the timber or over rocky country. Almost every man of the Arizona Rangers was a good trailer, and some of them the best that the Southwest ever produced. A man has to be born into the idea of trailing, and has to have an instinct for it and know the ways of bad men. If he keeps his eyes on the trail all the time, for example, he's bound to get his head shot off. If he loses the trail, he has to know how to find it again.

There's things any man's sense will tell him. If a rustler steals stock and starts out in a certain direction and in a hurry, which he is, he's likely to keep going that way unless he gets the notion that he's being followed. Signs that a trailer watches for are hoof prints of the animals, boot marks of the rustlers, whether high-heeled or not and what shape, and the droppings of the animals, and the ashes of the fires in the rustlers' camps. By the condition of the ashes and the nature of the droppings a trailer can tell how old the trail is. Contrary to popular opinion, broken branches on trees and bushes don't mean much of anything. I've talked to many Apache Indians about this, and they say too that they don't pay much attention to broken branches. Can't tell much of anything by them broken branches. And the Apache scouts are suppose to be the best trailers in the world. Nor is the use of a stream of water very important in covering a trail. First place, in the desert, there aren't very many live streams, and in the second-place, if you quarter systematically you can pick up the trail somewhere along the banks of that stream.

By quartering I mean cutting back and forth across the desert, after a trail is lost, until it is picked up again in soft dirt. When you're quartering you move crosswise, but at the same time forward too.

A good trailer takes a heap of interest in tracks. How many animals are there? What kind of shoes are they wearing, and are some of the shoes cork-tipped to keep the animals from slipping, like so many of the horseshoes were? He'll even get down and measure the size of the hoof prints with a piece of string. That way if other trails cross the one he's following he'll know he's on the right trail, and he'll know also when he finds the right men and the right stock. And he'll notice if the rustlers are wearing high-heeled or low-heeled shoes.

A trailer knows that a man can travel only just so long in the desert without water, and then he has to make for a watering hole. If the trailer is familiar with the country, he knows the location of the various watering places, and if he heads for the nearest one he's likely to find out that the rustler has been there before him.

But a trailer isn't hunting down a defenseless wild animal. He's hunting for a man with a trigger finger just the same as him, and probably with a greater inclination to use the trigger finger. In other words a trailer has to look out for his own skin, and can't go along with his nose buried to the ground like a man reading a book. He's got to wait till dark to get his water and make his fire so his smoke won't be seen, and like the rustler he builds his fire small, just enough twigs to boil his coffee and broil his meat. And he doesn't go tearing up to every ranch he comes to for chuck and water. As like as not, the rancher may be in cahoots with the outlaw, and anyhow what that rancher hasn't seen won't be told. The trailer even avoids the ranches except when he must have water, and then he doesn't ride up and ask for it unless he's sure who lives there. He waits till after dark and then sneaks up slow and careful. He won't use the wheel and bucket to bring up the water from the well, because the wheel might squeak and give him away. Instead he unties the bucket, fastens it to his catch rope, and lowers it that way, hand over hand.

The rustler is going to try to ambush the trailer if he can, a danger that should always be watched for. When the rustler strikes a rocky ridge or a slope of timber country, he's going to get his horses out of sight and come back to fill the trailer full of lead. But a good trailer goes around that black mesa to right or left and picks up the trail beyond it.

Outlaws have other tricks to fool the law men with. An outlaw who knows his business will usually wait until a heavy rain to rustle stock, and the rain will wash out his tracks, usually before the stock is missed and pursuit started. When a rustler is being trailed hard and badly pressed, he'll head for the timber in any direction, and when he strikes it swing round ten, twenty-five miles, reversing his direction. When a rain comes along, rustlers will swing at right angles off their tracks for many miles, with the rain covering their tracks, and then will head once more in the direction they intend to go. And after they have camped in what they think is an important place and are going on, one of them will dismount and come behind them for a mile or two, flipping a rope back and forth, or some pine brush, erasing the trail. But when an experienced trailer comes on the marks of such sweeping, he knows what's happened and can follow just as well as if the trail was there.

All these points of trailing and what to expect and what to look for a man can't just pick up and learn. He's got to be growed into them from his boyhood and from much experience. Some of my knowledge of cold trailing I picked up in the Indian country when I was a boy, and some I learned while I was a cowpuncher on the M&O, and some when I was a forest ranger. I had a good deal yet to learn from the Apaches when I became stockman and line rider for their Reservation. By the time I was appointed Special Ranger for Apache County, I was regarded, I can say without boasting, as the best cold trailer in that corner of the State, and I was given assignments other men wouldn't take and got a reputation for never returning without my man no matter how long I was in the brush after him. I have been put on a trail as much as three and four weeks cold and managed to follow it.

These three rustlers of Indian horses managed to trick us. Their trail from the highline camp near the border continued east toward the San Francisco River, about twenty miles away. We followed it, and near the Frisco River we spotted a lone horseman. We had got way around to the east of him, and as we'd lost the trail awhile before, we thought we must have overridden the rustlers and that they were behind us.

I put my spyglass on this lone rider. We didn't have field glasses. This spy-glass was the old-fashioned kind, like the ones the English seaman used to use. I've forgotten now where I got hold of it. "That's him, all right," I says to the others, "the tall one." I handed the glass to them, and each took a squint and agreed with me.

"Let's get him," Jeff Kidder said and spurred his horse into a gallop. Roundtree and I followed after him. But about the same time as we saw him, the outlaw spotted us, broke away, and ran his horse back toward Arizona. He had a good horse. We kept him in sight, four, five miles and then we lost him. But his trail was plain. That is, it was plain until he struck the heavy timber. There we lost it for awhile, and lost precious time. When we finally found it, we discovered he had turned east once more to rejoin his buddies. Only then we guessed the trick of leading us back had been played on us deliberate to give his confederates more time to get away with the stolen horses.

Once more we pushed his trail hard eastward, and on the second day we struck again the trail of the stolen horses, which to our surprise headed east a ways, and then all the tracks turned back toward Arizona and the Blue. This just goes to show how much trouble outlaws will go in order to elude officers, and how much of a trick it is sometimes to chase rustlers and bad men. We turned around and a second time headed back toward Arizona, moving fast until the trail became warm, and then we slow-trailed them—stuck very close to the trail and were cautious at any possible place for ambush, keeping our eyes up as well as down.

By this time we had figured out that they were driving about twenty-five head of Apache Indian horses and about eight head of ranch horses, which turned out later to belong to three different ranchers.

About noon that day we came to a little valley where they had stopped and eaten something, building a fire in the open. All signs there told us that they didn't think they were being followed any longer, so we pushed fast and in the afternoon we came in sight of them and Oscar Roundtree hollered at them, "You better surrender, you bastards."

They were about three hundred yards away, so I pulled out my spy-glass to get a better look at them. At that distance they thought it was a rifle, and they pulled into the open and began to cut down on us with their six-shooters. There didn't seem to be a rifle among them. However, they were fair accurate with the six-shooters, making pretty good linear shots but undershooting, and the slugs were hitting rocks and going zip-zoo-o-o-o as they ricocheted, all around us.

I can't quite describe the feeling you get when you're under fire, with bullets whining and cutting close. First you feel kind of shaky and frustrated, and then suddenly you're mad as hell. "Down!" Roundtree yelled. We slid down the backs of our horse with our rifles out as we went down, but even with all our speed the outlaws got in four or five shots apiece before we were ready to fire.

Jeff Kidder was a killer, and looked cool as he threw his rifle down on one of them. But just then I got my sense and poked his gun sideways. He turned toward me, roiling mad.

"They haven't any rifle," I reminded him. "It'd be cold blooded killing. They haven't a chance with six-guns at this distance."

"Why, damn you, Pearce! Them sonsofbitches—"

"I know I'm a cowman and you're a gunman, but Rynning—"

"Sure," said Roundtree. "We'll foller them. I don't give a damn how many shots they fire with them pop guns."

The two of us cooled Jeff Kidder down. By the time we started again, without us ever having fired a shot, the rustlers was well out of sight in that rough country. Again we trailed them, keeping so close that sometimes we spotted a glimpse of them only a quarter of a mile away, and through the spy-glass we could see how hard they drove the stolen horses. Encumbered with all that stock, they couldn't go as fast as us. And they didn't have any chance, with us pressing so close, to turn off somehow and hide their trail.

Back they continued toward Arizona. Near the Blue they abandoned all the stolen stock, figuring that we were cowmen and that we'd be satisfied to leave them be if we recovered the stock. We were more interested in the men, and left the stock to graze where it was while we continued after them.

We reached timber country, where it was snowing and the cold piercing, and then the snow changed to a clammy rain that fell steadily in a drizzle and soaked us through, and the wind blowing through our wet clothes made our teeth chatter. Toward evening, what with the rain covering somewhat their trail and obstructing our vision, and with darkness coming on, we lost them once more.

We found a half tumbled in, deserted cabin, with a leaky roof that plopped drips of water steadily as the rain continued all night. But to us in that forest and wet as we were, it seemed like the best hotel room we'd ever slept in. We built a fire and dried out our clothes, hobbling out our horses, and there we passed the night, mostly smoking and talking and keeping warm and listening to the rain patter on the roof of that little old log cabin and thinking how lucky we was not to be out in the downpour.

"This'll wash out their tracks," Roundtree sighed. "They got away."

I wasn't so sure. "They don't figure we'll be following them, so they won't be so careful. They'll keep their direction, I'll bet."

"Joe's right," Jeff Kidder said. He didn't hold any grudges about my jarring his rifle.

"Maybe," Roundtree said.

Smoking and talking we passed the night, and we were up long before daylight, and had our breakfast eaten, our horses unhobbled and saddled, our packs made up, and were ready to go when the first gray crawled into the sky.

With just enough daylight to see by, we did some quartering, and like I had said picked up what was left of the trail, still continuing almost due west of the Blue. Near sunrise, three or four miles from where we'd spent the night, we came in sight of a little log cabin and could see smoke curling bluish gray out of the chimney. The cabin was in a clear little valley where timber hadn't grown.

"Must be them," I said, and the others thought maybe I was right.

We left our horses in the timber, tied to pine trees, and taking our rifles we crawled on our bellies through the bushes and scrub and tall grass toward the house. We must have traveled near a quarter of a mile that way, and pulled up behind a log where a lone pine tree had once been. Here we got to studying, and talked.

Kidder and Roundtree were all for sneaking up to the house, pushing open the door sudden, and throwing down on them.

But such a procedure didn't make sense to me. When everybody is all excited like, if the outlaw doesn't throw up his hands pronto, a nervous Ranger is likely to pop at him. Or in a panic the outlaw may make a grab for his gun and kill the Ranger. But if everything is calm, the outlaw will likely stay calm and surrender. I've seen it happen that way many times before and since.

"We just stay here," I suggested. "They're bound to come out some time. And the house is in the clear. They can't get away. We'll just wait 'em out."

This didn't make sense to Kidder, but Roundtree agreed, and Kidder was in the minority. We waited, talking in low voices, building cigarettes and smoking them. We didn't have as long to wait as might be. By and by we could hear them talking. Evidently one of them had got up early to make the fire, and now the other two were just getting awake. Sudden like the door opened and two of them came out holding steaming cups of coffee and studying the sky, trying to figure out whether it was going to rain any more or let up.

"Now!" I said. The three of us stood up together with the hammers all full-cocked and our rifles pointing at the two.

Roundtree hollered, "Throw up or we'll cut you in two."

The short one dropped his cup of coffee and reached upward like he was trying to get hold of something up there he couldn't quite put his hands on. The tall one just stood there a moment, getting sight of us, and then hollered back, "Who are you?" Like the other, he packed his six-gun, but he made no grab for it, seeing we had the drop on him.

"We're Arizona Rangers. Throw up and don't ask so many questions."

The moment Roundtree said Rangers, the tall one's hands went into the air. "Now tell your pardner in there to come out with his hands up."

The tall one complied. The arrest was over. They were scared to death, and as we walked down on them the tall one hollers, "For God's sake, don't shoot. We won't make no trouble for you."

"You bet you won't," Jeff Kidder said through his teeth. "You made enough of it already."

While Jeff and I kept our rifles on them, Roundtree turned his rifle down and walked behind them to disarm them. This is something Western movies and books sometimes get mixed up on—the disarming of a man. You'll see in a movie a sheriff walk right up to a man from the front and unbuckle his belt and let his gun fall. That way that bad man can grab him quick, use him as a shield. And his partner can't open up at the bad man because the sheriff is standing between them.

We Rangers had had quite an extensive course of instruction from Rynning on how to handle bad men and when to handle them and how to disarm them. In addition I'd had my own little preliminary course from some of the Hash Knife punchers.

To disarm a man you should step behind him; and you should never pull his gun from the scabbard because that puts the gun closer to a quick grab for it. You should reach around his waist from the rear, unbuckle his belt to let his whole artillery drop at once, and then step quickly back. After this is done, you order your outlaw to step forward from the belt, and then you go along behind him where he can't kick you or make a sudden lunge at you, and pick up his weapons.

After we had disarmed the three outlaws and piled the guns into a little heap, Roundtree searched them from head to foot. He made them pull off their boots, their hats, their shirts, taking a pocket knife away from one.

After a preliminary hearing before Old Judge Bochley (a justice of peace down on the Blue), Roundtree and Jeff Kidder took the three outlaws to Clifton, while I took a couple of ranchers with me and rounded up the stolen horses. I returned those belonging to the three cattlemen, and the others were driven by a cowboy back to the Apache Reservation.

CHAPTER XVI.

BREED OF THE OUTLAW

I NEVER FELT MUCH ABOUT religion until after I'd married and settled down and began to think about the more serious things of life, other than gun matter and trailing and cows. I don't think any of the Rangers knew I was a Mormon, or would have cared if they had known. None of us was strong on church and Sunday school, though when a Sunday and a church was both handy at the same time, we might go inside long enough to deposit fifty cents or a dollar in the collection plate with the thought that if any towns on earth needed a sky pilot and religion, places like Douglas, Clifton, and Globe did. Some of the boys maintained they'd been to church a few times, but if they had it was so long ago they'd forgotten.

My early training did stick with me in some ways, though. At times when I was in real tight places and would have sold my chances of eternity for a glass of beer, I'd find an old song running through my mind for no reason at all. It was one that George H. Goddard, a speaker and singer in the Mormon Church used to sing when he made his annual circuit through Arizona, and it went in my mind just the way he used to sing it with his strong voice when I was a boy: "Who's on the Lord's side? Who? Now is the time to show. We ask it fearlessly. Who's on the Lord's side? Who?"

There was something else from my religion that I remembered and it is probably the reason I am alive today. It was the story I'd heard in church many times, the promise made by the great Brigham Young when he sent Jacob Hamblin out among the Indians as a peace maker. "Jacob Hamblin, I promise you that inasmuch as you will not shed the blood of the Indians called Laymanites, your blood will not be shed by them." It held good. And it held good for me too, and seems to me good sense as well as religion.

I haven't been the bravest law man in Arizona history by a long ways. In fact, I've sometimes questioned to myself whether I was fitted to my kind of work at all. And I haven't made as many arrests as a great many others, and I haven't developed any reputation as a killer. Maybe this last is my only real claim to reputation. All my life I've kept in mind Captain Rynning's instructions—that it was up to us to bring our man back, not to kill him—and the instructions of Brigham Young to Jacob Hamblin. It might seem cowardly to some, but where four Rangers were available for the arrest of a single man, it seems to me not courageous but damn foolish for one Ranger to try the arrest just to get a reputation. I've never hesitated to use fair means or foul to get a man, feeling it was better to outwit him than fight him, because my job wasn't to show how brave I was but to make an arrest. Always I've kept in mind I wanted to keep his skin free of puncture if I could… and more important, my own.

I've had acquaintance with dozens of outlaws, Mexicans and whites. Mostly they're of the same breed and like qualities, and get to be outlaws in gradual stages. A rustler is a man who has graduated in the art of driving off horses and cattle over rugged mountain trails, through deep canyons and heavy timber, and is physically fit for the most extreme kind of hardship, going without water and food when necessary, lying out in rain and snow, riding forty-eight hours at a stretch without sleeping. In most ways he's just a little in advance of the other fellow, even in brains.

After the young rustler—and most of them are mighty young when they start, not much more than boys—has stolen various brands of horses and driven herds of cattle off the range into new country and sold them, he is likely to become an outlaw. Marketing in the early nineteen hundreds wasn't so difficult. The large cow outfits along the border were willing to buy blotched brands because they could get the stock cheap. Same way with cattle along the border marketed in the northern part of the Territory. In some cases, the rustler would drive his stolen goods as far as he could get from where he stole it, sometimes as far as Cheyenne, Wyoming or Colorado, where the brand wouldn't be recognized and he could use a fake bill of sale to prove ownership.

A fellow will turn from rustler to outlaw because he knows he's in bad and can't be any worse off. He's after money now, money any way he can get it, and is not averse to strike at a payroll, a bank roll, or a U.S. mail stage, or even a train.

Outlaws are great ladies' men—no one in their class this way. And they're great gamblers. They take their chance on stealing something for nothing, and likewise on the turn of a card or the flick of a wheel. And, of course, they're heavy drinkers. Even on a job when they come into a town, they'll take time off to drink and gamble and make up with the misses, who usually admire them because they dress well and dance well and seem dashing.

But outlaws and rustlers, when they've been in the business long enough, wear a brand. Rustlers always know rustlers. A couple of bunches come into a town, complete strangers, and in no time at all you'll see them roistering together. How? By the way they walk, talk, dress, act. Everything about them gives them away.

One reason I think I've been a successful law man is being able to recognize rustlers and outlaws, almost at a glance. I have many times seen a man walking straight from me and not seen his face, and yet I could tell he was likely a rustler. Because they was cowboys, they walked bow-legged, wore high-heeled boots. So you couldn't know them by these common articles. But they had gun interest. Always fiddling or touching the handle of their six-gun, or just staring at it. And they walked like an Indian. They kept noticing what went on on both sides of the road, and every once in a while they'd turn around to see what was going on behind them. They had a very slow, deliberate walk, with head hunched on their necks, like something was worrying them, and they seemed uneasy and nervous. In a crowd, they wouldn't let anyone get behind them; they always managed to edge around so they were facing the crowd with their backs to a wall. They didn't talk much, but made good listeners.

Of course the above was the typical hardened outlaw or rustler, and he was usually caught in the end. Another kind, harder to catch, was the calf rustler of wet stuff (nursing calves), who usually owned a little outfit of his own and increased his herd by stealing calves from the big outfits.

* * *

There was a third kind of rustler or outlaw that was more pitiful than the others, the one that got into trouble by accident or circumstance, and was forced to stay an outlaw.

That kind was poor Mal Jowell. I'd known him since he was a kid. He was about twenty-three when he got into trouble, a fine looking fellow, almost handsome, very friendly and affable and popular with the girls, a good cowhand and well liked by everybody.

Montie Slaughter was Mal Jowell's cousin. Old man Pete Slaughter ran several thousand head of cattle on his place on the Black River, and his five sons, of whom Montie was the oldest, rode for his outfit. The Slaughters of Black River were kin to John Slaughter, famous sheriff of Tombstone, who built himself a record as a heavy contributor to Boot Hill Cemetery there. So all the Slaughter boys had hot blood like the one that shot up the dance hall, Christmas, and was fools for trouble. But Mal Jowell came into the trouble very indirect.

One day Montie racked into Springerville, looked up a number of his cowpuncher friends, and they got to playing poker and drinking heavily. Montie quarreled with Sheriff Ed Beeler and got himself killed, shot through the stomach. A coroner's jury acquitted Beeler. The Slaughters were never quite satisfied with the jury's verdict. Mal Jowell came down from Montana where he'd been working, and went to riding for old man Slaughter. He stayed at the ranch mostly, worked hard, said little.

About eight months rolled by. Then word reached Springerville that Ed Beeler had been killed on his ranch twenty-five miles away. He had driven his team and wagon through the gate, got down to close the gate, and was shot three times. Pat Slaughter and Mal Jowell were seen in that locality the day of the killing. It was plenty obvious who had done it.

Pat Slaughter stayed in the country waiting to take his medicine, and nothing was ever done about it. But Mal Jowell vanished. He turned up near Helena, Montana, where a sheriff tried to arrest him for extradition to Arizona and got lead as an answer. A little later Jowell was captured near Lone Tree, Wyoming, charged with the murder of the Montana sheriff.

He was returned to Helena, tried and convicted of the murder, and sentenced to be hanged. Yet on the train taking him to prison, he made another desperate effort to escape. It was successful. He jumped headlong through the train window with the train running forty-five miles an hour. Somehow he worked his way down to the Slaughter ranch on the Black River, secured a fresh mount and chuck, and vanished into the forest.

I knew Jowell well. Before the trouble he had eaten off my table at my ranch in Greer; he'd ridden the range with me, helped to brand my calves and drive cattle to the railroad. Now I was with the Arizona Rangers when the news traveled around my country that Mal Jowell had returned. Any of the Rangers would have given a couple of front teeth for the name of capturing this young Dillinger. But we all knew, likewise, he was a desperate man.

Captain Rynning sent me occasionally up from Douglas into the forest to scout around to see if any wanted men were in hiding there, as the mountains had a reputation for concealing outlaws. It was natural the Captain picked me as he knew how well I was acquainted with that region.

I stopped overnight with Toles Cosper on the Blue River, the same that had helped us out when we trailed the rustlers of Indian horses. He was glad to see me again and shook my hand hearty. Next morning at breakfast he said, "Now, Pearce, it don't sound very good for a feller to tell on a man he himself wouldn't try to catch. But I don't think this boy Jowell is down in Mexico at all. I think he's up near Hannigan's Meadow."

Hannigan's Meadow is a spring and clearing on top of the Blue Range, near where the Coronado Trail now runs. Then no one—except a few hunters in the fall of the year and cowhands in the summer time—went up into this country, unless it was someone on the dodge.

"What makes you think so, Cosper?" I asked. "That Jowell is one *hombre* I'd just as soon not go lookin' for."

Cosper nodded. "I know because I got a camp outfit up at Hannigan, and two punchers with a mount of saddle horses each. This Mal Jowell stays with them nights."

"Stays with them!"

Cosper nodded grimly. "That's right. The boys kind of like him, see. But they're uneasy for fear some officer'll ride up while he's in camp, an' mebbe they'd get killed, and them plumb innocent of anything."

"Why don't you have a try at arresting him?" I asked. Cosper was a deputized sheriff of Greenlee County, but only so he'd be an officer in case of trouble in his own neighborhood.

Toles Cosper grinned. "No, I'm not interested, Pearce. Anyhow I kinda like the damn fellow. So long as he don't bother me, I don't care to go botherin' him."

I thought a while and suggested, "Would you care to go along with me and try our luck?"

Cosper just wouldn't get interested. "Not me. That feller ain't comin' out of there alive."

I hunched my shoulders, shrugged. "I'm not just sure I care to try to handle him alone, but I'll go up there anyhow."

After breakfast I took the trail from the Blue, pushing up the slopes and hogbacks from the valley floor into the cool forest that I knew so well, with the leaves of the aspen and needles of the blue spruce still wet with morning dew. It was dusk when I reached the clearing of Hannigan's Meadow and saw Cosper's outfit there—several of his saddle horses, and two big, fine-looking grays grazing with them that bore strange brands and was sweaty with old dry sweat and saddle marks, telling me they'd been ridden that day. The punchers' tent was the west side of the *ciénega*, and I rode over to it.

The punchers were in camp already, one of them Toles Cosper's son-in-law. They looked me over, invited me to get down and unsaddle and have dinner with them. And their friendliness continued while we ate and talked around the red camp fire, circled by the dark smudges of the ring of pine trees, until I asked them, "I hear Mal Jowell is up in this neighborhood."

They got quiet then and hostile and looked me over closely. Even though I'd put away my Ranger badge, they were suspicious. I laughed. "Him and me are old partners," I said. I went on to tell about how he'd sometimes helped me on my ranch at Greer, and soon I had them believing me.

"He's around, all right," one of them said.

"Coming in tonight?"

The other said no. "Be around tomorrow morning. You better lay up with us, Joe, and then we'll ask if he wants to see you. He figures on riding down to the Slaughter ranch tomorrow."

I stayed the night with those two cowboys, feeling a little nervous in my sleep, not knowing exactly what I would do when the showdown came. Next morning while we ate breakfast, the outlaw came out of the timber carrying a rope in one hand and a rifle in the other. He spotted me right off, turned around, and started back.

But one of the boys hollered at him to wait and went over and told him I was Joe Pearce and wanted to see him. He remembered me, and sent word back it was all right if I'd leave my guns off.

That two-hundred yards to him across the meadow seemed like a mile. When I got close to him and looked at his eyes, I knew he wouldn't fire at me unless I made the first move. What a change in a man! In just a few years he'd turned old, with gray hairs and wrinkles and a hard squint to his eyes. His clothes were torn and almost in rags, his hat brim floppy and shabby and dirty, his boots run over with holes in the toes, hair grown out almost to the shoulders, beard long and scraggly. And he walked loose and swinging instead of the straight even walk he'd had when he was younger. A hunted man! There wasn't any romance to his life the way the books would have it. He lived hard and mean and dirty and was scared to death and wishing only somehow he could get on the good side of the law. But he couldn't.

"Hello, Joe," he says. "How'd you know I was here?"

"I can't tell you that," I said.

"Are you alone?"

"I look it, don't I?"

"Never can tell," he said suspiciously, somehow managing to look all over the clearing (to see if I had any confederates hidden) and yet at the same time to watch me. "We'll walk a piece into the timber," he said. "There we kin talk without interruption."

We went in a ways and sat on a log, him on one end and me on the other, still not trusting me. I've never seen a man so careful. I didn't have a chance to take him. Sitting that way, him uneasy and jumping up and pacing around and then sitting down again, he told me some of the things that had happened to him, and we talked of old times. All the while he held his rifle crotched in his arm.

Finally I saw it wasn't any use to hide my identity longer. "Mal," I says, "I'm an Arizona Ranger now."

His teeth clicked together; his face turned a ripe tomato color. "Why, God damn you dirty sonofabitchin' bastard..."

"Easy," I said. "I didn't come up to arrest you. You're still my friend. But you been seen here by outside people. It won't be long—"

"If I'd known you was a Ranger, I wouldn't 've shook hands with you or let you within a mile of here."

"Mal, you listen. The Rangers will be after you, you stay in Arizona. A half dozen will come up here and trail you down. I wouldn't give a nickel for your chances. They'll capture you or kill you. If I wasn't your friend, I wouldn't tell you this."

"Maybe," he sneered, but just the same growing more friendly.

"The best thing you can do is go back to Montana and stand trial. They'll be easier on you if you give yourself up."

"I can make it down to Mexico."

"Not likely, with all the Rangers after you."

He got gloomy silent. We walked back and had breakfast with the cowboys, and he was glum and silent all through breakfast. While he was saddling up one of his big horses, he hollered to me, "I'll think about your advice, Joe. I'll sleep on it."

"You better take it."

He was saddled and rode off and that was the last I saw of him. But in the end he took my advice. He rode all the way back to Montana and gave himself up, and his sentence was commuted to life imprisonment. Finally he was released and died outside the prison walls.

Mal Jowell was the third kind of outlaw. I've never felt sorrier for any man in my life than I did for Mal Jowell as we sat on that log near Hannigan's Meadow and he told me his sad story.

CHAPTER XVII.

SLEEPERED CALVES

Two jobs took me back to the Tonto Rim Basin and Bloody Basin and the Pleasant Valley where as a boy I'd been whipped by Hash Knife gunmen and promised to come back. Fate took a hand in bringing me back to help clean up the region.

Everybody knows that a calf rustler is a sly *hombre*, and because of the nature of his trade, it is hard to catch him with the goods. Captain Rynning in his books tells how, when suspicious of rustlers one time, he cut small slits in the throats of just-weaned calves, the gullet where the thick folds of skin is, and put in Mexican dimes. Later when the calves had the wrong brand on them, he was able to identify them with the silver pieces and thus apprehend the rustlers. I caught Andy Longfellow much simpler than that—or Carol Wiltbank or Andy Long. These outlaws from Texas had various names, and you could never tell which one was correct. Andy was a cold-blooded, slippery fellow. Later, after I'd had my dealings with him, he got into trouble with his brother over a calf and shot and killed him. That was the kind of man he was.

The Rangers had just finished cleaning up Tombstone of some trouble there, and Captain Rynning sent me to Phoenix. Sometimes us boys went on the train, for we all had passes on every road in Arizona and would sit in the Wells Fargo mail car and chew the fat with the clerks. With me I carried my saddle, bridle, spurs, Winchester, Colt, and blackjack. We had the blackjack for use in saloon brawls when necessary, but never used it on the range.

My first stop was Phoenix. There I went as directed to the office of H. Harrison, then secretary of the Arizona Livestock Board. He says to me, "Pearce, the range up there is pretty dry this year, and cowmen don't want to round up their weak cattle for calf branding. You know what that means."

"Sure," I said. "It means an army of rustlers to get to those calves first."

"There's been complaints," he says. "You know those folk up there, and you know the Bloody Basin and the Tonto Basin country. If you can catch one or two of 'em with the goods, the others'll lay off."

That was one of my jobs. The other was given me by the Governor of the Territory, Colonel Brodie. I went to his office next. He was a big man, and cordial, and offered me a cigar, which was a scarce commodity in those days. "Joe," he says, "it's the same old trouble between cattle and sheep men along the Verdi. There's been a couple of killings already this year. You been a sheep man and know the country. You go in there and make peace with those people. I'll leave it to you to handle it any way you like, but when the sheep move north to the summer ranges, there's likely to be hot guns." The Governor had given me my second job.

On the way up north, I ran into a third job by accident.

I hopped the train from Phoenix to Prescott, stayed there overnight, and next morning took the stage on which I had no pass and had to pay good money for my fare. In Camp Verdi, I bumped into a constable by the name of Frank Smith, and he told me of rustlers going through the country picking up valuable mules, which they would take to the mining towns and sell, where there was always a demand for mules. Frank Smith didn't know quite what course of action to follow. Over a long drink of tonsil varnish, I told him that I was a ranger sent up into the country to catch rustlers of various descriptions.

His face lost some of its worry when I told him that. The Arizona Rangers had already developed quite a reputation. "If you want to fall in and take a hand, I'll go with you and help you trail 'em down," he said.

It was agreed, and he rustled me a horse on which to throw my saddle. We took the trail right down the Verdi River, and succeeded in picking up the tracks where this mule rustler had driven off his most recent bunch, the bunch that Frank Smith had heard about. The rustler had chosen rough country, and it was hard going and a cold, cold trail, but the mules were sharp shod, and we managed to hold to the cold trail.

Smith and I trailed that rustler for three days, laying up at night to let the horses rest. Just at sundown on the third day we located him in a sheep camp where he'd gone because he'd run out of chuck. But there sat four men around the campfire, and it was a question which was sheep herders and which rustlers. (We had figured out that there was two rustlers driving the mules.)

We rode straight up to the camp, after I had previously given Smith directions what to do, for he was green at handling outlaws. I did not want to try an ambush; someone is too liable to get killed in an ambush.

"Get down," one of the men said friendly.

When you hear that greeting, it's always best to get down in a hurry, for to stay on your horse means you haven't come on friendly business. We had ridden up, like I planned, so that stepping down on the left, we had the bulwark of our horses between us and the outlaws and herders. As we swung out of the saddle, we threw down on them.

"Hands up," I said.

We caught them all off guard, and they were easy to disarm. We knew the outlaws from the herders by the fact that the herders had no six-guns. That night Smith sat up and guarded both weapons and the camp, while we put handcuffs around the ankles of the rustlers, and I handcuffed—rather ankle cuffed—myself to one of them. Of all the nights I've slept, that was the worst, the most uncomfortable, with that metal eating into my flesh every time my sleeping partner moved or stirred about.

Next day we took the two rustlers to Camp Verdi, where the J. P. put them under a five-hundred-dollar bond each.

* * *

That little side business attended to, I went on about my main chore, riding to the ranch of John and Pete Latourette, who owned one of the biggest cow outfits along the Verdi. Red-faced John Latourette was mighty glad to see me when I told him who I was, and pumped my hand up and down. "The place is yours," he told me. "What do you aim to do?"

"You think you've lost stock?"

"I know damn well I have."

We talked it over for a time and decided the best way to go about it was for me to hire out to him as a cowhand, so the boys wouldn't get suspicious, and keep my identity hidden until I struck signs of rustling, with the foreman understanding enough of what was up so I'd have freedom to move about the ranch as I pleased. This settled,

John Latourette furnished me a mount of good horses, while I locked up my Winchester and best and put my Colt in my jumper out of sight.

The big bosses of the outfit returned to Phoenix. I went to work as a cowman, doing what all the boys were told to do for a few days, but soon beginning to widen my activities. I scouted back into the Bloody Basin country, named for an Indian fight, and soon extended my activities as far east as the Tonto. All of this was rolling grassy country below the Rim. Then I struck sign, and plenty.

I was miles from the home ranch with a pack horse and outfit, which the foreman had explained away somehow to the boys. I was always keeping sharp sights for anything not natural, using my spy-glass some, and through the glass, I spotted a mounted man driving a calf ahead of him, and the calf was on a rope! That in itself was very suspicious, but not proof or anything.

At a long distance, maybe a mile, I followed him, keeping track of him through the spy-glass, and yet I was far enough away so he was not likely to see me. Suddenly he vanished out of sight entirely. We were in fairly rough country, and I took it for granted he had dropped down into some kind of wash or canyon. I jabbed spurs and loped along until I came to the place where he had disappeared.

Here a neat little valley opened down below me, a pretty pasture with green grass at the bottom and rim rock forming a natural fence almost around the top. Where the rim rock was not sufficiently steep, the rustler had built in roughly a fence of natural timber posts and wire. Leading into this perfect hideout was a lop-sided gate tied with rawhide and now closed. The rustler had vanished.

But the pasture below was spotted with a large batch of calves, maybe thirty or forty. I untied the rawhide fastening and rode down the trail to the bottom of the valley and went here and there among the stock, examining brands and condition of the calves.

Some of it was wet stuff—that is, calves in the process of being weaned from their mothers, while doggies is the big calves that have already been weaned. And there were some doggies here too. Some of the stuff was fresh branded and peeled, showing it had been done recently. Some bore no brands at all; some showed skinned legs where they'd been hobbled on one side so that they couldn't keep up with their mamas, and that way weaned on the range and then stolen.

Every Ranger carried a brand book for just such a contingency, a record of all the rightful brands of cattlemen and sheepmen in the Arizona Territory. I pulled out the brand book from my outfit and checked on the fresh-looking brands on the stuff here. Part of them was shown by the book as belonging to the gent named Andy Longfellow, the name of my suspected calf rustler. Others had been sleepered, that is, branded with a brand not of record in the Territory of Arizona. This kind of brand was also sometimes called a "slow brand."

I was fully satisfied in my own mind that this stock had been rustled, yet my case might not hold in a court of law, which is very particular on proof, and I had no absolute proof. This just illustrates the difficulty of apprehending a thief of calves not already previously branded. All the signs were there, yet who was to say that Andy Longfellow had not been branding his own calves, and he had a right to put any kind of brand he wanted onto his own property.

All the way to Pleasant Valley where I would find the nearest J.P., I cogitated this problem. And it was only toward the end of that thirty miles of riding that something entered my *cabeza* which should have been there all along. Some of that stuff was mighty "wet!" Maybe... maybe...

Bob Samuels, the J.P. in Pleasant Valley, heard my story and sent an old livestock inspector, G.O. Scott and my brother-in-law George Stubbard, back with me to drive the stock to Youngtown, while meanwhile word was sent about to the ranches in the neighborhood of what was in the wind and would they round up their cattle that were in that section and drive them over to Youngtown.

By the time we had driven the calves to Youngtown and thrown them into a corral, quite a few of the stockmen had gathered there to inspect the stolen stock, and a round-up was already in progress. The steers, so far as was possible, were left on the range. We were interested only in cows, and especially in cows that had lost calves.

When we drove the calves into the corral, you could hear remarks going all around. "I think that one's mine: she's got the signs," and, "There's one of mine—I bet a dollar," and so on. It may seem hard to believe that cattlemen can recognize their own stock, but it is so. If they have only a small outfit, they get to know individuals in it, even calves, just like you can recognize humans. Usually they can tell by the flesh marks—some white, some spotted with white feet, some red and white in a certain pattern.

For the larger outfit, there's another way of identifying. Each different outfit is usually building up a different strain of cattle—in those days some sort of mixture of the Chihuahua type of Mexican cattle, and some would have red Durham bulls and some the Herefords. An old narrow-headed bull that was fathering a herd would usually have narrow-headed calves. And there were other peculiarities of different strains such as the shape of the horns and the shape of the ears. A man could usually recognize a head from his particular stock. But again, even this recognition is no proof in a court of law. There's only the brand as the real mark of ownership; a blotched brand is a pretty sure proof of theft.

But there was something else too. A calf that isn't quite weaned is going to find his mama, and he isn't going to make up to any other little critter's mama. He knows his own feed bag no matter what brand he wears. That was my plan. When we had all those cows from the different outfits off the range being held there at Youngtown outside the timber corral, we turned them calves loose among the cattle. The bawling calves that were still "wet" went straight for their mamas—five of them. And this was sure—incontrovertible proof of the theft of the new brand on that calf and the brand on the mama didn't match. Of course, in this case they didn't.

I now had proof of theft and knew what name the thief went under and had seen him at a distance. But the thief was still at large. The J.P. drew up a warrant for arrest in the name of Andy Longfellow and put it into my hands.

With a rest overnight, I tied chuck on behind my saddle, enough for several days—jerky, coffee, bread, salt—all rolled into a blanket, and I returned to the little rock-rimmed valley to try to pick up the trail.

It led north. It took me upward toward the Tonto Rim, through badly broken up, rocky country and heavy timber so that much of the time the trail was hidden by dead pine needles. It was a hard trail to follow, and a slow trail that I lost often and had to quarter often to pick up. Evidently after his last foray onto the ranges of his neighbors for unbranded calves, Andy Longfellow had decided to lay up in the high timber until things had quieted and it was safe to drive off the stolen stuff.

I guess I was on that trail two or three days. One morning about nine o'clock, deep under the shadows of the great Tonto Rim, I spotted smoke. I knew I was near my man and went along carefully so as not to be taken by surprise. By and by I came in sight of his camp. He was stooped over the fire, snaking a frying pan with some bacon in it, and evidently didn't have much worry about being followed, for his rifle was leaned up against a tree about ten or fifteen feet off. I packed a six-gun, however.

It was obvious he didn't know who I was and had no idea he was being followed, so I decided on what might seem to be the boldest and most dangerous course to follow, but what is really the safest. I rode straight up to him peaceful like, not making any move to throw down a gun on him.

He reckoned I was just a wandering cowpoke. "Get down," he says.

I got down. "Sure," I said. "Cookin' breakfast. Smells damn good."

"Have some," he invited, glancing up at me and then looking at his bacon, which was turning brown and shrinking up in the fry pan.

"Don't mind if I do," I says. "You Andy Longfellow?"

At that he jerked up, setting his frying pan on the ground. At the same time I was showing him the star of the Arizona Rangers. A badge is sometimes a lot more effective than a gun. First, the outlaws had respect for the Rangers and their shooting. But even more, a man hates trouble with the law. He might kill another cattleman and convince a jury it was self defense, but an officer is always in the right, so that shooting an officer can lead to only one thing if he is caught—hanging. "I've got a warrant for your arrest on a charge of cattle rustling," I told him quietly. "You better be careful and not make any blunders with shooting irons."

"I'll go with you," he said.

"You don't have to put up your hands. Just stand there quiet and I'll walk over to you and take your guns." All this time I had not drawn my six-gun. I walked over to him, and breaking the usual rule because this was a different case, pulled his gun out of its scabbard. Then I walked over to the tree and threw the cartridges out of his Winchester, putting the empty gun back into his saddle scabbard.

"Now that's done," I says, "I'm hungry." Outlaw and law man sat down before that campfire and ate a breakfast of cakes and bacon together, and talked of all the various things that cowmen talk about, mostly whether the range was improving and how much rain could be expected this month or July.

That day and next we rode back toward Youngtown, and both of us slept peaceful that night, but me with the guns and his word he wouldn't try a break for it. I returned him to Youngtown where he was given a hearing and placed under bond.

CHAPTER XVIII.

SHEEP ON THE MOVE

Spring was breaking now, and the sheep were on the move, thousands upon thousands of wooly-looking gray sheep plodding steadily northward, from the lower mesas where they had wintered to the mountainous ranges of summer grass. Up along the Verdi River, which flows into the Salt, they moved northward out of Bloody Basin and Tonto Basin, bound for the timber country of Pine Flat above the Rim. Thousands upon thousands of sheep passing each day, and each herd cutting a wide swath out of the thin and drying range grasses. This was almost the exact center of the Territory of Arizona where they moved.

Sheep on the move and cattlemen worried. By this time, the spring of 1905, the range had been pretty well divided between sheep and cattle, and sheep men stayed in sheep territory and cattle men stayed in cattle territory. But when the sheep moved northward in semi-annual migration, they were bound to cross here and there sections that belonged to cattlemen. Trouble again. Not as bad a trouble as in my youth, but the same kind of trouble with the same reason... sheep and cattle trouble and gun trouble.

This year was especially bad because of the drouth and the dry condition of the range grass. Sheep go along slowly, edging through a range because they can't be hurried, destroying the grass, swath after swath, until there is nothing left for the skinny cattle in a drouth year.

The Latourette ranch headquarters stood near a ford of the Verde River, deep in the great canyon that swings north-westward, a fifteen-hundred-foot canyon, wide here, and the flat mesas high above the river bed. Latourette cattle grazed the high mesas behind the ranch on the eastern side of the Verde. Up the western side, the sheep were coming, grazing and plodding along under dozens of herders. And near the Latourette ranch, they would be driven down to the river for water; and they would cross to graze up the east side if they were allowed because grass on the eastern mesas was in better condition than on the western—grama and alfilera grass. The Latourette cowboys would save that grass for their cattle, I knew, even behind the whining of slugs.

It was time for me to return to the Verde and be where the trouble was likeliest to break: the ford at the Latourette ranch. There I was when a cowboy racked in and hollered that he'd spotted sheep south making this way, and everybody was certain they'd be brought down to water. It was Newman sheep, from Phoenix-way, on the move northward, three-thousand head of sheep.

"We'll give 'em a warm reception," said one cowboy.

The others agreed. The foreman agreed. No sheep would cross the Latourette ranges this spring. They strapped on gun belts, and oiled their Winchesters. When the first of the sheep reached the shallow Verde River and put their noses into the cool water, the cowboys of the Latourette outfit were lined up on the other side, squatted on the bank like a row of roosting turkeys, determined that no sheep would cross the Verde.

I hadn't said much up till then. There wasn't much I could say. The boys had a right to defend what was theirs. But only a few days ago, up the Verde, a cattleman by the name of Gene Packard had been killed by sheep men and his body thrown into a mess of cacti.

When the sheep began to come, I said, "It's plain you don't want the sheep to cross."

Some of them laughed; some just grunted.

"I've got orders from the Governor there's to be no bloodshed. But I understand your position fully, having once been a cattleman myself, and I still have a few head up at Greer. But the Governor wants peace. Let's stack the guns here and leave me handle this."

The foreman of that outfit was a rawboned Texan who believed that right of force was a lot louder talker than the right of law or ownership. "Like hell we will."

"All right," I said. "I'll go over and see what the foreman of this sheep outfit has to say."

The foreman was a nice fellow, a white man, and listened to my talk, and cocked back his frayed hat and looked across at the menacing cowhands of the Latourette outfit. "It ain't necessary to cross here," he agreed. "We'll drive back to the mesa and go up the west bank."

"Way back." I had already shown him my badge and my letter from Governor Brodie.

"Way back," he agreed. "We don't want no trouble. We can make it all right."

But it wasn't just a single herd of sheep; it was herd after herd, day after day, all poking along northward, making different trails to get new grass, for the sheep cut it low like a lawnmower had been run over acres of ground. Sheep on the move.

Next day it was ten thousand head owned by the A. and B. Schuster Company of St. Johns and Holbrook. Ten thousand head bouncing and walking and thumping down the long trail from the rim to the river for a drink of that precious water. The cowboys were lined up waiting for them, just like the day before. The cowboys just sat there waiting, with their guns showing conspicuously, and not saying anything, but really saying a good deal more than if they'd been shouting.

Down came the sheep. Once more I proposed that they stack up their arms and let me handle the situation, as was my duty, but they still didn't have the confidence in me. Once more I waded across the shallow Verde, sploshing along in my boots, to have a palaver with the Mexican foreman. He read the letter and listened to my talk, and agreed to keep to the west side of the Verde on his way northward.

The third day a great herd swung down toward the river, six or seven thousand head of bawling sheep belonging to Harry Scorse. There sat the cowboys waiting, and hopping and ambling along down the trail came the sheep. Suddenly I got mad—those punchers and their guns. For two days I'd turned the sheep back, and through no help of theirs. I've seldom been mad in my life, but that time I was.

"Lay your guns down," I said, and I put in a few cuss words to make it emphatic. "There's no need for 'em."

The boys just looked at me, some of them sneering.

I went down the row of them, and one after another, I kicked or knocked the six-shooters out of their hands. After I'd done three that way, the rest got up and moved out of my way, not caring to open up on an Arizona Ranger.

"You get on back to the ranch," I says, "and leave this to me. Next time any of you come down here I'll throw your guns in the river. The time to come down here is when I don't do like I say."

Those boys went disagreeable back to the ranch, and I crossed the river and once more made arrangements, this time with Harry Scorse's foreman that his sheep should keep to the west bank. Other herds came, and I turned them off, and they went just as willingly when I showed them my badge and my letter as they had with a whole row of armed cowboys on the other side of the Verde to bar their way.

Sheep on the move northward—today in the spring they are still on the move, not quite so many, but plenty of grazing sheep on their way northward to the high timbered ranges. There's no shooting any more and little disagreement, and the little of it that happens is settled peacefully in the courts of law. Sheep and cattle trouble was on the way out in 1905, and I think I did my small share there on the Verde to help to put a final end to it.

CHAPTER XIX.

SQUAW KIDNAPPING

Soon after I reached the Apache Indian Reservation, a lot of funny things happened: my meeting Loco Jim again, and then bumping into one I regarded as the son of the Apache Kid (though I never had the proof), and finally a squaw being kidnaped.

It was almost like going home, that appointment on the Reservation. My full title was United States Line Rider To Patrol the White Mountain Indian Reservation. I had several friends on the Reservation who had some influence and who secured the appointment for me, and I was grateful for several reasons.

Gun matter wasn't as strong in my head as it had been. After all, I was nearing thirty-three years old, and by that age the fascination of a gun is waning, and the pleasure too of long days and nights of hard riding in rough country, if that can be called a pleasure, and of arresting outlaws and bringing them to justice.

As a Line Rider, I wouldn't be on the move quite so much around the Territory; at least I'd be near my own country and in striking distance of Springerville, where a certain Minnie Lund was working as a cook for rich cattle folk. That was my second reason. This Minnie Lund was growing up, and not the same girl that had made fun of me in Nutrioso when I was courting the school miss there. I didn't think this was a strong reason, as my interest hadn't seemed to reach that stage as yet, but I know now it was the strongest of my three reasons for quitting the Rangers in 1906 before they had been disbanded by executive order, their job done.

At that time my third reason seemed the most important. During the time I was a forest ranger, I had fallen in love with a certain part of the forest deep in the mountains, a place overgrown with thick grass and with adequate springs of cool mountain water, and I had taken up the land and started to run cattle on it with my own brand, at first a "JP" and then a "P" on the left hip. My cows were mixed Hereford and

Chihuahuas, with a couple of not too good bulls, for fine bulls were hard to get. They cost sixty dollars and shipped from Springer, New Mexico, or even as far away as the Denver country.

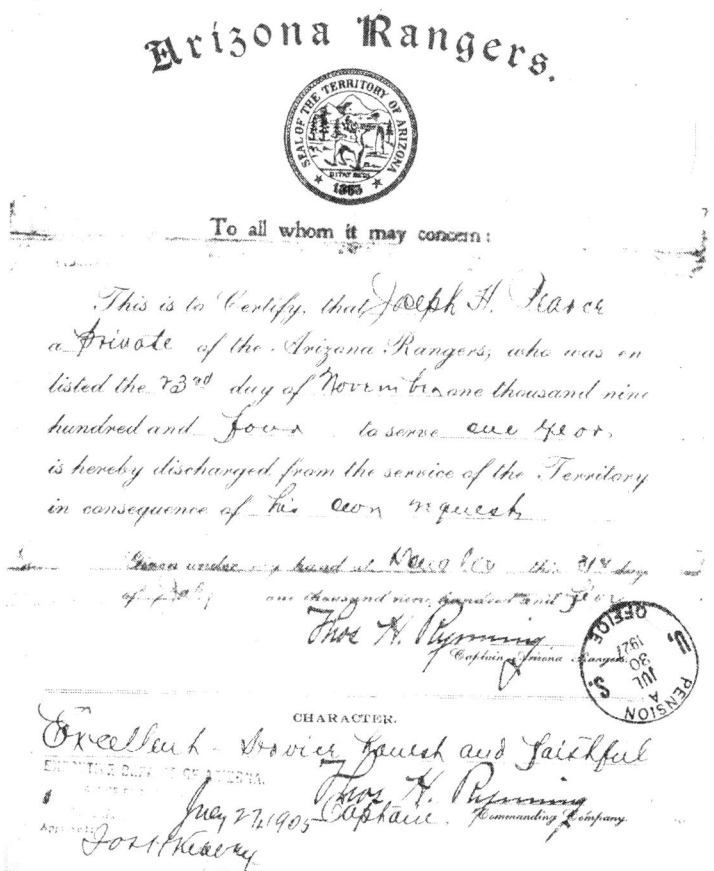

That was in 1902. By the time I left the forest service to join the Ranger company, I was running my cattle in an association, like the cowmen often did. There were seven of us running our cattle together and taking turns at looking after the cows, except at round-up time.

Usually when it came my turn, I had to hire a cowhand to take my place. However, round-up time I tried to be on deck. From 1901 to 1906, I was running between a hundred and two hundred head and marketing a few head every year.

The timber country had one disadvantage for running cattle, and it wasn't lack of water or feed, which is the disadvantage of many ranges in Arizona. It was the cold. The spring of 1905, the snow fell a foot deep at Springerville on the level and far below the altitude of the forest, where many feet fell and stayed on the ground covering up any possible food. The cattle died by the hundreds from both starvation and cold, and I lost almost half my brand. The Reservation job would keep me closer to my cattle at Greer where I could look after them.

My job as line rider for the White Mountain Reservation covered a good many duties, with a number of Apache scouts or native police to serve under me. In 1906, ranchers were making young fortunes out of grazing their herds on the reservation lands, which included some of the best range in the Territory. Most of the reservation was in high country of oak and some into the pines, with many fine grasses and, best of all, the brouse, or oak brush, the best cattle feed in the world. Many large outfits like the Chiricahua and the Double Circle bordered on the reservation lands and certainly wasn't especially particular if their cattle roamed over the boundary of the reservation and fattened on reservation forage.

The government concluded to collect a dollar a head for every cow using reservation lands and turn the money over to the Indians. I was to collect this fee. In addition, wild horses roamed the reservation, of no use to anybody, and I was to do something about cleaning them out, and also attending to the purchase of cattle for the Indians to take the place of the useless horses. Finally, though incidentally, I was to be a kind of police for the reservation grazing lands, where there had been many disputes and some gun play. Just before my appointment, for example, Henry Barrett and Prime Colman had had a large argument, ending in gun play, on their rights of grazing on reservation lands. Barrett was hit in the stomach with a rifle bullet. Colman was shot in both legs. Barrett, dying, had clubbed Colman over the head with his rifle saying, "Well, I guess that finishes the sonofabitch, but he's got me." Barrett died. Colman recovered.

Such things didn't look very well for the Agency, and I was to see that they didn't happen.

* * *

Directly the appointment was wired from Washington, I resigned from the Rangers by letter, telling Captain Rynning I'd toted a gun a long time and it was getting too heavy. Then I rode over to Fort Apache. Today Fort Apache is quite a town, with graded streets and wooden houses, service stations, and even a barber shop, with more recently painted in front of the word *Barber*, a *Beauty &*. Such is progress. The Indians go tearing around the narrow dirt roads of their reservation in their old jalopies at top speed. If there's anything worse than a drunk Mexican driver of an automobile, it's a sober Apache Indian driver. He don't give a damn about you. It's every man for himself and you get out of the way or...

But in 1906 the Apaches was just beginning to be civilized. Fort Apache consisted of a main office building and the rows or barracks for the Negro and white soldiers, blacksmith shops, stables and corrals, and quartermaster's building—all thin wooden buildings painted white. The Apaches at the fort lived in the hogans of wooden poles, brush, and sometimes skins, which were scattered here and there in camps on the tops of the grassy knolls and mesas, usually a wagon drawn up close and the horses grazing not far away, hobbled, of course.

Not all the Apaches lived at the fort. They came and went, and they moved about the miles and miles of reservation as the mood took them. But it was understood that certain parts belonged to certain tribes or families. At certain intervals the Indians would visit the fort to get their rations. To the government, the Indians were known by number, like A 13, D 3, and so on. Permanent at the fort was the Indian police and their families (the police numbered twenty-five or thirty). And when I came, a school had just been built and there was talk of educating the red-skin, but it didn't at that time go much further than talk.

I put my outfit on a pack horse, saddled up, and rode from Springerville, where I had been staying, down to Fort Apache, where I introduced myself to the Chief Indian Agent, C. W. Crouse, a nice young fellow and very anxious to cooperate with me. He told me that he was going to put three of his best men directly under me as a kind of bodyguard, while I could call on the police at any time. My duties were to be what was necessary. Then he led in Pinal and Kataga and said to them, "This man is your boss." Next he sent out his interpreter and in a few minutes Loco Jim entered the door.

I recognized him right off. He had changed a good deal since I had last seen him as a boy, tall and lean and strong. He was old now with some gray hairs and a slight stoop to his shoulders, but his face was still young and his expression alert. When he spoke, I remembered his voice, even after the lapse of many years.

With the Indians gathered around, I stood up in the center of the circle and talked, and an interpreter translated what I said into Apache. I'd learned from Father, and some from scouts Sieber and Horn, that if you want to make a good impression on Indians, you should never talk sitting down. And you should talk slow and dignified, just as slow as you can and hold your subject. And if you smoke, you should smoke very slowly, letting the smoke out of your mouth as slowly as it will move.

We smoked now, and I talked. Because Loco Jim could talk only a little English and I only a little Apache, I said to the interpreter, "Ask Loco Jim if he remembers the time he hit a man with a rock. Then he ran away and came to a sheep camp, and there a boy fed him and gave him a bed to sleep on."

Loco Jim studied awhile, saying, "M-m-m," to bring back the memory. I stood there smoking as slowly as I could, and he raised his head and looked flat at me, still studying. He walked over close and says in English, "You him." I could see his eyes light up with recognition. Suddenly he threw his arms around me. When an Indian gives a man a hug that way, it means something.

He said through the interpreter, "We were friends when you were a boy. We are still friends." And we stayed the best of friends to the end of his life. He was the bravest and finest Indian I've ever known. Where his grave is, on a mound two miles north of Whiteriver and near the highway, I would like to see a marker put. There he lies buried between his two faithful wives, and the grave unmarked and the mounds being leveled off by weathering, and soon all trace of the spot will be gone.

If for nothing else, his memory should be rewarded some way for his loyalty at the Battle of Cibecue. When most of the scouts, at a signal, turned on Captain Hartig and his command to massacre them, Loco Jim was one of the few that remained loyal and fought against his own people, just to teach them, he said, that they must learn to be at peace with the United States.

* * *

Only the best of poker players got into the game with the first sergeants of the troops. I could hold my own with them. But I wasn't near the slicker that Antonio Apache was, for he handled cards like an expert, talked English like a college graduate, and hinted that he played in games in Chicago when neither Hoyle nor money could win. I told him that at poker he was one of the seven wonders of the world. He never seemed to cheat, but just knew the game.

I got to know Antonio Apache pretty well. He came from no one knew where, and hung about the Agency a good deal of the time, or drifted down to Globe and back again, and seemed to have plenty of money. Often he came to my little wooden house to eat and sleep, and he talked so educated that I suggested he'd been to college. "Sure, I have," he said, but that was all. I couldn't get much out of him.

At the time he was courting one of Chief Alchesay's daughters in Apache style. Chief Alchesay had some of the best land on the reservation, and Antonio Apache told me, "I'm going to marry her and get myself a nice piece of land and settle down. I've been around enough." Ruth Alchesay had been married once, and her husband had died, which made her less desirable to most Apache braves as a wife. In addition, she had been thrown from a horse, broken her leg, and ever since walked a little lame which also was a set-back to marrying an ordinary Indian. But Antonio Apache wasn't an ordinary Indian. He wanted a piece of land and a grab at old Alchesay's wealth when the chief died.

He wooed and won Ruth Alchesay and married her Apache style, and then they were remarried by the Indian Agent in American style, because the Government had begun insisting on such ceremonies. He went to live at her hogan; but he was still around the Agency a great deal, looking for poker excitement and conversation with white men.

One day I was riding south of the fort over the grassy rolling slopes, scrub oak country, and I came upon Antonio Apache holding his horse some fifty yards from an Apache family camp of two hogans, and two women cooking over the open fire. I looked to see what caught his fancy, but didn't see anything special to gawk at.

"Hello," he says, and kept on looking. Then I figured out he was staring at the young Indian woman, dressed the same way all the Indian women dressed, a red skirt just like a curtain with five to ten yards of cloth in it, gathered in at the waist and ruffled, hair twisted around like a piece of rope, and loaded down with jewelry, silver bracelets and rings like the Navajo jewelry, and weighted down with a heavy string of turquoise beads around her neck.

This young Apache miss was good looking and no question, with smooth brown skin, a little lighter than the ordinary.

"Come on," I says. "You already got one wife."

Antonio Apache grinned. "It's not impossible to have another. The only trouble is, Joe, she's married."

"How do you know?"

"I can tell by the way her hair is fixed."

He sighed and wheeled his horse away, riding back toward the fort and me riding on about my business.

I had long suspected Antonio Apache might be the son of Apache Kid. I don't know exactly why I had this hunch—it just struck me that way. So I tactfully led up to asking Antonio this highly intimate and personal question by talking a good deal about the Kid, telling how I had seen him, and saying that he wasn't near as bad as he'd been painted.

He spent a night with me, and next morning I decided was a good time to spring the question. "Tell me who you really are," I suggested.

He grinned and shook his head. There he sat with his back to me drinking coffee.

"Well, I'm going to make a guess as to who you are. I know you're an Apache by your face and by the fact you can talk the lingo."

"It'll be all right," he says, "just so you keep on thinking it, and not saying it."

"You're a son of Apache Kid."

There was a long silence. At last he broke into the silence: "Let's have another cup of coffee," he proposed. He never denied he was Apache Kid's son, and I'm confident today that was his identity.

Not long after this conversation, word was brought to the fort that an Indian woman had been apparently kidnaped from her hogan, for she had been missing two days. I discovered the missing Indian woman was the one that Antonio Apache had been staring at so steadily. And what worried me still more: Antonio Apache, son of the most famous of kidnappers.

CHAPTER XX.

COLD TRAILING A KIDNAPPER

One often hears or reads in history about the fame of Apache trailers. This kidnapping furnished a good example of how efficient they could follow a trail. When we arrived at the hogan of the young Indian women, the native police were already there making an investigation. They had already discovered that her best dresses, shoes, saddle horse, and her jewelry were still at home, and so had concluded that she had not ridden off herself, but must have been taken by force.

My three Indian stockmen and scouts, Wyatt Katagie, Frank Pinal, and Loco Jim were the best trailers, and took the lead in the actual trailing. They and a couple of others dismounted and started to trail the woman on foot, while the rest of us followed on horseback, leading the Indian's horses by their bridles.

The trail was hard to follow, and sometimes the scouts got almost down on their bellies trying to see a little mark that the woman had made. This way we went slowly down the sloping land until we reached the Whiteriver, and here the scouts explained she had crossed the river from rock to rock. On the other side was a willow thicket, and near this thicket my Indians discovered in the soft dirt a perfect footprint.

That was an important discovery. Carefully the Indians measured that footprint from heel to toe, and across the heel and across the toe.

"New shoe," said Loco Jim.

"How you know that?" I asks.

Frank Pinal, who was younger and could speak better English explained, pointing to the track, "Not worn on the outside. Old shoe show wear. Not so deep as inside."

Here at the river we made other discoveries. The scouts found the place where she had been cutting willows, neatly laying them in a pile to be used later in weaving baskets after they had been skinned and soaked. Here Wyatt Katagie picked up a black-handled butcher knife with which the woman had been cutting the willows. All three of them searched about until they located also the print of a horse's hoof, steel shod.

Again the Indians took careful measurements on different sticks and marked each with some kind of symbol so that they had a perfect notebook record even though they couldn't write. They measured width and length, distance between the shoes and the heel at its outside, and the width of the plate. I've never seen such care and particularness as they used. They even got the stride of the horse and could tell whether the horse was a walker or a pacer and could almost describe the horse as if he were standing before them.

Now they showed me the bootmark of a man, and showed me that the sole had been sewed on because it was worn enough to show the thread marks. They measured the mark also, even taking the measurement between the thread mark and the outside of the sole.

"Big fight here," said Loco Jim. Bushes had been trod down and the footmarks of the woman and the man were mixed in a scramble.

Frank Pinal pointed up the slope. "He take her on horse after big fight." It was likely he had put her up in front of him and held her powerless while he rode away. Where the horse had passed through some bushes growing close together, the trailers stopped and studied those bushes carefully, and finally Loco Jim pounced on three or four hairs and showed them to the rest.

"Sorrel horse," said Frank Pinal.

Carefully they put the hairs into an empty sack which had once held Bull Durham tobacco. And now they went faster along the trail. It led upward from the river toward the south, through a rough, rocky country, vegetated with cedar, piñon, and juniper trees and thick-matted with underbrush. This is the worst kind of country to trail in. But the Indian scouts were equal to it.

Frank Pinal and Loco Jim took the lead on foot, followed by four others on foot. The rear four spread out so that they would find any signs that might not be on the direct trail. Frank called, "They fight a lot here." I was still mounted and, looking down, I saw at what he pointed: the tracks showed that the horse had been reined from one side to the other, like the man was jerking the reins here and there, busily occupied with something else. Often they called out that here a fox and at another place a coyote had crossed the trail. They missed nothing. They reported that here the woman had been holding back, but the man had her hand tight and was pulling her by force along the ground. Earlier they had pointed out that she had jumped down and the man had jumped down after her and chased her and brought her back. A little later he had got her somehow on the horse again, and once more they were riding.

I have seen veteran trailers from the Pan Handle at work, and the best trailers in the Ranger company, which was supposed to have the most skilled in the Southwest, and none was ever in the class with those Apache Indian scouts. They knew almost everything about the man's doings and could describe his horse as though it was standing before them.

It was growing late, the sun deep down in the west. The scouts went faster and talked their lingo about how worried they were for the woman, and as they went along, they reminded each other of stories of the Apache Kid and his doings. This had been the first kidnapping since his hey-day, but if he still lived, he'd be altogether too old to be responsible. Naturally what I gathered from their talk put me in mind of a certain Antonio Apache, who might or might not have the same propensities as his father. And it worried me some. I started twice to tell them of my guess that Antonio was the son of Apache Kid, and twice I shut my mouth tight. After all, I had no proof he was. And his disappearance at the same time as the Indian woman didn't prove him guilty. But it looked bad, mighty bad.

The trail led into rougher country westward. Two more trailers joined the leading pair, and we moved faster up the tall slopes. Evidently the kidnapper was headed into even rougher country, and country also where he was likely to find water.

The leading trailers stopped, pointed, grunted, talked. Here had been a real fight, the ground all torn up. Maybe the woman fighting for her life; it looked that way.

"She say she won't go. Bad. Very bad," said Frank Pinal. "Maybe we find her quick."

He was right. On a few yards, lying behind a nipple of rock protruding from the earth, the body of the woman lay. She was a nasty sight. Her dress was torn to shreds. Mats of hair, clotted with dirt and blood, lay here and there on the ground. Evidently her assailant had hold of her by the hair. And her skull was battered in.

The Indians sent a messenger back to the Agency to report what had been found and to leave directions that neither Indians nor whites be allowed to come into this locality because they might obliterate the trail. The woman's husband and family and friends were to be allowed to come with a stretcher to carry back the body.

Night had come down. It was too late to trail farther. We hobbled our horses and built a small Indian fire to cook our supper on, just enough wood to do the cooking and no more. And the Indians stretched out, eating and talking, and some of them lying upon the ground and groaning and even beating the ground with their fists, their anger was so great. If right then we could have laid hands upon the kidnapper, there would have been no cost of trial.

The talk rambled on, mostly in Apache, but some in Spanish, which the older Indians could talk better than English, and usually used when they were conversing with me. Talk was still of Apache Kid and speculation as to whether his ghost might not have returned and done this thing. But they were sure he hadn't. Apache Kid wouldn't have bashed in a woman's skull, even though an uncivilized savage according to most folks' estimate.

By and by some of the Indians walked out onto the top of a pine-covered knoll and built a big fire. I asked Loco Jim in Spanish what it was for, and he told me it was to ward off the evil spirits from this place, that evil spirits hate light of any kind, and never go around in daylight.

There was little sleeping that night. We sat and talked or dozed, waiting impatiently for the morning star so we could take up the trail of the killer. The country was dreary and a wind played spooky sounds and the fire shot out sparks, then died down. More wood was put on. That way the night passed. And eating in my mind all the time was the thought of Antonio Apache.

Finally I took Loco Jim into my confidence. I told him what I knew and what I suspected about Antonio Apache. He was silent awhile, forehead wrinkled as he thought, and then he shook his head. I was a little disappointed in a way, even though I liked Antonio, but Loco Jim exploded my theory entirely.

He explained that he thought this the work of a white man. An Indian would never kill a woman that way with a rock. He'd put a knife in her. The horse was iron shod, and by the nail marks, it had been done by one of the blacksmiths of the fort, and Antonio had ridden unshod horses. And he didn't think an Apache woman would have put up such a fight, leading to her death, if it had been an Apache that had kidnapped her and not a white man.

Next morning four of the woman's family arrived with a home-made stretcher and put the body on it, carrying it home for burial. No children were allowed to see the body, and most of the older ones were afraid to look at it, so it was a very poorly attended funeral.

Meanwhile, we took up the trail again, and it veered around and turned straight eastward, back toward the fort. The scouts trailed him clear to the fort, where the trail vanished. Though every shod horse in the post was examined, the killer was never found, which is not strange as soldiers were deserting right along, and any one of them might have done it.

The Apaches were convinced that some crazed soldier was responsible, and that no Indian could have done it. I don't know. I've never fully made up my mind, but I never will know. It's just one of those mysteries with no solution and will always stay a mystery.

CHAPTER XXI.

SKIRTS AND STAMPEDES

When I took up my job as line rider and stockman for the Reservation, the Apaches tended more to horse flesh than beer. There was a fine great range of theirs unoccupied except for useless wild horses, a range with an abundance of brouse, brush, grass, and weeds. Up to this time, the Government had not bought a hoof of cattle for them to help make them independent, and the few head they ran themselves was scrawny and of poor stock, mostly from Chihuahua and Sonora, Mexico—brindle, black, and pinto longhorns.

Crouse, the Agent, and I discussed the matter. For the first few months of my time on the Reservation, I had been busy collecting one dollar per head from the adjoining stockmen, also counting the stock at round-ups. That had been my chief duty. And I'd collected quite a tidy sum of money. Also there was other sources from which the Indians derived revenue. These funds were usually used to construct roads and dams and canals on the reservations, but there was still quite a few thousand dollars lying unused.

Neither Crouse nor me could see any good reason why this money shouldn't go to buying cattle for the families and tribes, maybe ten to twenty-five head for each family, depending on the size. Our request for this investment in cattle was submitted by Mr. Crouse to the Indian Office in Washington, and a representative, Mr. S. Connell, was sent out to make an investigation. With him I rode over almost the entire Reservation, and he was much impressed with the possibilities, and agreed with me that cattle ought to be bought and that the Reservation ought to be cleaned up of the wild horses.

Within two weeks I had orders to go to Wilcox and make a deal with the Norton Morgan Commercial Company for the purchase of one thousand two-year-old heifers and one thousand cows and calves—heifers offered at sixteen dollars a head and cows with calves at from twenty-five to thirty dollars a head. I wired Mr. Crouse the price, and he wired back to make the deal. This was in June, and the arrangement was made that we would take the cattle in July after the seasonal rains had started so that the grasses would be in good condition for the trailing. A part of the arrangement also was that I was to use my own cowboys, Indian cowboys. I paid down a two-dollar deposit per head and returned to the fort to make arrangements for my cowboys.

The buying of the cattle was only a beginning to getting them up to the Reservation and distributing them. Things went smooth enough at first. In mid-July I returned to Wilcox with eleven mounted Indian cowboys, and arranged for a chuck wagon to Geronimo; from there we would have to pack our chuck on mules.

Two trips were to be made. The first drive we would take the two-year-old heifers, and then return for the cows and calves. We started out upon the drive of two hundred miles. It was my idea to take things easy all along so that the cattle would be in good condition when we arrived.

The day's routine was this: each day we split the herd into two groups, five hundred to a group, and split the cowboys also, a half for each herd. This way the cattle had better grazing all the way, and we trailed them slow. Behind us came the chuck wagon, the cook already having been up since before the first sign of daylight, for by the time silver was in the east, we were on the move. The cook's job, in addition to furnishing lanky, hungry cowboys with steak and coffee and a few other substantial items, was to gather wood, bring water, make the fire, help load and unload bedrolls. At eleven a.m. we ate dinner, with two men holding the herd while the others ate, and then picking up their chuck afterwards.

At night we threw the herds together. Two men at a time did the nighthawking, all taking turns each night. We did a good deal of singing to keep those cattle quiet. It was strange to hear the Apache cowboys chanting out of the night as they rode about after the cattle had been bedded down. But the cattle seemed to like the chanting. And those Indians were good horsemen and good cow hands.

Everything went fine until we had crossed the Gila River and were heading north of Geronimo on the second leg of the journey with our chuck and bedding now on mules and pack horses.

Now these cattle were all wild-raised on the wide open ranges in the

Chiricahua Mountains between Wilcox and Douglas. They'd never even seen a corral. Their only handling had been the cow round-ups in the open. And any cattle, when driven over a strange country, naturally become uneasy and nervous and flighty, especially if they've been driven a little too far of a day in order to reach water and a good place to bed them down.

I was with the front five hundred, helping to keep them moving, and we were headed up a wide swail to the north when the Indian girls put in their appearance. They were riding wild and bareback after a bunch of mustangs and shouting shrilly. Bad enough that, to happen right in front of our lead cattle. But, in addition, they were dressed as all the Apache women dressed, in those five and ten yard voluminous skirts, always of a red color, all shades of red from maroon to crimson.

In the breeze those skirts spread out bigger than flags. Red skirts tearing across the landscape in front of the eyes of our jittery cattle, and coming toward them on a dead run. The leaders snorted, threw down their heads, whirled back on the trail, back toward the Gila River a mile away. Hell had let loose. The cattle milled and bumped into one another with horns cracking, and finally got straightened around and galloping the wrong direction with heads down and brains *loco*ed. This was a real stampede.

The boys and I rode with them, galloped parallel to the leaders and fanned and slapped our slickers across their noses and sang to them and tried to get in front of them to turn them back. Once we could get them milling, we would have them under control. But they were hog-wild and no luck.

The second herd saw them coming, and us singing and waving our slickers, and they got right into the spirit of the occasion. They lowered their heads too, turned, and bolted. A thousand head of cattle thundering down the swail toward the Gila River. When that bunch of cattle hit the Gila River, they splashed it dry, but for the sake of truth I might say that the Gila had very little water in it at the time, despite the summer rains. The river bed with its sandy banks on both sides slowed them down, and by the time the leaders reached the other side, me and my boys was there already, and started them to milling. We knew we'd stopped the stampede for the present.

But we knew, too, that after cattle have once stampeded on the trail, they'll do it again at the very least noise. Even the shaking of a slicker may start them off, shoving their noses to the ground and running completely wild. When they get that way, they follow one another over a cliff, or smack into the side of a freight train. We knew that from now on we'd have our hands full.

We drove them north to Dead Man's Crossing of the Blackriver and on toward Fort Apache. They were nervous but we kept them in control, and it was with a big sigh that I finally watched them bedded down in a camp on the Whiteriver just a mile north of Fort Apache. This would be my last night in charge of them; next day they would be off my hands. I'd already sent one of the boys ahead to let the Agent know when we'd arrive, and hundreds of Indians had gathered at the fort, each family to take charge of their share of the cattle.

As usual we were up well before dawn and all mounted and grazing the cattle leisurely along the river toward the fort. Just as the sun came up… boom! The sound echoed along the canyon and smacked the ears of the stock. It was the firing of the cannon at dawn. It happened every morning, but I'd forgotten about it.

Down went their heads! Just as before, they turned and milled and started back up the trail, spreading out into the rough country, humping over cedar trees and rocks and along rough natural gutters. We spread out with them, every man of us cutting with our spurs, and in a wide circle we rode to get control of them, while they sprawled and stumbled and lumbered on.

This was much worse country for a stampede than the other had been, but in a way it was in our favor as well because it slowed them down, and we were able to put a stop to the stampede quicker than the other one. None of the cattle were killed, but several were crippled and a great many of them dehorned and bleeding from the broken splints.

The drive of the second batch of a thousand—the cows and calves—went along without undue incident, the female of the species being just naturally better behaved, I guess. We got the two thousand head onto the Reservation and divided, and from them have come many, many thousands of Indian cattle.

From McNary every year is shipped more than two thousand steers, sold by the Indians, and many hundreds of fat old cows. R 14, for example, an Indian cowman on Cedar Creek, has been very successful in the stock business, having such a fat bank account that when the Government asked for its first subscription to Liberty bonds, he was able to buy ten-thousand-dollars' worth.

That's quite a change in the short stretch of a few years. From naked bucks in breech clouts burning ranches, stealing, scalping whites or roasting their feet over fires, to patriotically buying Liberty bonds. Quite a change.

My next job was to clean out the wild horses.

CHAPTER XXII.

WILD HORSES

It would have been one thing for me and my scouts to have ridden over the hundreds of square miles of the Reservation and shot down the wild horses. It was quite another thing to catch them and bring them in alive. We had to use many tricks, and some of them I've never heard about elsewhere, for they were invented on the spot.

Some of these wild horses were branded animals that had run off from their range and got mixed up with a wild bunch and taken to wild ways. But most of them was mavericks—that is, born wild on the open range and never known the feel of a saddle or hackamore, the cut of a rope, the word of a man. They only knew enough about a man to be afraid of him. When I say wild horses, they was really wild like any other wild animal.

But the government wanted them taken alive. Though a maverick is seldom a satisfactory horse, there was a market for the mares to mother mules in Louisiana and Texas, with the proceeds going to the Indians; and there was market for a few of the animals to the stockmen of the Territory. This suited me, for I have never approved of slaughtering them and sending them off to factories to be turned into chicken feed. What an end for a fine wild horse—turned into chicken feed!

Having been around horses all my life, I have a pretty soft place in my heart for them. Some folks don't believe me when I say that I have seen tears coming out of horses' eyes when they was mistreated, but it's a fact. I have been in chases after rustlers where the easiest way to make a catch was to shoot down the horse and put the man on foot, and I have known others to do it, but I have never been guilty. I would almost rather shoot the rustler than shoot down his good old faithful saddle horse.

I estimate there was some five thousand horses running loose on the Reservation, some of them belonging to adjoining ranchers but having gone to the wild state, and the rest just belonging to nobody. Our assignment was to catch as many as we could of the wildest.

The place to catch wild horses is at the springs where they water, and like other wild animals, they quench their thirst at night, so night is the time they must be caught. The way we were most successful, and a method often used elsewhere, is this: We built a pole corral at the spring out of any timber that was handy, with a gate which would close and fasten, but which we, of course, left open till the animals had been corralled. Leading up to this gate in the shape of a V, with the point of the V at the gate, we ran string out in wings a half mile to a mile in length. All along this string we fastened bits of colored rag at intervals.

Sometimes we'd ride out and pick up and chase a band of wild horses until it got into the V, and then down it to the corral. Strangely enough, the horses would seldom break the string. However, this method, though commonly used, is hard on your own horses over rough country. A simpler way, and just as successful, is to station a man at the gate of the corral, where he lies awake all night… or sits if he wants. The horses come to water and walk along into the corral, and when they get inside, they snort in surprise. If the sentry happens to be dozing, this wakes him up. He closes the gate and fastens it. The next morning comes the job of removing the animals. As additional inducement to lead the horses to their capture, we'd put salt along the wings and salt licks in the corral. By this method I've caught as many as twenty-five horses in one night.

Another method we devised (that required less preparation) we used with some success. We would fence off several known watering places so that the animals would have to come to the watering places where we had our traps set, places where the trees were thick. Here we'd fasten our ropes with loops in them to green saplings, and then we'd get set to stand guard, for a horse is likely to choke himself to death in one of these traps if the man isn't handy to rope his forefeet and bring him down and tie him with a hackamore.

The horses would come up and get their heads tangled in the loops, and then what a commotion! Whang would go the rope as it zinged and the sapling swayed low with the horse in full, frightened gallop.

But the tree was green and though it would bend, it wouldn't break. The rope, half-inch seagrass rope, would hold a bull elephant.

Another method I tried did not end very successfully. We had caught a wild mule in our corral, only one out of a known bunch of thirty or forty that I'd been laying for yet couldn't seem to catch. An idea stuck in my *cabeza* and I tried it. We made a dummy man out of an old coat and pair of trousers and fastened together with rope so it wouldn't come apart, and this we tied to the back of that wild mule and turned him loose kicking and bucking and then tearing off at a dead gallop.

We chased him as best we could, but soon were out-distanced. He found his band all right, like we had intended. Someone saw that mule and dummy man ten miles from where we'd let him loose, him trying to catch up with the band, and the band at full gallop trying to get away from the mule. Two days and nights he ran them over the wild country of the Reservation, and when we finally caught up with them, you've never seen such a band of tame wild horses in your life, all petered out and slowed down to a walk, the easiest to catch and drive of any stock we captured. The only catch to this method, and why I didn't use it again—most of the horses was ruined as saddle horses by that chase, the bottom completely knocked out of them, and never the same again.

Once a wild horse is captured, only half your job is done, and the second half is likely to be even harder than the first. A corralled wild horse feels so regretful about his imprisonment that if any humans are around, he won't eat or drink for two straight days and nights. But if he's left alone, he'll eat after the first day and night of captivity. The mares were, of course, the easiest to handle, even though as wild as deer, and bucking and pawing when a hackamore was first put on them. They'd soon cool down. You would naturally think that wild horses would be hard to break to saddle, but that is not as often the case as otherwise; a wild horse won't have learned the trick of bucking like a horse used to human ways. Most of these wild horses, after being roped and brought down and a hackamore put on them, would be easy to drive and lead. It seems that once they're away from their wild ranges, they lose the desire to be independent.

We had most trouble with the stallions between six and ten years old and a few of the old mares, but especially the stallions. They would rear, then hang back, and plunge and kick, and try to bite anyone that came near them. We had a way of cooling them down.

That kind it was unsafe to rope afoot, and even when they was roped from horseback, they'd sometimes lunge at your saddle horse with their teeth bared and their heads back and every hair standing stiff on them. After we had them down, we'd lead into the corral a large jack burro with a leather halter around his neck. We'd fasten another leather halter around the neck of the stallion, and to each leather halter we'd tie at the end a strong three-foot stretch of rope. When they were necked together securely that way, we'd turn them loose onto the open range. Fight! They'd go at one another with their teeth and bring blood; they'd try to turn their rumps to kick. They'd roll on the ground and butt and kick and roll some more with squeaks and bellows and all sorts of snorting noises, and kicking up the dust in a cloud.

Maybe you think it was cruel to the burro to tie him up that way to an animal twice his size and leave him to shift for himself. But such was not the case. He wouldn't fight unless the stallion fought, and stopped fighting when the stallion quit. I've never known it to fail; in one to three days the burro would come back to his home ground leading that stallion all cooled off and ready to behave. Cowmen use this trick sometimes to tame down wild range steers, long horns and all, and the burro always wins. He's a tough animal in a fight, the burro is.

* * *

Both my scouts and I spotted *Negro* early in our campaign and wanted that stallion bad—a big, coal-black horse ranging down on the Cibecue near where Highway 60 now runs from Show Low to Globe. He was wild as an antelope, weighed about twelve hundred pounds, and had come from fine American stock. In his band were about forty mares, all mavericks. That stallion would be a prize for anyone.

We tried every way I knew how to get him. I had as many as five and six Indian cowboys at one time after him, trying to drive that one horse into the wings of our corral, but he was too wary and eluded them one way and another.

It became a game with the Indians, and perhaps with the horse.

The Indians were all anxious to own him, and I wanted him, and the Government wanted him for the dollars he would bring. Time after time he eluded us, and then at last one night, we got him. We had set a dozen of the nooses to green pine trees, young ones, and were waiting near a water hole, with most of the other water holes shut off.

We heard a loud snort, then a whistle like the whistle of a train, a crashing of bushes and thudding of hooves, and finally the thump of a heavy body brought to earth. There was enough moonlight from a sliver of a moon to see what we had caught, and the Indians set to shouting. "Big horse! Big horse!" they yelled.

Negro put up a good fight. Behind his weight the rope would sing and pip like a blacksnake as he hit the end of it and went down. But he was up like a spring coming back. Almost a dozen Indians were there trying to rope him from on foot but not get close to his sharp teeth and hooves. One of them finally swung a loop around his forefeet and down he went, and with a whoop the redskins were on his big and quivering black body. They got the hackamore on him and tied him to a tree with a rope six feet long, leaving one Indian standing watch to be sure he didn't tangle that rope around the tree and hurt himself.

Next morning we tried to make up to our prisoner, talking Spanish, English, and Apache to him, but he just didn't seem to savvy any of those languages. Any man came near him, he made a lunge with bared teeth and eyes shining full of the devil. If we rode a horse near him, he'd swing round to get his hoofs in proper aiming distance. Finally we put two men on horseback with a rope each to the hackamore and led him out to open country to handle him.

For two weeks this horse would try to kick or bite every man that brought feed or water to him. And he did the longest stretch of fasting of any wild horse I know. But we finally broke him to lead and ride, which was a real achievement.

However, both the Apaches and I was disappointed that we could not have him, for if we tried to keep him on the Reservation, we knew that at first opportunity he would break and head for the open range along the Cibecue. He had to be sold, taken out of the country far enough away that there would be no temptation to try to return.

About this time there was to be held at the fort an auction of condemned cavalry horses, and to this auction came stockmen from all over the Territory to get horse flesh cheap. *Negro* was thrown in with the rest, but was auctioned off separately, after it had been explained just where he came from and why he was being sold.

Bush Crawford, a horse dealer from Globe, bid in *Negro* at two hundred dollars. The following spring *Negro* was seen by some Apache cowboys ranging wild and free along the Cibecue, even though there was a brand on his hip. His band of mares had all been caught and shipped to Louisiana, but there was *Negro* back home and seeming to enjoy himself alone. The last I heard, he was still the property of Bush Crawford and still free and grazing the good Indian grass on the banks of the Cibecue.

It seemed to me fitting that it should be so. That was where the big black stallion belonged.

CHAPTER XXIII.

APACHE QUIRKS AND WHIMSIES

I've had campfire acquaintance and some friendships among all the tribes of Indians in northern Arizona, and the Apaches seem to me to be the lowest average mentally of any of the tribes. The Hopis are well ahead of the Navajos, to my notion; some ways they are almost white. The Navajos are smart—above what amounts to their cousins, the Apaches. The Apaches seem more loggy stupid.

Many a tracer has lost good business by speaking to an Indian before being spoken to. The Indian doesn't like it. He will stand around awhile without saying anything, and then will speak, and then it is the white man's turn to speak.

I've asked many an Indian who has been Christianized which religion he likes best, the new one or the old one. And whether he's a Hopi or Pueblo, Navajo or Apache, he always answers that the old one suits him better than the new. This attitude must have been pretty discouraging to missionaries like my father or Jacob Hamblin.

In my dealings with them, I've found all the tribes honest, especially the Apaches, where honesty is a mighty strong code. It had to be. They lived their lives in the open, with no padlocks for their hogans and no place to hide things away, and honesty within the tribe was as natural as eating. If a white man is ever dishonest with an Apache, and has made a gain by such dishonesty, it will take him years to overcome the hate of the Indian. But if he has made no gain by his dishonesty, then the Indian will ignore it.

I have often left items in the care of Indians, sometimes for months; and when I came to get my property, it was always returned and was in the same condition that I'd left it. One time, for example, I left a saddle with an old Apache squaw on the south part of the Reservation and told her I'd come back for it in two weeks.

I returned on time. She was cooking a little jerky and coffee and invited me to eat with her, which I did. We sat outside the hogan and ate and I asked her, "You still got my saddle?"

"Sure," she said. She could speak a little Spanish. "Still have saddle."

"No one run off with it?"

"No. No white man here in two weeks. Saddle all right."

You can see from this what a good opinion the Apaches have of the white man's honesty.

When I arrived at Fort Apache in 1906, the only buildings were the fort and the houses of white people attached to the fort. The Indians, as I have explained, lived in scattered hogans of skin and grass, or sometimes covered with wagon covers or pieces of old tents. About this time the Government began a program of building houses for the Indians, insisting that those who had the advantage of some schooling be exemplary and live in these houses to show the rest of the tribe what being civilized meant.

The Indians would not live in the houses. They continued to live in their hogans. Some of them explained to me that the floor was too hard and it wasn't healthy in the house, and that a stove was not made to cook on but to keep warm by. The only way to cook was on a fire outside.

They just didn't like the houses. Even today, though a great many of them do have houses, as you go through the Reservation, you'll frequently see a neat little white house and a couple of rusty looking decrepit tepees near to the house, and the Indian families living in the tepees, while the house is practically empty, or is used to store feed and grain.

* * *

When a school was first opened (about the time I came), taught by young American misses, the Government had the dickens of a time making the children come to school. Under orders, the parents would bring the children in their old wagons or on horseback and leave them at the dormitory—it was a boarding school with food, of course, furnished free to them.

During the night, most of the children would vanish from the Big House and scamper home. Sometimes it was as far as twenty to twenty-five miles to their home village, but even the young ones would set out in the night and walk it home.

Next morning the school rooms would be practically empty and Crouse would call me up. "You're a truant officer today, Joe."

"Fine," I'd say. "Give me the names of the brats."

He'd read off a long list of names of children and parents and then give me the numbers of their parents: G 14, three children; F 21, one child; and so on. I'd take Loco Jim (usually) with me and set out to track down the children.

These children were as wild as deer. And they were afraid to death of any man with a badge. Usually all I'd see of them in a camp that day was a little dust going over a bank. But sometimes the braver ones would stand and holler, *"Tu-bugin-cida!"* (I don't know who you are.) And then they'd break and run.

We'd visit each village, find the parents, and tell them in Spanish—I would—that their children must go to school. Most of the older ones could understand Spanish. But they'd shrug their shoulders and say they didn't know where the children were. "Children gone. Not here till night."

We always went truanting prepared to stay overnight, and often enough the children would lie out in the brush all night long. But by the next morning they'd had enough of it and would come in to their parents with their heads bowed and crying and weeping and begging not to be sent back to the Big House.

But the parents knew they had to obey the Agent. The children always went back with us, and then in a few days we had to do the whole thing over again. Funny bunch. Now it's different from that. The Apaches seem to have a little more appreciation of education.

* * *

When I was a line rider, the bucks of the tribe went about clothed as they had been in the early days—breech clouts and shirt and moccasins, and a band wound around their long stringy black hair, usually a bright-colored band with sometimes a feather stuck into it. Their hair was their pride and joy, the longer the better. Long hair was a part of their religion, for the god in the sun had once given them eyes and well-shaped mouths and long hair and horses to ride.

Somehow a rumor got started around the Reservation that an order had come from Washington saying they must cut their hair. Likely there really had been such an order, I don't know. The Government has sent out some funny orders one time or another.

First I knew of it there was a mob of twenty or thirty noisy bucks around the front of my frame house one morning. I went out to talk with them. They told me why they had come—the haircut order—and that they had heard I was the man to enforce it, and that was why they had come to me.

I shrugged my shoulders. "I don't know anything about it," I told them.

They went on to elaborate. They understood that if they didn't cut their own hair in two weeks, they were to be chased down, their hands tied behind with wire, and their hair cut off with sheep shears.

I told them I'd check into it, and then I forgot it. But the bucks didn't. There was a great scarcity of bucks on the days assigned to draw rations. They were hiding out in the brush and sending their squaws to get rations.

After a time had passed, some of them came to my house again and wanted me to write back to the Big Chief and tell him that they wouldn't have their hair cut off. I told them I would do it, and then I high-tailed it over to Crouse's office and told him all about what was up, and that he'd have a few dozen tribes of Indians migrating from his Reservation if he didn't put their minds at ease.

Crouse said, "You go back and tell them that such an order hasn't come. And if it does come, it will never be enforced on this Reservation."

That satisfied the bucks, and things were calm again, and the men began to come in for their rations, which they liked to do. It was always a great treat to them to get together with the other families and gamble and talk. The Indians themselves came around to the white man's way, and as I have said, upon the Reservation now is a beauty and barber shop.

When I drove the two thousand head of cattle to the Reservation, it wasn't the first time that the Indians had had stock. There was a mighty important reason why the Agent divided the stock into parcels for each family. Previous to this, the Government had bought six or seven hundred head of sheep. The chiefs of the tribe had decided that rather than divide the sheep, it would be much easier for the different families to take turns herding the sheep.

If you think those fellows didn't like mutton, you don't know much about Apaches. The herding moved along from month to month, with no stockmen checking to be sure the sheep had salt and to tend to the dipping and shearing. The herd diminished rapidly.

About the time I came upon the scene and was loitering in the office of the Agent, an old Indian woman entered, wadded up into her six or seven yards of dress and carrying her blankets on her back. She had a loud complaint to make. She had not completed her family's time of herding the sheep.

Through an interpreter, Mr. Crouse asked, "Why don't you finish it?" He couldn't understand this strange love of herding sheep.

"You buy more sheep," she said.

Mr. Crouse got to his feet angrily. "You have no more sheep?"

"No."

"What has become of them?"

She evaded the question. "They are all gone. You buy some more."

And Mr. Crouse couldn't get her to tell what had become of the sheep, but, of course, he knew and I knew. Each family's turn at herding had been a time of mutton gorging and much slaughter and much drying of mutton jerky. No wonder the old woman objected to losing time on her family's turn at the sheep business.

So when the cattle arrived, no one in authority even suggested the idea of communal ownership. And I'm afraid that's about the way communism would work among the whites too—everybody grab as much as he can.

* * *

When the first wagons were issued to the Apaches, they were made in Moline, Illinois, and shipped with harnesses on the Atchison, Topeka, and Santa Fe to Holbrook, about a hundred and fifty miles north of the Reservation. Thirty or forty wagons were included in the first shipment, and the heads of families notified to go to Holbrook with animals to drive back the wagons.

Now, not a saddle mule or saddle horse or burro belonging to the Indians had ever been harness broke. But the Government didn't take this into account, and the Apaches, tickled that they were to have bright-painted new wagons, didn't take this into account either. A cavalcade of them rode to Holbrook and gathered in a great camp beside the railroad track, mighty colorful with the women in their bright red dresses of all shades and the men with the bright-colored headbands, and all the teepees and tents springing up from the ground in a great clutter.

One by one the wagons was unloaded, and when a flock of them had been removed, the Apaches went to harnessing up their stock. Mules and horses bucked and shied, but the Indians was persistent and got those jittery horses and mules harnessed down.

About that time a west-bound freight train chugged along the tracks, slowed down for Holbrook, and the engineer looked out and spotted what was going on. With a grin, thinking it a good joke, he pulled down that whistle cord and held it open. Every horse went off like a shot over the white dusty flats. It didn't make any difference what direction, just so the wagons went bouncing and dancing and jarring those that happened to be seated and had hold of the reins. Others, on the ground, had the reins jerked out of their hands, and still others, halfway onto their wagons, was spilled off. It took all the leather and copper rivets on the A & P west of Kansas City to patch those cheap harnesses.

This wasn't the end of the trouble. The wagon brigade reached the rough country south of Holbrook near the old Cooley ranch. The Indians had noticed that when going up hill, ten men held the wagon back considerable and the horses had to strain a heap. Already they'd thrown away their brake bars, no finding any use for them in the flat country.

At the top of the hill, they put their heads together and got to figuring and decided that if ten men held a wagon back going up hill, twenty men out to be enough to hold it back going down hill. They decided to experiment with one wagon, and twenty men got in it. Fifty yards down the slope, men and wagon and horses ended up in a mad scramble, but with nobody badly hurt.

They took no chances with the other wagons down that hill. They cut small pine trees and fastened them to the back of each wagon so that the pine trees dragged along the ground and braked the wagon down safe.

* * *

The medicine men were the biggest men among the Indians and the hardest for the Government to shake them loose from, though by now the success of the Government doctors has just about convinced them their own medicine men aren't much good. Sometimes now they use both medicine men and doctors just to be on the safe side.

The medicine man was usually just a little superior in brains to his fellows, and somehow aroused faith in his ability to call down the Big Spirit into the bodies of those that might be burned, sick, or hurt, and to drive out the devils and evil spirits. This was their main hold: to cast out the devil, get this devil into their hands, and run to the door of the wickiup and blow it out of their hands into the wind, so that it'd be blown away and never come back. I saw them once get seven devils out of a sick woman who was so poor and skinny that she didn't look like she could hold even half a grown one.

I saw the treatment of a little nine-year-old girl who had been badly burned. The medicine man that had been called in pounded a weed between two stones and put it on the burn and then sang, "Ho, ho, ha, ha, hi; ho, ho, ha, ha, heo, heo, heo-o-o." When he wasn't very successful, he called in another medicine doctor. That was another trick they had that isn't beneath the practice of modern medicine. The more doctors, the better chance the patient had, according to them.

I notified a doctor from the fort and went with him to the hogan. The medicine doctors were resentful; I think they felt their power slipping even at that time with the influx of white medicine men. We had to threaten them with arrest in order to make them leave. The army doctor healed the little girl and she lived, but the Indians maintained that the medicine men had already put her on the road to recovery so it was easy for the army doctor to finish the job.

The idea of magic in the medicine men went right along with witchcraft. Many believed that certain old women of the tribe were witches.

In the old days, these women were killed because it was believed that the only remedy was to destroy the body and that would destroy the devil.

Even when I was at the post, though, the tribes wouldn't harm the witches if they would leave and go way off by themselves somewhere on the Reservation. Many a poor old squaw has thus been forced to go off from her people and shift for herself.

Many believe in ghosts, which especially hang around the dead and around the hogans and houses where people have died. That is the reason they like to burn the teepee where a person has died, and there was no great harm to burning an inexpensive tepee, but this was quite a problem when people began dying in the more expensive government houses and the Indians wanted to burn them.

In my time the Apaches had, and still have, the usual vices common to the rest of mankind—prostitution, gambling, and drinking. But because they don't have the resistance and will power usual in most white men, they go to considerable extreme in the last two, while prostitution isn't too common, though enough that syphilis has made inroads among them. The cause of prostitution is easy to understand. Among them a man can divorce his wife by simply up and leaving her. She is removed from the marriageable market, for a buck will never marry a woman so divorced, but will marry a real widow. She can go back to her folks if they'll take her in, or she can become a prostitute. The soldiers at the fort were responsible for the spread of syphilis among the Indians.

The Apaches liked their liquor. They are fondest of the white man's whiskey, but this is not easy to get. And next they prefer *mescal*, commonly drunk in Mexico, which is made out of the leaves and roots of century plants, allowed to ferment after boiling, and then distilled. But this is difficult to make, takes a long time, so their most common drink is what they call *too-lie-pi*. This is made very simply by boiling corn and water in a big five-gallon can, straining off the water, and allowing the liquid to ferment for seven or eight days. Without any further work, it is ready to drink.

It tastes a little like beer, has about the same amount of alcohol in it, but has a much more lasting and sometimes disastrous effect if a great deal of it is drunk. Bucks, squaws, and children all drink it, but, of course, the bucks go to extreme, and it is full of fighting propensities.

There's hardly ever a big *too-lie-pi* party without someone getting into a big fight. The bucks go after each other with butcher knives if guns aren't handy, and strike for the intestines or the groin or the outside of the leg. If they get good and drunk, they sink into a stupor that will sometimes last as long as three or four days.

Drinking and gambling go together, and I've seen a man wager his teepee or his last horse or even his wife over the results of a foot race or a horse race or the toss of gambling sticks.

CHAPTER XXIV.

DRINK AND THE DEVIL

The government was fully cognizant of the immoral conditions among the Apaches, especially the drinking of *too-lie-pi,* and wished to put a stop to such. For this purpose they sent out special agents at one time or another, but the agents met with little success. One case in particular I remember with a laugh—the case of Mr. Olander Olson, a special investigator of the Indian Department. He was a nice enough fellow, though very efficient, and took me to task for my neglect in not putting a stop to *too-lie-pi* drinking.

"You have not done your duty, Pearce," he said. "Haven't you ever tried to raid their stills and places of drinking?"

"Yes, sir," I said. "Once. But once was enough."

"You did not have success?"

"No, sir. Only a little valuable experience."

"I'll have to see what I can do," he says. "I must be able to report to Washington that I have broken up at least one *too-lie-pi* camp. Will you go with me?"

"I don't know much Apache," I told him. "I know the name of a dollar and a horse and a few things like that, but I can't talk much."

"At least you can take me to one of their camps?"

"Sure," I said. "But you can't change their appetites, no matter how many *too-lie-pi* camps you raid."

Mr. Olsen remained firm, and the Agent sent out orders for horses, already saddled, to the entrance of the agency. We mounted, and I led Mr. Olsen off southeastward. We reached the region of scrub oak and blackjack pines and I guided him through the timber to a well-concealed camp I knew of.

We rode straight into camp. The Indians didn't pay much attention to us as we came up. The center of the clearing was free of children. There was several teepees around, and the men lying about basking in the sun, and some was playing the white man's card games of monte and casino. On a level track a little distance off from this central camp was a track with some fine horses hobbled near—black and sorrel and pinto, sleek little ponies—and several was lining up for a race on which would be bet money and horses and blankets.

Back in the pine timber beyond the race track, I knew there was a group of bucks playing the favorite Apache gambling game. This consisted of a long cane with notches and numbers cut into it, which was laid about twenty feet in front of the players, and a wooden wheel that was marked and numbered. The manner of play was to roll the wheel toward the stick so that it would fall on the stick. Bets were paid according to numbers and marks on the stick and on the wheel.

In the center of the clearing between the teepees, two enormous squaws worked over the open fire. One of them must have weighed a hundred and eighty-five pounds and the other a good two hundred. I looked at those squaws and then at slim Mr. Olsen and felt sorry for him.

The big squaws was handling the *too-lie-pi*, which was being drunk by everybody in profuse quantities, spilling around worse than hornets' nests. On the fire was a couple of cans of the new stuff cooking, while on the ground near the squaws was several five-gallon cans of the finished product.

Mr. Olsen dismounted, humped over to where the *too-lie-pi* was being made, and without any warning, he kicked over a can of the finished product and a can that was cooking on the fire. The *too-lie-pi* ran over the ground and vanished. Mr. Olsen bravely would have finished the job if those enormous squaws hadn't got him first. He went down to the ground under a mass of Indian woman flesh. Next I saw of him in the mass of arms and legs was the hundred-and-eighty-five pounder sitting in the middle of his back to hold him down, and the two-hundred pounder laying on with a doubled rawhide rope at the place where the chastisement is supposed to be the most effective.

I ran over to help if I could. Mr. Olsen howled. The squaw continued with the beating, and no signs of let-up. "Tell them to get off," he hollered at me.

"I don't know how," I said.

"Tell them something," he yelled. "Joe, tell them to quit! Pull them off me!"

"Well," I says, "I don't know as it's a healthy time to interfere."

Mr. Olsen howled and kicked his feet, but the two-hundred-pounder kept whanging away. "Give her money," Mr. Olsen yelled.

That was a good idea of his. I put my hand in my pocket and pulled out a couple of silver dollars. The squaws glanced at the money disdainfully and continued their form of torture. I added another dollar and another to the ante, and still they whaled on Mr. Olsen. When I reached six silver dollars, they laid off and took the money.

The Government Special Investigator got shakily to his feet, with both hands held to the seat of his trousers. He staggered toward me. "Let's go, Joe," he said huskily. "But if you don't mind, just lead my horse. I'd rather walk."

On the way back to the fort, Mr. Olsen got to laughing over what had happened. "You know, Joe," he says, "I'm now fully qualified as an Indian War veteran, and upon my return to Washington, I shall immediately file application for a pension."

After that the Apaches went on drinking their *too-lie-pi* in the *too-lie-pi* camps unmolested.

* * *

Long before prohibition, there was bootleggers on the Whiteriver Reservation, some of the smoothest that ever hit the West, plying their trade among the Apache Indians. These Indians always had money somehow, and their taste for *too-lie-pi* and *mescal* was only exceeded by their taste for raw American whiskey. It seems that a white man is supposed to be willing to walk a mile for a Camel, but those red-bellies would actually walk ten or fifteen miles through timber country for a glass of whiskey. One bootlegger in particular I remember well, a dark complexioned, stubby little man who spoke Apache fluently and was on the best of terms with the red-skins. I think at some time or other he had been married to an Apache squaw as quite a number of white men and Mexicans did—some, because it meant an easy living from the Government.

We called this bootlegger Frenchy. He owned two pack and one saddle burros, and his method was to buy in Holbrook two five-gallon kegs of cheap whiskey. Then he'd load his chuck on one pack burro and his whiskey on the other, and over the whisky he'd fasten his bedding to conceal his goods. From Holbrook to the mountainous country of the Reservation he would never travel the highways, but would keep to the brush and away from all roads and trails. Most of his traveling was done at night, while he laid up during the day in some vegetated canyon or draw or coulee and that way escaped detection.

Once on the Reservation, he would go to the southwest corner about where Highway 60 now enters, down toward the Cariso and the Cibecue. He always selected a place to peddle his whiskey in a clearing surrounded by dense growth of trees and thickets, but never near a cliff or canyon, knowing the Apache weakness to fall off anywhere when he is drunk. When everything was ready, Frenchy would send out an Indian cowboy to notify all Indians of that locality that he was ready near some certain spring in the hills where he would dispense his goods.

Here the Indians would gather in swarms around the kegs, which had been placed upon a log or rock a foot or two above the ground. Not till five o'clock would Frenchy begin to sell his liquor. With him he carried a glass or cup that would hold from two to three ounces of the stuff, and no Indian would be given a second helping until all were served, that way whetting the bucks' appetites for more.

He was clever in his selling. The first drink cost each Indian two-bits apiece. Time for the second, and Frenchy's price had raised from twenty-five to fifty cents. The third would cost each buck a dollar. And beyond that, if the Indians stayed on their feet above that point, drinks ranged from two dollars to a saddle horse. Frenchy succeeded in driving some pretty good stock out of the Reservation. It was always a lot easier to sell those last drinks than the first ones at two-bits. By dark, most of the Indians were drunk, and Frenchy would quietly slip through the trees, leaving the bucks to their next day's hangover.

He'd been following this business successfully a number of years, never caught in operation inside the Reservation, when I became a line rider. One of my Indian stockmen told me one day that Frenchy was to make a visit and invited me to go along, thinking that I would enjoy the drinking orgy. I decided then and there that this was to be the end of Frenchy's bootlegging. I went with the cowboy.

When we arrived, the Indians was some of them already drunk and Frenchy was filling his cup for the others. To avert suspicion, I went up and had a drink and then a second, and continued to watch his method of operation. He wasn't afraid of me, even though I was a white man, thinking I was a renegade married to a squaw.

By and by I walked up to him and showed him my badge. "You're under arrest," I said.

"All right," he said. He didn't make any move to grab a gun or put up any resistance, and I didn't pull a gun on him.

I took him back with me and turned him over to an officer in Fort Apache, and he was locked up in the guard house to await a hearing and trial. There he was among a bunch of soldiers, most of them incarcerated for drunkenness, and no one regarding him as any different from the soldiers.

At that time the Government was building a road across the Whiteriver just a half mile west of Fort Apache, and mostly the prisoners in the guard house did the work as a kind of chain gang. Frenchy took his place alongside the others swinging a pick.

It seems one day there was three soldiers guarding the fifteen or twenty men in a chain gang working near a break in the canyon with a thick grove of willow trees and underbrush not more than ten or fifteen yards away.

Frenchy waited his opportunity—that is, for one of the guards to pass between him and the lower side of the road, which was about ten feet down off the bank. As the guard paced between him and the bank, he made a sudden lunge, pushing on the guard and grabbing the rifle as the guard tumbled over and rolled down.

French jumped down after him over the bank and went like a rabbit toward the willows and underbrush, where he disappeared before the other two guards, further away, knew what had happened even.

Frenchy did not return to his old lucrative work on the Reservation. The last I heard of him he was dealing a monte game in one of the saloons at Globe. His disappearance was a day of mourning for the Indians.

CHAPTER XXV.

COURTSHIP, MARRIAGE, ETC.

My courtship of Minnie Lund was carried on at long range, while me a line rider on the Apache Reservation and Minnie Lund, now twenty years old, trying to help her family out (twelve children in it) by working as a cook in Becker's kitchen in Springerville a hundred miles away. Thirty-three, thirty-four years old I was, and a more successful Romeo than I'd been with the Nutrioso school marm.

A time comes along in a man's life when he no longer hankers to be as wild and free as a range maverick, when the thirst for adventure cools, when he yearns for a saddle and a bit in his teeth and a load to carry, and a corral to be shut up in at night. He hears of all his friends getting married. He's really lonesome in the single state, and a lump comes into his throat when he gets to thinking of himself and feeling sorry for himself.

I was in the mood to be a Lochinvar. *[EDITOR'S NOTE: In a poem by Sir Walter Scott, after being rejected by his beloved's father, Lochinvar arrives uninvited at her wedding and steals her away. "So daring in love and so dauntless in war, have ye e'er heard of gallant like young Lochinvar?"]*

And Minnie Lund wasn't altogether averse to my advances. I was a long-legged cowboy person, with a grin and good nature and old enough to know my own mind and maybe to seem a bit romantic, though unpolished, to the young miss. I courted her in Becker's kitchen, and Mrs. Becker often enough shooed me out for interfering with her girl's work.

I remember well enough the time I proposed to her. We was standing outside the kitchen door, and it was late, all the light of the house out, but enough moon for me to see Minnie good and to see the fresh look she always wore, like a summer breeze from the north, and her clear skin and smile.

"You know," I says, poking the toe of a cowboy boot at the ground, "I think maybe I need a cook more than Mrs. Becker."

She changed color. She knew what I meant well enough, but pretended otherwise. "What do you mean, Joe?"

"Well," I says, "you think you could throw hash for a cowpuncher with a big appetite?"

"What cowpuncher?" she giggled.

I kissed her then, but she jerked away and with her face turned from me, says, "You better ask my father."

"I need a cook worse than Becker's."

"You ask father."

"I'm asking you."

"You got to ask him first."

When I tried to kiss her again, she turned and ran from me up the steps. Crash! Bang! Crack and clatter! Minnie went tumbling headlong among a mess of pots and pans that had been in the kitchen. We'd plumb forgotten. It was Mrs. Becker's trap. You never knew where she was going to put them, but she fixed it so's she'd wake up and find out what time the girls that worked for her was coming home. She looked after their morals pretty strict, feeling responsible.

As I was helping Minnie up, and Minnie laughing, Mrs. Becker poked her head out of the window. "Is that you, Minnie?"

"Yes'm."

A pause. "You know what time it is?"

"No'm."

"Two o'clock. It's a scandal. You tell that Joe Pearce if he keeps you out this late again he can't come to see you any more. You hear that, Joe?"

"Sure I hear it," I said. "But I better tell you now, Mrs. Becker, maybe you're going to lose a good cook."

"Hmph!" she said and slammed the window shut.

Minnie and I stole a kiss and she whispered, "You be sure to ask Pa." I promised her I would.

It was just before this proposal that I was feeling love sick and sad (and you can get just about as sick that way as really being sick). I wrote a poem. I was pretty discouraged at the time. Dick Summers says it isn't much of a poem, but I wanted to put it in my book just the same. Here it is:

> Makes no difference now what kind of life they hand me,
>   I'll get along without you, that's plain to see.
> I don't care what happens next 'cause I'll get by somehow.
>   I don't worry because it makes no difference now.

It was just a year ago that I first met you.
  I learned to love you and thought you loved me too.
But that happened in the past and I'll get by somehow.
  I don't worry because it makes no difference now.

After all is said and done I'll soon forget you,
  Although I know it's going to be quite hard to do.
Let things happen as they will because I'll get by somehow.
  I don't worry because it makes no difference now.

We were married soon after I proposed, after the grapes were ripe and harvested. Minnie's Uncle Ed, a Mormon bishop at Greer, performed the ceremony. But that didn't entirely satisfy Minnie, nor did it satisfy me fully either. We Mormons believe that unless a couple is married in a temple, the marriage is good for only the time here on earth; but if you are married in a temple, then the marriage becomes sealed forever, for time and eternity. Three years after the first ceremony, we made the long trip to the Tabernacle in Utah, at the time the nearest temple, going by rail to Denver, and by rail from Denver to Salt Lake City. There the church officials performed the sealed ceremony.

Marriage brought a good many changes in my life. Soon after the ceremony, it was necessary for Minnie to house tame me, stressing all the rudiments of that form of training. My table manners wasn't much, because table manners around a campfire don't exist. Though they're not to be bragged about even now, they suffered a little improvement. I was accustomed to forking potatoes and meat right out of the skillet and onto my plate, and this habit was broken.

The worst habit breaking me from was sleeping in the open. I just couldn't get comfortable on a bed, especially in the summer time. I'd spent my life sleeping on the ground; on hot nights I thought I was smothering. One night soon after we was married, I went outside with a blanket and went straight off to sleep on the hard ground that felt so comfortable and cool, but my slumbers was rudely interrupted. I jumped up yelling and wiping off my face and out of my eyes what remained of a bucket of cold water. Habit number two was broken. And many other habits came in for their share of change. Smoking and drinking vanished. These were not hard to break as I'd learned not to let bad habits get a mortgage on me and was not a heavy indulger in the usual human vices.

Minnie made me a good wife. She had always been her father's "boy," all her early life doing a good deal of plowing, hoeing, heavy work, cattle driving, raking hay, mowing with a mowing machine. When she was ten years old, she had driven a team of four horses ahead of her father's sulky plow. And she had learned from her mother all the tricks of cooking and preserving, and all the different medicines that the Mormon mothers use; and she has been a midwife many times for other Mormon women. When the babies began to come, she knew already just how to handle them, having had so much experience with her own brothers and sisters, while I thought I was going to break my first boy in two when I picked it up.

She could handle money and hang onto it and onto property better than I. When we were married, I quit the Indian service. We bought ourselves a piece of land in Eagar, two miles south of Springerville, and here we settled down. We built the house that we still own; Minnie planned it. She helped to lay the adobe bricks that went into it. When I was cattle buyer, she rode with me to purchase the cattle, and she was a good cattle buyer, and a good cowboy, for she rode the range with me for two years, helping to drive many herds to market.

Soon after we were married, I got the notion to make some more money somehow and bought a piece of land near St. Johns, thirty miles from Springerville. I had the idea to raise a few horses and a little alfalfa, and try to sell the horses along with my steers from Greer and Eagar, but the way it turned out, I raised more hell than horses.

For seven long years I lived almost alone on this ranch and farm, while Minnie lived at Eagar, and we only saw each other at infrequent intervals. And when I wasn't ranching at St. Johns, I was on the trail into the Indian country tracking down rustlers, or here and there cattle buying for some butchers at Winslow, or acting as livestock detective for the State Sanitary Board.

It was hard on Minnie, bearing and rearing children, doing the plowing, hoeing, cultivating—handling the Eagar ranch like a man and doing a woman's work, too, but taking it like a soldier and standing the strain with her strong body. And not complaining.

I complained. Right after I bought this ranch at St. Johns, which Minnie hadn't wanted me to buy, it stopped raining. I got it into my head, after worrying day and night for nearly seven years about the money I was losing, that it might be a good notion to sell the place. It took seven years for that to sink in.

I struck up a deal with thrifty young Mr. Dennis Heap. When he gave me the check for it, I says, "There's one thing I was to do before I go, you don't mind."

"Go right ahead," he offered.

I went to the barrel of water that I'd hauled from St. Johns for cooking and drinking purposes. I dipped in the bucket, brought out a slopping pailful, walked to the house, and flung the water onto the roof.

Young Dennis stared at me, puzzled. "You crazy, Joe?" he wanted to know.

"Hell, no," I says. "I just wanted to see if that shingling job of mine would turn water. I lived here seven years and never seen them shingles tried out."

EDITOR'S NOTE

"It Makes No Difference Now"

In 1938, Texan country musician Floyd Tillman had his first major hit, a song called "It Makes No Difference Now." He later sold the rights to Jimmy Davis, who also claimed a degree of authorship. The song has since been performed by musicians such as Gene Autry, Marty Robbins, The Supremes, Fats Domino, Ray Charles, Willie Nelson, and Merle Haggard. Joe unpretentiously says he penned the words before 1906, over three decades before the song's rise to fame.

CHAPTER XXVI.

COWS

THE CATTLE BUSINESS IS A precarious adventure, as I have discovered from my own experience, never having made much money out of it. When the Hash Knife outfit unloaded its many thousand head of cattle from the Pan Handle country of Texas, dumping them off from the freight and stock cars at Holbrook, Winslow, and Flagstaff, that was a new epic in the cow business of the Territory of Arizona.

In those days the grass was tall enough to mow with a farm mower like alfalfa. The cattle began at once to fatten; you could almost see them fill out and grow sleek. Other big outfits saw the apparent success of the Aztec Land and Cattle Company, and moved into eastern Arizona: the 24, the Long H—known by their brands—Cooley and Hunning of Show Low, the Chiricahua, the Double Circle of Eagle Creek in Graham County—these moved in following the lead of the Hash Knife.

After a few years the fierce blizzards of the high country began to take their toll. They were so severe and the snow so deep in 1888 that thousands of head of cattle died. I have seen them die.

I have seen cows gathered in small herds, moving away from the slantwise blizzards that blew raw against them. They would drift until they were many miles off their range, and not knowing where any water was. Helpless, they stood in clumps among the cedar and juniper and piñon, humped up and waiting for the storm to break, the calves standing shivering by their sides and slowly dying. Snow was eighteen inches to two feet deep and no bare ground with grazing likely to show up in from one to three weeks. No rancher of the high country weans his calves in the fall of the year.

Finally the cattle would work their way to the small swales or arroyos where the snow was not so thick, and paw down through the crust to find rabbit brush and greasewood, sage, and the dried blossoms of the stock of the oose. For some, this was enough to save their lives and the lives of their calves. *[EDITOR'S NOTE: An arroyo is a small canyon or gulley with steep sides cut into the ground by running water. A swale is a stretch of land that lies lower than the surrounding area and is often wet.]*

But others had to die. I have seen in small coves and timber breaks the cattle piled up dead, fifteen to twenty of them in a single place. The mothers usually died first, the calf staying with the mother and standing as long as he could and then flopping down beside her. If the calf died first, the mother would remain, for a cow is one dumb brute that will stick to its offspring as long as it has life. She would graze close about the calf until she starved, and then she also would die.

Before the cold of 1888, the Hash Knife was branding more than ten thousand calves a year. That bad winter cut down the output considerably, but the Hash Knife was still running a good business. There was no limit to their broad open ranges, their cattle drifting as far south as the Gila River, and west to Tonto land, both on top and under the great room, others straying to the eastward as far as Gallup, Zuni Village, and way north into Hopi land.

But the Hash Knife ended in bankruptcy, as did many other large outfits. Bad winter after bad winter killed off the stock. This was the largest cause of failure. But rustlers maliciously took almost as large a toll as the weather. Cowboys regarded it as less of a crime to steal from the larger outfits than the smaller, as was natural to think. Punchers in the pay of the Hash Knife outfit itself were often the worst offenders.

The case of Johnny Palmer and John Williams of Holbrook and Winslow is a good example. They were Hash Knife cowboys sent out to winter camps where they was supposed to keep the big calves branded. These men were furnished chuck and grain and horses by their outfit, yet instead of branding the calves in the Hash Knife, they started their own brand. That winter they branded several hundred head of big calves into this brand and also the brand of smaller stockmen. Come spring, and they undertook to ship their brand of cattle out of Winslow, trying to bribe the cattle inspector to let them do it and failing. Next they tried to ship their herd from Holbrook and failed. Finally the company allowed them to ship a few of the calves, but took possession of the rest, and let the cowboys go, not pressing charges which were very difficult to prove, though it was pretty well ascertained that these rustlers was of the low breed of mankind that would shoot down the mother cows in order to get the calves, to avoid the chance of rustling being proved against them.

Johnny Palmer and John Williams are just samples of rustlers practically caught bloody-handed. How many weren't caught at all? The Hash Knife herds diminished.

No blame to the big outfits—before the time of the Arizona Rangers when the law was thin—for hiring gunmen solely and particularly for the purpose of discouraging rustling. These gunmen had as their only job just to ride among the cattle in the open range and keep their eyes open. The Hash Knife had quite a few.

The Double Circle, north of Clifton, had one gunman that was quite a character—old Uncle Heck, a small and sandy complexioned man with very mild blue eyes, slow talking and slow walking, with head always bent forward like he was in a deep study. I got to know him when I was in the forest service and made the rounds of the cattle outfits to keep tally of head using the forest lands.

I also got acquainted with a man by the name of McAllen, known as "the pianer picker." This McAllen had come into the country from no one knew where, and had taken up a homestead about twelve miles from the Circles, as they were called. He built himself a small log house, a small corral to catch his two saddle horses in; and inside the house he installed a small organ, packed out of Clifton on a horse. When the boys came by to see him and he was short on chuck, he fed them up on music.

Now this pianer picker, McAllen, started up a little iron called a brand and proceeded to brand the Double Circle calves in his iron. Five years rolled around, and he owned a couple of hundred cattle. The Circles in general, and Uncle Heck in particular, thought he was picking up mighty fast. Uncle Heck had his eye on McAllen.

One night I was staying with the pianer picker and a number of the Slaughter cowboys up that way. It was fall of the year and still warm enough to sleep out. Each of us selected a pine tree and unrolled our bed. Someone must have spotted where each one put his bed.

About daybreak bullets began to spat all around, clipping the coffee pot, plunking into trees, but most especially hitting in the region where the pianer picker had his bed. He jumped up and ran for cover, then began screaming and hopping around. He'd been shot in the wrist and the hand. One of the Slaughter punchers rode after a doctor, but just out of curiosity, followed the trail from McAllen's log cabin.

Two miles away, this puncher rode up on top of a knoll and there was Uncle Heck sitting peaceably on a rock smoking his pipe.

"What you doin' here?" the puncher asked, knowing Uncle Heck's reputation.

"Wall, I'm huntin' hosses. What you doin'?"

"I'm huntin' doctors," says the puncher.

"What's the trouble?" Uncle Heck wanted to know.

"The pianer picker got shot in the hand an' heel this mawnin'."

"Well, how do you reckon that happened?"

"Do'know. We was all asleepin' roun' camp an' the shootin' started. No one hit but the pianer picker."

"Now ain't that all too bad," says Uncle Heck. "Lucky he's got plenty of cattle to pay the doctor bill."

The puncher rode on for a doctor; Uncle Heck rode down to the Circles. In a few hours Uncle Heck returned with a dozen Circles punchers. Uncle Heck says, "Possession is nine points of the law, boys. Get to work." They rounded up the pianer picker's cattle and drove them to the home ranch, where a Double Circle was put on their hides.

McAllen never returned to his cabin. So far as I know, what remains of his little organ is still there in the cabin.

* * *

Beside rustlers and cold weather, the wild wolves were a menace, more to sheep than to cattle. They preyed in gangs on the sheep and took a heavy toll, especially during the lambing season when the ewes and lambs were put in small *atajos* herds and left out at night with nothing more than a small campfire or a lantern to scare off the wild animals. A single lobo wolf I have known to kill as many as twenty-five lambs in one night.

The wolves were big and fierce and seemed to be afraid of nothing when they were hungry. When I was at a horse round up, twenty miles west of Taylor, one of our horses strayed from camp and lay down a distance off. We found him with a wolf at his belly pulling out an intestine. We shot the wolf and then shot the horse to put him out of his misery.

It is supposed that one of these lobo wolves—some light-colored and others almost black, with long bushy manes and tails—will not attack a man, yet I have known such to be true. Mr. Elisha Everett, a farmer of Springerville, was plowing in his field just about dusk when a large wolf came skulking up, slipped under the fence, and tried to pounce on him. Everett kept the wolf off with his whip while he maneuvered around until he got one of the horses unhitched and rode it safely back to the farm house. By the time he returned with a rifle, the wolf had gone.

Wolves will not attack calves and cows if there are sheep handy, which seem to fit their appetites better. The largest loss of cattle came indirectly when hydrophobia broke out among the packs of lobos. If they bit cow or calf in an attack of hydrophobia, no matter how small a scratch they made with their teeth, the animal would invariably die. It might live along for weeks and sometimes months, dwindling away to skin and bones before it keeled over.

The hydrophobia scourge thinned out the packs of wolves, killed them off a lot more rapidly than hunters and trappers could have done, until scarcely any remain.

Though drouth never hit the northern and eastern part of Arizona in the high country the way it did the southern part, yet other dangers and menaces, as I have shown, made the cattle business a hazardous gamble from start to finish, as big a gamble as faro or Mexican monte. Chill blizzards, rustlers, and the huge lobo wolves thinned out the cattle. The big outfits broke up one way or another, and the smaller outfits took control. Of late years there's been an increasing tendency, though, for big outfits to come in and buy out the smaller cattlemen.

CHAPTER XXVII.

TRAILING INTO INDIAN COUNTRY

In 1907 I was appointed County Ranger in Apache County, a special office under the direction of Sheriff Peralta. It was my job to clean up rustlers. From 1907 to 1913 I divided my time between the little ranch near St. Johns that failed so badly, and riding trail to rustlers at the border of Arizona and New Mexico. I made good money as a county ranger, what with a steady salary and rewards. It amounted often to two hundred a month and enabled me to support my St. Johns ranch in style, while Minnie supported the family mostly with her ranch and farm work at Eager.

The White Mountains of Arizona and the Mogollon Mountains of New Mexico were at that time and still are probably the wildest and lonesomest stretches of country in the United States. And the Indian country—the flat plains and sometimes rolling hills, and the tall gaunt buttes in northernmost Arizona—run them a close second. I was one of the last to ride trail on outlaws and gunmen because they chose the uninhabited region when other parts of the country had been cleaned up.

Sheriff Peralta and the three members of the Board of Supervisors had the confidence that from my long experience I was the man for the job. Would I do it? Could I do it?

"I'll try to make a hand," I said.

That satisfied them.

I had many exciting experiences as a county ranger trailing over the dreary Indian country, where one can ride a day at a time without ever seeing a human face, or even anything moving at all, and gets comfort and companionship out of spotting the tracks of a covey of quail or the footsteps of a white-tailed deer in the dust.

Bill Stamps brought me one of my most exciting chases. I was home at Eager to visit with my family when he came. The big Cross Bar outfit had headquarters in Springerville, two miles away, and he was foreman of the outfit. He rode up to Eager, rousted me out of bed after nine o'clock.

Bill was mighty excited. "Joe, some bastard's run off a batch of our best cutting horses."

Now that was mighty serious. A cutting horse requires almost as much training as a circus horse. He has a special job to do and must be trained to do it—to ride into a herd and cut out the strays and all the steers and leave the cows and calves so the calves can be branded. He must be well reined, must have the lithe movements of a cat, turn on a dollar, be very intelligent. In other words, he must know his business.

A good cutting horse will take an interest in his job like any man. You send him into a herd and start toward any animal, and he'll take up from there without your ever touching him again. He'll trail that brute to the outside edge, and there he'll run and bump into the animal to give it a boost away from the others—all this and his rider never touching rein or putting spur to his belly.

It's easy to see why an ordinary good saddle horse is worth perhaps seventy-five dollars, while a good cutting horse is worth two, three hundred dollars on up.

"That's why I come down here and rolled you out," Bill Stamps said.

"That's not so good."

"Worse than that," Bill said and spat tobacco juice, "along with the cutting horses, this bastard took Midnight."

"Now that's serious," I said. Midnight was a prize whip stallion used for breeding purposes, worth fifteen hundred dollars if he was worth a penny. "You want to go tonight?"

"We ought to," Bill said. "I had the boys cut this bastard's trail a piece till they saw he was headed off the mountains toward the Indian country. I need every hand at round-up, so I come hightailin' it down here to pick you up."

"Be with you in a minute," I says. I went and kissed Minnie. She hadn't wanted me to go back into the law business; she worried about me every time I was trailing, knowing the gun trouble I was always liable to get into. It wasn't that Minnie ever said anything. I could tell by her set face and dogged look, while her mouth pinched down. One thing she always made me promise—because she took her religion mighty serious—that I would never kill anybody under any circumstances.

I always promised with mental reservations. If it come to my skin or the outlaw's hide, just the natural instinct of human preservation would make a fellow act first and think of his religion afterward. At least that's what I aimed to tell her if it became necessary, for it was the truth.

She had a secret reason for not wanting me to kill anyone that I was to find out later.

I kissed her. "Now you remember, Joe."

"Sure," I said. "I'll remember."

I kissed all the kids, all six of them. None of them woke up, not even the baby; and I kissed the baby twice because I had a fondness for babies, and somehow I had a feeling that this time I might get into more serious trouble than usual.

In less than half an hour, we were in the saddle. We rode all night through the foothills and into the timber country, the horses finding the trail almost by instinct while we knew we were right by the dim outlines of the hills that showed pale as ghost hills against a star-spattered sky.

We reached the round-up camp in the dim morning just as the cook was hollering, "Roll out, you buzzards. Come an' get it."

We unsaddled our horses and grained them while I went around questioning the punchers to get the straight of the situation further if possible than Bill Stamps had been able to give it to me. It seems that some few days ago a floater had drifted into the camp, just like it happens in the round-up camps often—punchers without a job come drifting in and stay with the camp awhile half hoping to get a job and half hoping they won't. The cattle country swarms with the likes of them, boys with itching feet and a lazy no-good feeling to their natures. They stay a while and then about first pay day the hills look too inviting to them, especially after waking and thinking they've spent the night eating coyote meat with a pack of lobos from the taste in their mouths and the condition of their heads. This Beasley fellow seemed like that, the boys said, until come the first heavy rain and he had vanished and so had the stallion and the cutting horses out of a big pasture.

What was he like? Well, a quiet-mouthed fellow that hadn't had much to offer about his business. He looked like almost anybody except that he wore a rattlesnake-skin around his stetson and was a mite shorter than average and carried his gun low. His gun looked greasy and old.

At mid-morning I rode northward out of the round-up camp with full directions as to where the boys had dropped the chase. I picked up sign easy enough where it led off the mountains and followed it northeastward to the boundary between Arizona and New Mexico. This was a rolling, hilly country, with once in a while a sheer ravine breaking off from the higher hills. Its points were heavily timbered with cedar and piñon trees, while lower down were grasses and small scrub. The trail was old but could be followed. It led toward the Zuni Mountains in New Mexico, which was then a rendezvous for rustlers. The mountains made a nice place to hide away, right in the middle of the Indian country with all its fine and only half-protected herds of horses and cattle. And from these mountains the rustlers could either choose to go northward to Durango to market their horses or south to the Mexican border.

In the trailing I had spotted Midnight's round hoofprint easily, almost like a fingerprint and different from the others. About this time the going must have been rough for Mr. Beasley because I came on his cold camp, picked up a rusty nail and a discarded shoe. He must have carried horseshoes and nails and hammer with him, for here in camp he had shod the whip stallion and two of the cutting horses to make the going easier over the rough ground, and he had used shoes with cork tips, not taking any chances on the valuable horses slipping and breaking their legs in case of rainy weather.

Right then I got more respect for this rustler. He wasn't any amateur. For me the cork tips had an advantage also; they made the trail easier to follow. That was why he had not shod the animals until he was sure he had shaken loose all pursuit.

That night I rode into the little Zuni village of Ojo Caliente. These Zunis are like the Hopis—short, heavy-set people that live in communities and farm and herd rather than follow the nomadic life of the Navajos. Their huts were of mud and branches pasted together, some built of stones, while not far from the village their fields sloped toward the river, fields of black loam now thick with corn and the roasting ears in ripe fine conditions, while their peach trees were heavy with fruit just ripening.

Indians are not friendly with strangers. Children scattered pell-mell and vanished like dust-blown leaves into the houses; no women were in sight, but I could see their black eyes shining intently as they peered at me from the dimness inside. The men continued to sit indolently outside their houses, hardly noticing me. But the dogs took plenty of notice. A thousand of them came yapping and barking and acting fierce and unfriendly around the heels of my skitterish horses.

I pulled down in front of the bigger houses where an old man was sitting pensively. I scattered the snarling curs with a shout and turned to the old man. "You seen a white man last day or two with plenty of horses?" I asked.

The Indian just stared at me.

"You talk English?" I asked.

He shook his head slowly.

I was stumped, for I didn't know any Zuni, and certainly this red-man seemed disinclined for talk. But while I stood there thinking what to do, the children began to edge bashfully to the door of the hut, curiosity getting the better of their timidity. One of them was a young girl, perhaps sixteen years old, not exactly pretty but quite handsome. Like her people, she was heavy-set, but she wore an American dress and American shoes and had ribbons, a dozen of them, tied into her black hair. I knew right away that she had been to government school.

I whipped off the red-silk bandana from around my neck and walked toward her, holding it out to her. She started to retire, but I guess that bright color was too much for her, and she smiled and took the gift.

"You talk English?" I asked.

She nodded and said, "Some."

Now I got along all right with the Zunis. I showed them my county ranger badge; a badge will always impress them, and they took me for a white man of some importance. I told them I was after a horse thief. I described to the girl this fellow Beasley with the greasy looking gun and the snake-skin band; I described the black stallion. The girl translated everything I said to her father, while from other huts the Indians wandered over and listened to the exciting talk.

Beasley had passed through the village a day and a night ahead of me. They were sure of the man. And he had been driving at least a dozen horses. They had fed him and let him sleep here, and he had left during the night, taking with him a blanket and some stolen grain.

"I won't treat you that way," I told the girl laughing.

The Zunis were now entirely friendly. They fed me peaches, green corn, and squash for my supper and gave my horses grain and hobbled them for me. Late in the evening they showed me to an empty little hut, and the girl told me that it was mine. Before dawn two Indians mounted bareback came to the hut and woke me, helped me to saddle up and make ready, and then rode ahead of me northward to show the trail that the stranger had taken.

Between Ojo Caliente and Zuni Village lies a country of hummocks and sand dunes often cedared on the crests, exceedingly difficult country to trail in; and I could understand the courtesy of the Indians in helping me to trail this land. Beasley had gone slow through here—I could tell by the space between the animals' tracks. He had circled Zuni Village to the east and in the flat country beyond the sand dunes he had headed straight toward the blue Zuni Mountains twenty-five miles away.

At this point my Indian guides halted and pointed first toward the mountains and then toward the trail. They meant to tell me they thought they were no longer needed, and I nodded my agreement and gave each of them some tobacco to pay for their trouble.

I took up Beasley's trail at a gallop, for this was not hard country to trail in, fairly level ground, and when there were ridges, the passes seemed clear-cut as he was holding to the direction of the Zuni Mountains. I made good time and toward evening rode up to a little spring in the foothills of the mountains. Here was a pretty little *ciénega* or valley thick with green grass from the white water that bubbled out of the side of the mountain, coming up from underground through fissures in the rock. *[EDITOR'S NOTE: A ciénega is a place at the foot of a mountain or inside a canyon where groundwater reaches the surface causing a wet, marshy area. These often evaporate rather than draining into a stream.]*

Here Beasley had camped. I found the ashes of his dead fire, and scattered about it were the gnawed cobs of roasting ears and peach pits, the green corn shucks and some of the corn he had fed to the horses.

But there was no reason why I shouldn't make such a pretty little valley as this, shady and cool with willow trees, my own camping ground. I heaved off the pack, unsaddled my saddle horse, hobbled them to let them loose in the thick green grass.

Then I made camp for myself. I always made a small Indian fire on the trail, just big enough to fry my bacon and boil my coffee. The coffee chugged pleasantly. The bacon sizzled and spat. I was hungry and tired. But I was elated. Signs here showed the rustler only a few hours ahead. By tomorrow I ought to overtake him.

It was deep blue twilight, the evening walking over the ground in crooked purple shadows. It was so quiet that any sound not belonging to the quiet would have made me jump. I heard something and jumped, getting out of that firelight as fast as a monkey.

"Hello," a voice called.

CHAPTER XXVIII.

THROW DOWN

When I am in camp, my Winchester is never very far away. I backed off from that fire, leaving my nice bacon just ready to eat and my coffee began to foam and bubble and ready to drink. I was out of the range of it and with my Winchester crotched under my arm when a young man rode up.

"Howdy," he said.

"Same to yourself," I said. "Get down."

He studied my Winchester. I could see he was a presentable young man, dressed the fanciest—a shade on the dudy side with a large white Stetson hat and silk shirt, new looking boots that must have cost twenty-six dollars the pair. He had a high forehead, looked intelligent. All in all, he didn't fit with the description of the man I was after, however. There wasn't any snake skin band on his hat and he was taller than the boys had told me Beasley was.

Yet I couldn't be comfortable about him. Any man in the neighborhood of the Zuni Mountains—white man—had no good business there unless he was a law man. I read him as a real outlaw.

"I come peaceful," says this fellow.

"*'Ta bueno,*" I said and lowered the muzzle of the Winchester. "Get down."

He pulled down. Ruefully he looked at the fire where my bacon had burned and my coffee boiled over and both made quite a stink. "What're you doing way out in this wild-man's country, *amigo?*"

I said, "Just passing through, stranger. Cowhand from down Texas on the drift. Any cow outfits hereabouts where a man could get a job?"

He snorted, eyed me coolly. "I ain't quite satisfied where you're from," he said.

"I been working near Flagstaff awhile."

"I'm pretty well acquainted around there."

"I ain't satisfied as to your business either," I threw back at him. "What you doing in this red-belly country yourself?"

He laughed short. "I'm a drifter, too," he said. "How about some chuck?"

I nodded. "Throw off your stuff. We'll make a night of it together."

He seemed a good-natured fellow, willing to take a hand, but I didn't trust him a mite, though I really had nothing against him. He might be an outlaw, or again he might be a law man like me and not willing to show his play right off.

While I fixed a new pot of coffee, he fried some more bacon, and did a right good job of it too. Each of us watched closely every move the other fellow made. My saddle was close to where I had unrolled my bedroll and one of the first things I did was walk over and shove my Winchester into my saddle holster, which was of heavy leather reinforced with a brass ring at the mouth and very slick on the inside so that I could draw it out almost as easy as a six-gun. I had had it made special in a saddle shop in Douglas when I was a ranger. Lying there alongside my bedroll, it would be handy if I needed it during the night.

I noticed that as I poked the Winchester into the holster this stranger with the white stetson tapped with his fingers on his wide belt close to the handle of his gun as if he was itching to use that gun. All the time he wore a kind of half smile, the cynical kind that twitches the corners of the mouth. Smiling fellows like that are often very clever and very dangerous because they are so deliberate.

While we ate, he asked, "Which way you headed tomorrow, Joe?"

"North. You going that way?"

Well, he didn't quite know yet. It depended. He was just drifting like me, looking for a place.

The more I talked to this young fellow, the less I trusted him. I pumped questions at him, not acting too curious, mostly about cattle business, and then later about the Navajo reservation country to the north and the Colorado country. He knew Durango mighty well, and he was right familiar with the various watering holes on the Navajo Reservation. In my own mind I had him tagged for a rustler, but there wasn't any proof—and I was sure that he wasn't Beasley, so he wasn't my business.

He had no bedroll. I was certain I wasn't going to sleep with the jasper. So we sat up and chinned, the fire dying down into red, glowing coals, the night chill, the horses restive. I could hear the animals thudding and champing off in the dark somewhere, but I couldn't see them.

Suddenly he stopped in the middle of a sentence. "Listen—" he says. Then, "You hear that?" He scrambled to his feet. "See him? See him?!" He ran toward the darkness, jerking out his six-gun and firing three slugs as he ran, and me watching and staring and wondering what it was all about.

He returned toward the campfire, panting and sweating, while he broke his Colt and put in three more cartridges from a hand-tooled expensive gun belt. I saw he was right familiar with his gun, for he spun the barrel so that the hammer rested on an empty chamber, and he put it back into its holster with a sliding, easy motion as though his gun was his friend and not something to be afraid of.

"What'd you see?" I asked.

"Puma, I think. Didn't you see him?"

"No," I said.

"He was there as plain as day—near the horses. I saw his eyes. You can always see his eyes."

"Yeah," I said, not very convinced.

That was a long night. I sat for a spell with him by the fire, my back to a willow. Finally I lent him one of my blankets, even though I could have nicely used it, for no matter how hot the day gets in that mesa country, the nights are always mighty cold. I crawled into my own roll and pretended to sleep, but I kept my eyes open enough to see him and to watch him. And he was watching me like a cat.

I would swear I never closed my eyes all night long.

We ate breakfast while it was still gray, the birds hadn't even started to chirp. While he was cooking the bacon, I went over where he thought he saw the puma, but I couldn't find any tracks. I didn't say anything, and he pretended he didn't know what I was about, though he knew well enough.

"Well," I says while we were eating, "reckon I'll pull north this morning."

He nods. "Guess I'll break off and quit you here, Joe. I'm headed south."

We went to get the horses. Something I hadn't noticed earlier in the half darkness. The horses weren't around. They weren't anywhere in the little valley of green grass watered by the spring. Now that just didn't seem natural—even though they'd broke their hobbles they would leave it. I saw the half grin on his face, but I shrugged my shoulders, and the pair of us went to scouting around for them.

It took us most of the morning to find them and bring them back to camp where the saddles and my pack were. When we found them, I held up the broken hobbles.

"Rope's gettin' old," he says.

"They look like they was cut to me," I told him dryly.

"Who'd cut them?" He looked dangerous and serious then.

"Haven't any idea," I said sarcastically.

We weren't too friendly when we said *adios*. He rode south; I picked up Beasley's trail easy enough.

A mile from my camp I came on the remains of another camp, blackened coals, a couple of gnawed bones. I picked up a horseshoe nail. The puzzle of my friend was clear. Beasley had made camp at this point to shoe another horse, and the stranger with the white *sombrero* had been with him. They could see over the valley and had watched me come, and the man with the white stetson had left camp and come down to keep an eye on me. He'd decided somehow I was trailing Beasley, so he'd signaled with the three shots and Beasley had pulled up camp and vamoosed.

Sure enough, I soon lost the trail in rocky ground and couldn't pick it up, though I quartered for the rest of the day. I was a mighty despondent *hombre* when I made camp that night, knowing how I'd been tricked.

Nothing for it now but to ride over to Gallup, buy a little chuck, and return home.

* * *

Gallup in those days wasn't much of a settlement, a scattering of wooden dwellings and stores along the railroad track, a place where the Indians came to trade. The biggest place in town was the C. N. Cotton Store, and there I went to buy my chuck. I headed straight for the high board corral on the opposite side of the street—the board corral was necessary for protection of the stock in the bitterly cold winters that Gallup has.

I tied up my animals along the rack inside, pulled off pack and saddle, and was headed for the gate when I happened to look over another board fence that was just about the height of my eyes, a separate enclosure inside the main corral.

There was the bunch of them, the Cross-Bar cutting horses, their brands as plain as the nose on your face, and in addition the black whip stallion Midnight. With them was the little roan horse of the stranger that had spent the night with me in the Zuni Mountains. The roan was sweaty as though it had been ridden by somebody hightailing for hell.

I looked around. Nobody was in the corral. I pulled the Winchester out of my saddle holster and went straight across the street to the Cotton Store, where I went to the telephone and spun the handle. I asked to speak with Sheriff Roberts of Gallup, whom I knew personally.

Bob Roberts answered the phone.

"This is Joe Pearce," I told him. "I got some business for you. You come pacing down here pronto with a couple of deputies."

"Ain't no deputies in, but I'll be there. Where you at?"

"Cotton Store."

I left the phone and stood in front of the store watching. I didn't want those two horse rustlers to be getting away while Bob Roberts and I got together. He came down from his office in ten minutes. I described the two men we were after the best way I could—the tall one with the white stetson, and the short one with the snake hat band.

"We'll handle 'em," said Roberts.

"There they are now," I said.

Sixty yards off Beasley was coming out of the meat market with a package, walking slowly towards us, and the tall one with the white stetson was coming out of a restaurant with several loaves of bread under his left arm.

"All right, Joe," said Roberts. "I'll take Slim. You take Snake Band."

We walked south across the railroad tracks and along the main street, while they came together and walked toward us. I looked away so I wouldn't be recognized. Roberts turned his face and pretended to talk to me. The rustler scarcely noticed us as we passed one another.

Two paces past them, Roberts and I turned together the way we had planned. And with our swing we brought our guns up and ready to throw down.

"Put 'em up,' said Roberts sternly.

It was as simple as that. The boys raced one another to see who would be first up with his hands, and then I stepped behind them and pulled out their guns while Roberts held them covered. By lucky accident I captured my men and brought them back to St. Johns for trial, after they had outwitted me and made me look like a fool.

[EDITOR'S NOTE: Joe later added a page to his manuscript to supplement his story of Beasley. It is included below.]

WHILE PASSING THE NIGHT IN the Zuni mountains with the tall dude, I could see that he was a clever gunman. I read him as a real outlaw. He stood about 6'2", was very erect, had brown hair and brown eyes. He wore a pair of very high-heeled, shop-made boots and one of the highest-priced J.B. Stetsons on the market. He had a broad double cartridge belt—carrying one roll of .45's and another roll of 30x40's—and his .45 hung very low on his hips. His gait was very slow, his shoulders were broad and square, he wore a cunning little smile on his face all the time and talked very slow.

He wanted to talk about the men on the border. Since I had served along the border in the ranger country, I would shear him off and talk about Flagstaff. I was afraid he would catch me in a place where he would have me cornered about the men on the border. He walked with his head bent forward as if in deep study.

Even captured, Beasley would not divulge who he was. We had them both locked up in the Gallup jail but in separate cells. After two days' time we turned the dude loose. We told Beasley he was gone. We had nothing against him because he was not found with the stolen horses. Beasley then opened up and told us, "He goes by the name of Tom Capehart, sometimes Tom Low. He is the head of our outfit. He operates from Durango to the border."

Tom Capehart was one of the most notorious train and bank robbers of the Southwest and the leader of the notorious gang of rustlers. There was $5000 reward on him at the time and we didn't know it.

EDITOR'S NOTE

Tom Capehart:

It's possible that Tom Capehart and Tom Low were both aliases for an outlaw named Harvey Logan, who was nicknamed Kid Curry.

He was mild-mannered and likable when he was sober, and some claimed that he really was "the fastest gun in the west." He was a train robber, and in one raid he famously dynamited an express car. He rode with the Blackjack gang and later with Butch Cassidy's wild bunch.

After more than a decade of terrorizing the west, having killed at least nine lawmen, he was captured. He escaped, but a posse tracked him down, and a gunfight ensued. He was severely wounded and shot himself in the head rather than face capture a second time.

He is pictured below, standing on the right with his hand on Butch Cassidy's shoulder; the Sundance Kid is seated on the left.

CHAPTER XXIX.

I MAKE A HAND

During the summer of 1912, a telegram from the Indian agent at Black Rock began the most exciting man hunt I've ever been on. The substance of the telegram was something like this:

RUSTLERS RUNNING OFF SIXTY HEAD OF INDIAN HORSES. HEADED FOR BORDER. CAN YOU TAKE POSSE AND INTERCEPT THEM. REWARD FROM GOVERNMENT.

I knew what rewards from the government were like, and didn't care to gamble equipment and time of a posse of men. I'd go myself; that wasn't much gamble. And in addition I took Clay Hunter, a little squirt of a fellow who talked through one corner of his mouth. He was a puncher and trapper and had seen a good deal of the West. I thought that with luck Hunter and I could handle any situation that might come up.

We outfitted and started within an hour, riding northeast from Springerville into New Mexico, at a point a hundred miles below Gallup, where we hoped we might run into the rustler band. We had no idea who the rustlers were or what the stock looked like. But we did know we could spot Indian horses out of Indian country because they would be branded with the Zuni tribal brand and not a private brand.

Second day out in the scrub country of cedar and oak, rolling country with dark ridges, we spotted dust. Through my spy glass I could make out four riders bareback, trailing after one another.

"Indians," I told Hunter.

We rode toward the band.

Sure enough, there were four Indians: two Navajos and two Zunis, dressed in reservation fashion—the Navajos taller, wearing American shoes, their hair long and braided like a woman's, and tied in a knot on the backs of their heads, held in place by a red ribbon, while they wore flat hats with wide brims. Quite a get-up.

The Hopis wore ankle-length moccasins, blue shirts, their hair clipped at shoulder length or a little shorter and tied with a wide red band around their foreheads.

One of them, however, was not an Indian, but a renegade Mexican, who when a child had been kidnapped by the Apaches, sold to the Navajo tribe, and brought up by them. When he was a man, he had married a Zuni squaw and now lived with the Zunis as one of them. Thus *Jesus* could speak both Zuni and Apache, and could converse with me in Spanish.

We discovered that they also were trailing the rustlers of the Indian horses, and I saw no reason why we shouldn't join forces. We sat down and had dinner together and held a good long pow-wow Indian fashion.

I said, "These rustlers of your horses have a good two days and two nights' start of us, but I think we can catch them before they reach the border. My friend and I are paid to fight. You go along with us and help us to trail, and we'll do the fighting and maybe get your horses back for you. I haven't much grain and food, and neither have you, but we may have enough."

Jesus translated for them. They all sat and smoked little hand-rolled cigarettes and seemed to be thinking over my proposition for a long while, though that was just the Indian manner because they'd probably decided before I ever said a word.

After the smoke and the pow-wow, we started south. I took the center lead, two Indians and Hunter riding behind me, while two Indians, one on each side of me and a little back, cut sign—that is, watched for any evidence off the main trail and were ready to pick up the trail in case I should lose it.

The first night we made a dry camp and fed the horses what grain we had to keep up their strength. Hunter knew this country well. Because the horses were tired, he left them to rest and walked three miles to a watering tank he knew of to fill the canteen. He returned after dark, and all of us were mighty thirsty and grabbed the canteen from him. He grinned.

"Don't you want a drink, Clay?" I asked him.

His grin widened. "Naw," he said, "I had a big watering down yonder."

Then I poured out the water for the coffee into the big fire-stained pot. It was still light enough to see the dozens of wrigglin' pollywogs and waterdogs. "I thought that water tasted mighty funny," I shouted, grabbing my stomach while Clay Hunter laughed aloud until I thought he'd split his sides. The Indians looked solemn as owls.

We strained out the creatures through a piece of gunny-sack and poured the water into the coffee pot. We were going to reach a time on this trip when that waterdog and pollywog meat wouldn't have tasted so bad.

Next day trailing again through dry and uninhabited country, with the landscape hardly changing at all except for new cedar ridges, but they looked just like the ones we had passed. We discovered among other things that there were three men in the rustler bunch. We could tell by the different-sized bootheel marks in the rustler camp.

Cojo found the gun. When an Indian trails, his sharp eyes miss nothing. The old Navajo, cutting sign, spotted the place where one of the rustlers had left the main herd to rope a horse, and somehow the rope had hooked around the handle of his gun and pulled it out without his ever noticing.

Cojo brought the gun to me and I examined it. Here was our first possible key to the identity of the rustlers. It was a fine forty-five, pearl handled, with three notches cut into the handle. I unscrewed the pair of pearl handles, knowing that sometimes gunmen will put their names inside their guns, and sure enough I found the initials T.M. carved there.

Hunter saw them also and his eyebrows lifted. "Ted Maris," he said. "Hmph." And that was all. But we knew what we were up against. Ted Maris was a known rustler with known killings to his credit, a bad one, who later killed his own wife in cold blood. That was the kind of *hombre* he was. He had rustled from white owners in the White Mountain ranching country until it became too hot for him, and now inflicted his depredations on the helpless Indian cattlemen. We knew he was the kind of gent that would kill at the drop of a hat.

The Indians knew the name also, the minute they heard it from Hunter. They went into a huddle by themselves, pow-wowed awhile, looked very solemn. Hunter and I waited impatiently. Then *Jesus* came to me and said in Spanish, "We do not go further, *amigo*. It is far from our home."

I had a difficult time persuading them. I told them I was sure we could get the horses and mules. I repeated that they wouldn't have to do any fighting, but I needed them for trailing, and that at the first sign of trouble they could whip down off their nags and hide behind anything handy while Hunter and I did the fighting. At last they agreed to go on.

And they were mighty handy trailers to have about. I would just give them a highball motion and one or the other of them would swing into the lead and cover ground so fast it was hard to keep up with them—to say nothing of following the trail. A white man can never compete with an Indian as a trailer. I guess it's born in 'em, or perhaps it's their better eyesight.

We followed the rustlers into rough country, rolling hills and rocky draws and canyons, spotted with scrubby cedar. The sign was growing fresher and hotter. Old *Jesus*, riding in the lead, spotted a hide and head, where the rustlers had butchered a beef. He sprawled off his wiry little horse, all in one motion, and put his hand under the hide to see if it was still warm. He shook his head. No, we weren't that close yet. "One day ahead," he told us in Spanish. We had gained a day on them.

But our chuck was gone. That night we ate the last of the Indians' jerky, and for breakfast we finished off our coffee. From now on we must either rustle our chuck or go hungry.

The trail swung east, on the north side of the Mogollon.

That day the trail led us right up to a little one-room ranch with a small pasture to one side of it, a well out in front with windlass and wooden bucket. A couple of dogs came from nowhere to bark at us. This was a forlorn and desolate looking place, like so many of the small ranches in Arizona and New Mexico. None of the romantic atmosphere of the movie ranch house or the dude ranches that lately have begun to clutter up Arizona, with the babbling brooks and spreading cottonwood trees, their timber corrals and chutes and fine saddle horses and one-hundred and twenty-five dollar hand-made saddles.

This was just the place of some poor sucker, Mexican or American, trying to eke out a living in the only way he knew how. We thought it might be a place to replenish our chuck. It was the only human habitation we had seen in three days of travel.

In the pasture was a single horse. I galloped over and looked at the animal, and saw he was all sweaty and wore out. I rubbed the old salt sweat off his shoulder and then off his side, and out of the caked whiteness came a brand—the Zuni brand. Here is what it looks like:

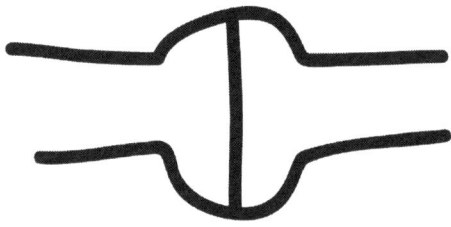

"All right, boys," I called, and signalled them up to the rickety door of the little adobe ranch house. I knocked. Nobody answered, but we could hear some rustling noises inside. I kept on knocking until my patience was worn thin. Then I hollered, "Open up, or we'll bust down the door."

An old Mexican, white-haired, trembling, looking scared to death, pulled open the door. He wore a gun, a six-shooter, but didn't look fit to use it. "Enter your house," he said in polite Spanish, though it was plain to see he wanted us a thousand miles away instead of inside his house.

But we went in. All six of us. We saw right off that there was no chance of getting supplies here. The house had an old iron bed that sagged in the middle, an iron cook stove with one leg missing, an old wooden table. That was all the furniture, no chairs or even boxes to sit on. A couple of rusty cooking utensils hung from wooden pegs in the adobe wall. It was plain the folk here ate direct out of the kettle and not from plates.

Two girls about sixteen and eighteen years old sat on the edge of the bed with their legs drawn up to try to hide the fact they were barefoot, but their black dresses was just too short to keep their legs hidden, and were full of holes showing brown flesh through them and no underwear or underclothing. Yet there didn't seem to be a stitch of clothing anywhere. They must dress that way summer and winter, and on the New Mexico plateau it is mighty cold in winter time, with deep snow. Nor did I see any food of any kind in that place except a half-filled gunny sack of *frijole* beans, and God knows we wouldn't want to rob them of that.

The girls were quite pretty except they were too thin to look healthy.

Picturesque? That isn't the word I'd use from my vocabulary to describe this dreary poverty and lonesomeness.

I questioned the Mexican. "Who owns that horse in the pasture?"

He shrugged.

"Who waters him?"

"I water him at the well."

"But you don't know anything about him or the men that rode up here?"

"No, *señor*."

"All right," I said. I showed him my county ranger badge. "I'm going to put you under arrest and take you with me to Springerville."

That made him talk. He told us how the three outlaws had come through with the band of horses and left the one in his pasture because it could not go on, promising him money if he took good care of the horse.

"Was one of them Ted Maris?"

"That is what he called himself."

"When did they leave?"

"Yesterday. They were in a hurry."

"So are we. Come on, boys. But you—" I turned to him. "I'll get the *caballo* later and maybe you too."

* * *

Now the trail swung east, on the north side of the Mogollon Mountains, which contain some of the wildest country in New Mexico. The trail kept sheering off the mountains, circling them, as it neared the pass through the mountains to the mining camp of Mogollon. It was easy for us to know what the rustlers had in mind. Mogollon was running full blast in those days, and in a busy mining camp there is always need of mules, without too many questions asked as to where the mules came from. By selling a few mules, the rustlers would get enough money to take them to the border.

We entered very rough country, hills and black mesas and heavily timbered ridges with cedar and juniper and piñon pine and occasionally long-leaf pine. We rode near enough to the camp of Mogollon that we could hear the detonations of the great blasts tearing off ore from the mountainside. Except for the one ranch, this was our first hint of civilization.

For some reason the rustlers avoided the mining camp. Perhaps they had spotted us trailing them. Or one of them might have had a sudden hunch that they were being followed. Men outside the law are superstitious. At any rate they kept to the rough country.

And we gained on them, for the trail was now really fresh and gave indications we were not much more than half a day behind. We could tell by the length of stride that the rustlers were slowing down, their horses beginning to weaken, while our own had the advantage of having been fed some grain at the beginning of the journey.

We were near enough that I felt it my duty to take the lead, and we rode with drawn rifles and with the understanding that when I swung my arm down everybody was to get off the saddle in a hurry and hunt cover. And whenever we struck steep incline or a hill or a bad piece of country, I would signal a halt and scout ahead in a wide circle to avoid an ambush. To conserve our horses, all of us dismounted and walked the horses up the steepest places. The Indians knew we were getting close to the enemy. Whenever we stopped to have a look around, the Indians would ride close, put their heads together, and Navajo and Zuni would sing a battle song, moving their feet in the stirrups to keep time to the chant.

By nightfall we had not overtaken the rustlers. We made a hungry camp, every man complaining of his belly and drawing in his belt. "It won't be long now," I said. We drank a good deal of water to try to fool ourselves that our bellies were full.

Next day at noon we struck a little spring and paused to water our horses. Usually we made them wait and cool off at least ten minutes before we'd give them water, and now we took this brief time to scout around and try to pick up signs. We found them. Footmarks near the water looked very fresh and damp. And the horse manure was fresh and green and warm to the touch.

"Two hours," said Cojo.

"Less than that," I said.

I was closer to right than the Indian. An hour later we came to a high, smooth knoll that commanded a sweeping view of the surrounding country, and I handed Cojo the spy glass as I had been doing so that he could look around.

This time instead of shaking his head sadly, he lifted his hand, shouted, "Acoo!"

Then he began to count, indicating fives with his right hand raised and fingers outstretched. He was counting the horses.

I snatched the glass from him and finally made out the little valley he was looking at. It contained a big pasture with horses scattered grazing all over the pasture, two houses near together and smoke coming out of the chimney of one of them.

I squinted at the sun. An hour perhaps before darkness. We laid plans. Instead of riding directly to the ranch, we would go in a wide circle and perhaps come on it from the other side. In the scrub we ought to be able to get up pretty close without being seen. The Indians would surround it, and I and Hunter would walk up to the door when the trap was laid.

This approach was even easier than I thought. With the Indians lying in the brush around the larger of the two huts, Hunter and I walked up to the door, knocked, and then jumped back into the shadows in case someone inside should open up on us. We heard the slow clanking of heavy spurs on the floor board.

We heard the squeak of the door handle. I nodded to Hunter. He looked a little scared. I guess I did too. You can't help it in moments like that.

"That you, Maris?" we heard someone say in English with a Mexican accent. Then in Spanish. "We are not friends any longer."

"*Vengas,*" I said softly.

Then the door opened. I stepped forward and grabbed, while Hunter threw down his Winchester. With gun in my right hand, I reached forward with my left and grabbed the fellow by the jumper, jerked him right through the door before he knew what was happening, and pitched him to the ground, where Hunter covered him with his rifle. Meanwhile I stepped past him straight into the house with my gun elevated to my right ear and ready to throw down in any direction. I knew this Ted Maris was nobody to fool with.

Another fellow crouched standing in the corner. He wore his six shooter low in the front of him, almost in the middle of him. He threw his hand down for the six-shooter.

"Don't pull it!" I yelled. "I'll kill you dead, you son-of-a-bitch."

He stood there still in his crouch with his fingers wiggling above the handle of that six-shooter.

"All right," I said sarcastically. "Put 'em up."

His hands popped into the air, and I let out a sigh that he didn't hear. I've never come nearer to killing a man than him. And there's always the chance I might have missed, and then he'd have killed me.

No one else was in the three-room adobe. We searched it through. And Maris was not one of our prisoners. They were both Mexicans, Dinicio Sanchez and Pat Gutirez, sullen as animals at being caught. Sanchez was a medium dark Mexican, square shouldered and heavy set with legs bowed from being born in the saddle. His lips were on the thickish side and ears turned down on the ends oddly. Pat was dark and Indian looking and had dreamy eyes.

"Where's Maris?"

At first they wouldn't talk.

Then Sanchez said, "We have a fight. Maybe he come back here. Maybe he don't."

I couldn't get anything more out of them right then. We searched them. We stripped them down until they were as naked as the day they were born. In Sanchez' boot in a little rubber case, we found a six-inch dagger. That was a little Mexican trick I had to be on the lookout for all the time.

Now I made preparations for the night. We had nothing to hold our prisoners very well—needed handcuffs. Contrary to popular notion a reata or a hobble aren't much good. They're too easy to slip off after you've worked the knots loose, and it's too easy for a prisoner to make a grab at you while you're tying him. *[EDITOR'S NOTE: A reata is a lasso or long-noosed rope used to catch animals.]*

Therefore I decided that I would take Sanchez in one room and Hunter take Pat in another, and we'd stay awake all night guarding our prisoners. It's a strange thing that a man alone is not nearly as likely to make a break as if someone else is there to kind of lean on for responsibility.

I had already called the Indians and directed them to search the second, smaller house, about fifty yards away, which they found empty. Meanwhile, one of them had killed and quartered a small goat that he found straying about the ranch, while in the kitchen of the larger building we found flour and beans and coffee. We made a huge meal of it—Hunter and I, the Indians, and the outlaws all eating together, while we kept our guns ready should the outlaws try to make a break. That Harvey House dinner tasted mighty good to our bellies after our long fast.

Darkness had crept in on us. Now I gave orders for the night. The four Indians were to patrol outside, guard the horses and watch for Maris. Hunter was to take Pat into the largest room where there was an old fireplace and a great pile of cedar and pine wood. He would keep the fire going. I took Sanchez into the small back room and lighted a tallow candle which I had found in the kitchen.

That was the way we passed a long night, with Hunter and I hollering to each other every little while to be sure we were awake. Every hour or so the Indians would walk one by one to the house and say *bueno* and then walk away again to their posts.

Somewhere near midnight I thought I must be dreaming at a sound I heard. I shook my head. I was awake all right. I heard a baby crying.

EDITOR'S NOTE

In March of 1943, Joe told a variation of the story from the chapter titled "I Make A Hand," and he published it in The Improvement Era. *It is in this alternate version that he mentions his nickname "Lone Wolf."*

CHAPTER XXX.

A BABY INTERVENES

Well, I had to find out where that baby was crying. I ordered Sanchez into the next room so that Hunter could guard both prisoners, and I stepped out into the cool desert night, with the stars as big as ten-cent pieces. In the open, the crying was clearer. It came from the little hut, off from the main ranch house.

I walked over to the hut and pushed open the rickety door. In one corner was an old wooden bed, in the center a table with dishes and cooking utensils. On the bed a woman lay with the baby in her arms, and she was crying almost as loud as the baby. A candle burned on the table.

"Pardon me, ma'am," I said. This woman was a pretty little Mexican girl, not much more than sixteen or seventeen, too young to be a mother, yet it was plain this was her baby and not much more than six or seven days old, I judged.

She stopped her weeping to look at me with big brown eyes that glistened in the candle light. She didn't say anything. She started right in to cry once more. Naturally I was kind of embarrassed and didn't know whether to back out or ask a few more questions.

"What're you doing here?" I asked.

"*Es mi casa*." [This is my house.]

"Where's your husband?"

She pointed in the direction of the other house. "You 'rest heem," she said in English. Then she told me her sad story in a mixture of Spanish and English, with many plaintive Mexican oaths such as *dios mio* and *ai, Jesus*. It seems that young Sanchez was part owner of this ranch and was as good a cowboy as any in New Mexico until he had fallen into bad ways and evil company.

Ted Maris had come along. There had been a good deal of talking one way or another, and Sanchez began to be absent from the ranch now and then. And just as their first baby was about to be born, he had gone on a long journey. The baby had been born during his absence.

He had never even seen the baby, and now he was arrested and would be put in American jail, and she would be left alone the same as a widow only worse.

"*Dios mio! Dios mio!*" she wailed.

"I'm sorry, *Señora*," I told her in Spanish. "He must go to jail." But I wasn't much of one to resist a woman's tears; they always sort of got under my skin. "If there's anything I can do for you now—"

"You let me see him, eh, *Señor*? You be my good friend, eh?"

Well, I couldn't see any harm in it, so I returned to the big house and came back with Sanchez pacing along in front of me. Some of his sullenness had dropped from him. He almost ran as he reached the door of the house, and when I came trotting in after him, he was down on his knees beside the bed and he was crying and the baby was crying and Dolores was crying. They made quite a chorus.

Now the Mexican girl got mad at him and called him a *ladron*—a thief. "Blood of Christ!" she wailed. "Why did I ever marry to you?"

Sanchez hung his head.

Next all the tears went out of her face and she began to whisper to him, and her eyes glowed. I couldn't hear the whispering because of the crying of the baby, but Sanchez didn't look quite so unhappy.

The girl talked to me. I could never catch Maris. He was a bad, bad man. He would never come near the ranch as long as we were there. He had eyes in the back of his head and went through the night like a cat and could shoot like a *Rurale*. Besides, I didn't know his hiding places. But Sanchez did. And they had quarreled and Sanchez was very angry at Maris. Sanchez would risk his life to bring the outlaw to me a prisoner if I would but let him go free, and his wife would promise me he would not do another bad thing as long as he lived.

I was tempted as I looked at those wistful, pleading eyes of the girl, and the tiny baby lying beside her. But I knew my duty straight enough. Sanchez had been caught with the goods and must be tried.

But couldn't I do some little thing for him?

Suddenly I thought, "Why not?" That old phrase popped into my head about setting a thief to catch a thief.

I said, "He must go with me. But I promise you if he brings me Maris I'll go before the courts of McKinley County and tell what he has done and see that his sentence is light. But how do I know he will come back at all?"

"On my life, on the Virgin, I promise you," the girl told me.

I felt I could trust her, and through her and that oath I could trust Sanchez. "First thing in the morning you go after him," I said to Sanchez.

* * *

And Sanchez brought him in. He was gone most of the day and about the time I was getting worried and thinking I'd been made a fool of, Sanchez and Maris came riding up to the ranch, Sanchez whistling triumphantly in spite of a shallow flesh wound in his right arm.

"Good," I said and nodded approval. I could see right off what a tough customer this Ted Maris was, a half-breed Mex, six-feet tall, very slender, very slow and deliberate with his movements, dangerous looking as he stared at you smokily out of sun-narrowed eyes.

It was mid-afternoon. We had not slept the night before; yet I knew there would be no chance to sleep for a good long while. Already the Indians had rounded up the horses and we were ready to go.

Hunter and I were mounted to ride behind the outlaws, with the horse ramada following us.

Maris wouldn't budge. He just stared at us with head lowered like a ructious bull.

"Ain't you going?"

"No," he said.

"Like hell you're not."

"I am not going," Maris said, "unless you give me a gun and let me kill this son-of-a-bitch Sanchez first."

I just chuckled. But the strange part about it was that he meant it. He was so mad at Sanchez for turning him over to the law that he would rather die right there than go along with Sanchez.

"That's the kind of feller he is," Hunter spat. "One side, Joe. Ain't time for foolishment and nobody'll ask questions." Hunter leveled his Winchester on Maris' belly.

The bluff took well. Hunter sounded mighty like he meant it. You could see the rebellion fade out of Maris' eyes. His eyes quailed in front of that steady rifle.

And when the hammer clicked metallically, he said, "All right. I'll go with you. But I don't forget things, Sanchez. First chance I get, I'm going to kill you."

"Poo. You ees nothing," Sanchez said.

We rode out into the afternoon and into the darkness that crept down off the mountains. We rode that night. The Indians and their herd of horses were too slow for us. We knew we had to stay awake until our prisoners were safely locked behind bars. With us we had taken grain and food from the ranch. We said *adios* to the Indians, and pushed on by ourselves. I took the lead to keep to the trail and Hunter brought up the rear with his Winchester always ready.

All night we rode. Hunter and I were hanging grimly to the saddle, for we were almost dropping with weariness. "We got to do it," I kept telling myself.

The next day was the hardest. The big sun sprawled over the desert with roaring heat, and the waterholes in that region were far apart. That hot July afternoon almost finished us. We had been two nights without sleep, three days. If you've never gone without sleep that long, you have no idea what it feels like. I just felt dumb. I felt just as dead all over as a log—couldn't even feel the horse moving under me, while my head seemed to float by itself in the heat. And I couldn't see very far ahead into the desert. The desert looked black.

Hunter and I rode now in the rear, separated about a dozen paces. I kept noticing that Hunter dropped forward over the pommel until he was almost touching the horse's mane. And then he would jerk up. He didn't know he had been asleep.

I rode over by him. "You been sleeping," I said.

He grinned slantwise. "So've you, Joe."

"Have I?"

"Every time I look at you, you look like you were asleep."

"They'll make a break for it," I said.

We talked about making camp, but that didn't sound good either. Either one of us tried to stand guard, he'd be sure to go to sleep. We were safer to stay awake in the saddle.

"We can make it all right," said Hunter. I studied the landscape. "Can't be far," he said.

"'Bout ten hours riding like this," I guessed.

"We can make it," said Hunter.

I decided he was right. "We'll keep calling to one another," I said. "That way maybe we can stay awake."

I hollered at the outlaws, and we pushed our horses harder until they looked soapy with sweat and white alkali dust.

Toward evening the country began to look familiar, the rolling grassy slopes of the high range near Springerville, almost treeless, and in the distance the White Mountains. Not one of the rustlers had tried to make a break for it yet, but they were watching us, even Sanchez, whose honor was not now at stake.

Hunter and I were now nearly dead for sleep, as we neared Eager, which is two miles from Springerville. And there was no jail at Springerville, the nearest being St. Johns, almost forty miles away. I could have gone to Springerville for help to guard the outlaws while we slept, but that extra two miles seemed like a million. I'd geared myself to last until I reached my home and no longer. Minnie'll take care of them, I told myself. I can't last out another five minutes. Hunter was asleep in the saddle.

We reached my 'dobe house at midnight. I herded the fumbling outlaws into my living room.

"Minnie!" I called. It didn't sound like my own voice. It sounded like somebody else calling. "Minnie!" I called again. It seemed like an hour, but was more likely five minutes. Minnie came down the stairs in some sort of dressing gown or kimono draped around her. She took one look at me.

"Why, Joe!" she said.

"It's all right, Minnie," I said. "Just dead for sleep, both of us. Is the shotgun loaded?" We held down on the boys while she went into the next room and brought back the sawed-off shotgun. This weapon was a 10-gauge model and I usually kept it loaded with buckshot for just such a time as this. It's a good weapon for the novice because if just one piece of the heavy buckshot hits a man, it'll knock him down, and if your aim is anywhere near a man the scattering charge will knock him down.

"Minnie," I said, "just this once you have to help me. You stand here and if any of these dirty snakes makes one little move to get away, you fire that gun at him. You hear?"

Minnie nodded grimly.

"You heard what I said, boys," I turned and told the rustlers. "Likely you've heard what a ten-gauge sawed-off shotgun will do to your belly if you get the whole charge." The outlaws didn't seem to pay attention; they were slouched on the floor and looked as though they were already asleep. Hunter staggered into the next room and he was asleep.

Everything looked all right. I'd done all I could. That's the last I remember. I don't even remember lying down. I guess I just passed out.

And Minnie stood there grimly from midnight until dawn with that sawed-off gun, alone in a quiet house with desperate men. But Minnie is the kind that can do it.

Hunter and I were up before dawn, and had breakfasted and were in the saddle bound for St. Johns by the time the sun came up. Minnie fixed breakfast for all of us.

At St. Johns we turned the rustlers over to a first lieutenant of the New Mexican Mounted Police. I kept my word to Sanchez about helping him at his trial, and he got off with a light sentence.

"Well, Minnie," I said after I'd got home and slept off all the tiredness of that trip. "You helped me out when I needed you

EDITOR'S NOTE

Here ends the story, on the 295th page of his typewriter manuscript.

While it is a beautiful sentence as it stands, there is no final punctuation. This suggests the story continued. (Joe's table of contents shows this as the last chapter, but it seems a page or two is missing.)

This leaves us to wonder about Minnie's secret reason for wishing Joe would never kill anyone, even in the name of the law...

APPENDICES

APPENDIX A.

A BIOGRAPHICAL SKETCH OF JOE PEARCE

Joseph Harrison Pearce was born in St. George, Utah, on September 4th, 1873, the third of an eventual eleven children. He moved to Taylor, Arizona, with his parents, James Pearce and Mary Jane Meeks, when he was four years old. He was baptized on July 1st, 1883. He grew up as a farmer and rancher, driving milk cows on foot. He got a fair education and later attended Brigham Young University for one year, until he contracted measles, diphtheria, and influenza, which interrupted his schooling. In 1897, at the age of 24, he taught school in Silver Creek and had twenty-three students, all Mexicans. In 1898, he taught school in Adair.

Over the years, he became an expert tracker, and the Indians called him "Lone Wolf" because he often worked by himself. On November 23rd, 1903, at the age of 30, he enlisted as one of the original Arizona Rangers. After a brief, distinguished career, he resigned in 1905. He spent the next six years as a Line Rider, after which he became Chief of Apache Police on the Fort Apache Reservation.

He married Minnie Lund on November 7th, 1906, in Greer, Arizona; they were endowed and sealed in the Salt Lake Temple on October 7th, 1909. Together they raised nine children. They eventually began their own ranch near Mount Baldy in Eager, Apache County, Arizona, which included a nine-room house, an orchard, some cultivated acreage, and a hundred head of cattle. They spent the rest of their lives together there.

Joseph likely wrote his autobiography in 1915, or soon thereafter, as the final events he mentioned happened in 1914.

In his later years, he served as vice-president of the Arizona Historical Society. But he never fully got gun matter and such out of his system: In 1949, at the age of 75, he applied for the position of police chief of Evans, Kentucky, and in 1954, now 80, he applied to the Border Patrol (where he indicated his age as "over 21"). He was not accepted for either position. He later served as a consultant for a TV series about the Arizona Rangers called *26 Men*. His final calling in the church was as a teacher in his High Priests Quorum.

He died at the age of 84 in Mesa, Arizona, on March 4th, 1958. Minnie followed him on March 1st, 1970, nearly twelve years later to the day.

They are buried in the Eagar Cemetery (block 50, lot 02, grave 13).

APPENDIX B.

MY LUCKY NUMBER 13

These are Joe Pearce's own words. The following is transcribed from "An Oral History Interview with Former Members of the Arizona Rangers" recorded in 1957, a year before Joe Passed away.

The reader may be interested to know that Joe pronounced the name Geronimo as a Spanish word, starting with an H-sound rather than a hard G.

Also, the following background will make the story a little more clear:

In the line of his duty as a lawman, Ranger Billy Webb killed Sam Bass. Lon Bass, the brother of the dead outlaw, ran a saloon attached to a home in Douglas. At a certain point, he threatened to kill Billy Webb if he ever entered the saloon-home again.

Some time later, Billy Webb and his fellow Ranger Lonnie McDonald heard gunshots fired at or near the saloon while on duty. When they entered the saloon to assess the situation, Lon Bass saw them from an adjacent room where he was dealing Monte. He stormed into the main saloon and commanded Billy Webb to leave or he would "beat the face off him." Billy Webb drew his Colt .45 and shot the saloonkeeper point blank in the torso. As the impact spun the man around, Billy Webb shot him again. Lon Bass fell, crying, "Oh my God!" and died there on the floor—with a round through his heart. McDonald was also hit by a bullet, which some said was a stray that had passed through the saloonkeeper.

Billy Webb was soon arrested for the murder of Lon Bass. He stood trial but was found not guilty.

I'LL TELL YA ABOUT NUMBER 13, my lucky number.

I was seeking adventure. I was young. I'd rode with the old Hashknife outfit at Holbrook, and I was in Holbrook when they brought in the first trainload of cattle from the panhandle of Texas.

It was 1885. I rode with the boys, and I learned to speak the language of the Texas cowboy. They was always fine fellows to work with, but they were pretty hard characters. The order of a .45—that's the language the boys spoke. The Hashknife boys were told that they were coming into a frontier country, about the time Geronimo was operating, and they came in well-armed to defend themselves. They also brought in a bunch of gunmen with them to keep down cattle rustling and to keep sheep off their range. There were probably 150,000 head of sheep running on the Hashknife range at the time.

There was a lot of cattle rustling going on in Arizona at the time, and they'd swipe Daddy's cattle. The rustlers got off with about a hundred head, and I didn't feel just right about that. My daddy's name was James Pearce, and we had a ranch over near Heber, on Pearce Wash, and right where the members who were participating in the Pleasant Valley War would come down and sup with my father. I got acquainted with the

Tewksburys and the Grahams and also many others who took part in that Pleasant Valley War.

Well, as I say, I was seeking adventure, and there was an opportunity after the Arizona Rangers had a fight with the Smith brothers on Black River, and two of our boys were killed—two rangers—Carlos Tafoya and Bill Matson. Well, I had an opportunity to fill the gap there, so I enlisted.

I was about twenty-eight. I was called to Douglas—the headquarters of the Arizona Rangers were then in Douglas. Captain Rynning was one of Teddy Roosevelt's Rough Riders. He was a lieutenant in the Rough Riders and was active in the Battle of Las Guasimas and helped take San Juan Hill, and was very close to Bucky O'Neill (the famous Bucky of Prescott) when he was killed—he was standing right near him.

Well, as I say, there was an opening to go in, and I had no star at the time, and Ranger Billy Webb had just killed an outlaw by the name of Bass, a brother of the notorious Sam Bass of Texas, that the Texas Rangers wiped out. Well, Billy Webb killed Bass in Douglas.

I had no star when I enlisted in the company, and after Billy Webb killed Bass, he was wearing star number 13. I had it in my head that it was really an unlucky number. The captain came over to headquarters one morning and said, "Joe, you haven't got a star. How about taking Billy Webb's number 13?"

There was about eight or nine Arizona Rangers in the building headquarters, and the boys raised up; they never said anything, but they began to shake their heads and move their hands: "No, no, no—don't do it—don't do it."

I said, "Well, Cap, how about putting it off until tomorrow? Let me think it over a little bit."

That night I paced down in Douglas, and there's an old lady there who could pretend to read the past and the future of anyone. I handed her a dollar, and I told her that I had lined up with a gang of gun-toters, and I wondered if that'd be a lucky or unlucky number.

Well, she asked me my age and what I followed, and I told her. And she said, "Now, young man, don't pay any attention to that old English adage that if a cat runs across the railroad track at night it means a wreck. There's nothing to that. You go ahead and wear star number 13, and it'll be luck to you."

And it was. I wore it through the years of service that I had, and if it hadn't brought luck to me, I wouldn't have been here to tell you about the Arizona Rangers.

APPENDIX C.

RECAP OF WHITE MOUNTAIN

Eagar, Arizona, Mar. 27th, 1947

Written by Joe Pearce:
Arizona Pioneers' Historical Society
Tucson, Arizona.

GERONIMO HAD BEEN CAPTURED. FOUR-HUNDRED of his band had been deported to Florida and Indian Territory. The wily Apache Kid, the greatest of all kidnappers, had been chased out of the territory into Old and New Mexico. The famous scouts Tom Horn and Al Seiber, who had served their country so well at Fort Apache and San Carlos, had rolled their beds and gone, as there was little in their line to do. The famous Apache Indian Scouts had been disbanded and replaced by a new title: Apache Indian Police.

There was no one in that immediate vicinity whom the U.S. Indian Office and the military of the Fort Apache considered fully qualified to fill the place of Chief of Police. I was riding with the Arizona Rangers at Fort Apache and incidentally met Colonel Bacon, Commander at Fort Apache, and C.W. Crouse, Indian Agent at Whiteriver. I was then offered the place of Line Rider and Chief of Police. Turning in my star to Captain Rynning of the Rangers, I immediately took over the responsibility of bringing law and order to the White Mountain Indian Reservation.

I entered upon the scene with from twelve to twenty men mounted and fully equipped as the original scouts. Some of them had served under Tom Horn and Al Seiber. There were a few Indians who wore only G-string and a red handkerchief around their heads, who would never come in to the agency, not even for their rations and allotted clothing.

* * *

Cattlemen were wrangling over their old grazing land on the reservation, which had been leased to them along a period of years, and there was an occasional killing. The Indian had few cattle compared with today, and the reservation lands were leased to the various stockmen for miles around who had not sufficient range. At times the cunning cattle rustler and horse thief would be chased out of the various counties by the sheriff and marshals and would seek refuge on the reservation, and it was my duty to see that they were either captured or chased off the Indian lands.

The Apache was a clever, cunning man when it came to trailing. The police took more delight in chasing a rustler off the reservation than they did by arresting him and holding him for trial, when we did not know the gravity of crime committed. Rustlers and tough gunmen were chased off the reservation under smoke and with no strong intentions of returning. This police patrol was a powerful little band when turned loose on the enemy, and at no time did I ever allow them to commit an unlawful act toward anyone.

They knew their right: They were strict in the observance of all rules and regulations. At times when they felt they were within their rights in exercising authority over their grazing lands and I did not see it that way—as the Indian way is not always as the white-man's way—I would restrain them and in a pleasant manner take the lead and round up cattle and horses and count them, and in some cases drive unpermitted cattle from the Indian lands while owners were protesting.

Trappers of beaver, bear, and wolves came on the streams where beaver were most plentiful and would hunt and trap without a license. We drove them away, with the admonition to stay away, which they did.

I was given three Indian stockmen to aid me in looking after all cattle and horses grazing on the reservation. Their names were Loco Jim, Frank Pinal, and Wyatt Katage. They were also assigned to me as my personal body guard. They were cool-headed, very honest, truthful, and dependable under any and all circumstances. Twenty middle-aged men, mounted and well armed, were placed as policemen under my command. It did not take long to get acquainted with each and every one of them, learning their particular ways and habits. There were no two of them alike, so in order to work with them, to learn their likes and dislikes, I had to get right down and study them out and handle them with caution.

*　*　*

They were used at times to round up outside cattle—that cattle allowed to graze on the reservation (the grazing fee at the time for permitted cattle was one dollar per head a year). Many stockmen would turn loose 500 head counted in and would have 500 more on their range near the unfenced reservation, and those outside would soon find their way onto the reservation. When I would go to the owner and ask to round his cattle up and count them, in some cases they would raise an objection and set forth all kinds of excuses that their cattle were poor or that it was too early in the spring for them. In fact they would refuse to have their cattle gathered by me to count. I would then summon my police, gather and count, sometimes finding from a hundred to five or six hundred head more than were permitted. We would hold the cattle till the overages were paid.

There were about thirty-five to forty thousand head of permitted cattle grazing on the reservation during good grass years, which meant that many thousand dollars to the Indians.

It was at times a difficult matter to keep policemen from fighting with hot-headed cowboys. I have acted quickly riding or stepping between angry cowboys and some of the more aggressive policemen. Had trouble started at times, there would have been bloodshed, but never a fight was stirred up while I was with my police.

One time I was going to a roundup on the Double Circle Indian allotment range and had about twelve men. They reached the roundup a few minutes ahead of me. One very heavy policeman, John Burk, weighing about 225 pounds, rode up to the roundup, and there he saw a cowboy riding one of his saddle horses. It was a cowboy who was a transient looking for work and was riding Burk's horse Buster. Without saying a word, Burk ran his horse up by the side of the cowboy, threw his arm around his neck, and dragged him off his horse, holding him with his right arm securely around the neck, carrying him about fifty yards, slowing up his horse, and letting the cowboy down onto his feet. The cowboy was so badly choked that all of the fight was taken out of him. Burk, dismounting, unsaddled his horse that the cowboy was riding, turned him loose to graze, and then proceeded to count the cattle. No stir was made, and business went right along. The cowboy rode about four miles to camp behind another man. We stayed with the Double Circles for several days, and the cowboy helped the cook from then on.

At this time the Double Circle and the Chiricahua cattle companies were the largest cow outfits in the territory, the two of them owning about 60,000 head of cattle (Chiricahua owning 35,000 and Circles 25,000).

* * *

One of the greatest pleasures to me—and at the time I was so proud of—was when troops were called out on a week's practice march, or a campaign across the reservation in order to familiarize officers and men with the reservation, or to look up an uprising among certain disgruntled tribesmen. I would take my place at the head of my police and scout, sending a small number of them to drive the troop pack mules at our rear on the trail. Commanding officers trailed close behind us.

Upon reaching the top of a divide or mountain, we would halt, dismount to let our animals rest, and look back on the trail, and there see a long line of troops following single file with their sabers glistening in the sun and strung back on the trail for miles, with rolls of dust curling into the air. Before crossing some small valley, this would give officers and men an opportunity to make a survey of the territory and topography of the country. Before arriving at Indian camps or small settlements with troops, I would send a scout ahead to warn them of our friendly approach. Had they not been warned, they would have been greatly perturbed, thinking that they were there for some evil and unwarranted purpose, and there would have been not an Indian to be seen, all taking to the brush.

The riding upon them with troops of this nature has caused Indians to leave the reservation around San Carlos. The history of the Indian Campaign in Arizona under General Crook and General Miles will show where 85 Indians left the San Carlos reservation and, crossing the international line with their families near Douglas, moved on into the Sierra Madre Mountains of Sonora. While I was riding with the Rangers, we had occasion to ride in the Sierra Madres, and we found a small remnant of the San Carlos Apaches still using their mother tongue. I had learned to speak some Apache and talked with them and could readily distinguish their words and accent.

* * *

It became my duty to keep a close lookout for forest fires on the reservation, which was usually caused by lightning, careless prospectors, visitors, and many times set by natives who were still under the impression that smokescreens would bring on rain. When the Indian crops were dry in June and July, the corn wilting and beans ceasing to grow, the women, who happened to do all the farming, would slip out into the heavily timbered hills and start fires then pray to the Great Spirit for rain, which would come about that time in the season, smoke or no smoke. And the medicine men would announce to their clan that the smoke and their supplication had reached the Big Spirit on high and he understood their needs and rain was to follow. When smoke began hovering low to the ground and a heavy shade would fill the air and the sun turn dim, we would ride out and climb high hills and would locate the raging forest fires.

Police and scouts would take food and bedding, axes and shovels, and ride to the fire and proceed to put it out. We would pitch camp at the nearest water and ride to the fire and back. The first thing we would do was to cut pine limbs and whip out the blaze while others would follow up and move all burning chunks and limbs back into the burnt land. There never was a fire so fierce and destructive that we could not put it out. It sometimes took several days to extinguish a fire. And after days of hard night-and-day fighting on the fire line until all were totally exhausted and sometimes short of food, I would (at the time all fires were out) call my men together to sit down in a circle. With them all slowly smoking their hand-made Bull Durham tobacco, I would explain to them, "The Big Spirit above well knew that your crops needed moisture before the smoke arose, and he will send rain in time to save your crops. Now warn all of your people asking them next year to withhold the making of fires and give the Big Spirit a chance to send rain without smoke." Many would comply, and gradually they outgrew the idea that smoke would bring rain.

* * *

To show you how clever the Indians were, when our scouts and police were patrolling the reservation, you could see small smokes from the top of hills. And back from the top of higher bluffs, you could see small fires to give warning to all of their people of the approach of pale-face or the white man. The flash of a mirror in your eyes from the hills meant, "Our eyes are upon you."

When I first took over the handling of livestock, many natives would swarm around me to get acquainted and tell their many troubles which were usually over their ranges. I would go to them severally and try and establish lines and watering places. There was an old lady came to me and said, "I have a complaint and it is the most important of all, for it pertains to food for my family." My stockman Jim was summoned as interpreter.

She started something like this: "You know the government bought 1500 sheep for the entire people. And instead of each family being given their share, they were were all run together, with each family taking turns in herding, which was two weeks. They have all had a turn but me, and now I am left out."

So we retired to the office of the Agent to put the matter up to him. She proceeded, "I want my turn herding."

"Well," replied the Agent, "go ahead. Here is a letter. Pearce, you send a policeman to the herd and allow this woman to take the herd over for two weeks."

"No that is not the idea. I want you to buy more sheep."

"Where is the sheep?"

"They are all gone, and I want my turn."

"Gone?"

"Yes, all eat up."

That was the brief experience of an Indian Agent buying sheep for the entire tribe on the communal order of handling them.

Now when you think that the Apaches don't like mutton, you just don't know.

The 1500 lasted just one summer.

APPENDIX D.

A BIOGRAPHICAL SKETCH OF MINNIE LUND

Minnie, the daughter of William Wilson Lund and Annie Elizabeth Wiltbank, was born at Nutrioso, Arizona, on June 8th, 1885, the night Geronimo and his band made their raid through the valley. She was born in a barricade—a small fort built for protection from the raiders. When she was young, timber wolves roamed in great packs, killing many cattle. Minnie was a pioneer child and helped her parents in the home. Her mother was a cheese maker of considerable fame. The cheese Minnie helped her mother make sold at a premium on the local market and found its way to the tables of the big cow outfits.

Minnie loved music and had a beautiful voice. She learned to play the guitar and took part in the home entertainment that was so popular in those days. She sang in a small choir and was an ardent dancer—a perfect figure on the floor.

At the age of 21, Minnie worked for Gustav Becker and his wife, Louise, and that's when she began courting Joe Pearce. She and Joe were married on November 7th, 1906, in Greer, Arizona, by Ellis Whitney Wiltbank, Minnie's uncle (who they called "Uncle Ett").

While Joe went to Whiteriver as a government scout, Minnie continued her schooling at the academy in St. Johns with her younger brother Marion. They lived in Clifton that year. When Joe and Minnie's first child was six months old, the small family traveled to Salt Lake City and had their marriage solemnized in the temple on November 7th, 1909.

That spring, they were the first to cross Black River into Greer, where Minnie's parents had moved back in 1904. Minnie and Joe purchased two town lots from William Eagar—amid the beautiful White Mountains of Arizona. They also bought and sold cattle with Joe's brother Jess.

Minnie had nine children—seven boys and two girls: Alta, Donald Kent, Milton Armond, Ivan Shannon, Zola Elizabeth, Vinton January, William Pratt, Grover Wilford, and Sherrel Nile.

After 51 years of marriage, Minnie became a widow on March 4th, 1958. She continued to enjoy good health until 1963, when she broke both legs. She passed away March 1st, 1970. She left the legacy of her great posterity.

APPENDIX E.

MINNIE: BUILDING THE HOUSE

The following was hand-written by Joe's wife, Minnie, and later transcribed for this edition.

We bought three acres of land from W.B. Eagar.

We started building (Dad and myself). We got the house laid out the way we wanted it. Then we started digging foundation. It was four-foot underground. Then we had to haul rock to fill it up. Old Richard and Lizzie was our team.

When the rock was hauled, it was warm enough to start making adobes. We got John Norton and his brother Dave to help. We went on the south side of the cemetery where they always made adobes. There we made half enough. They were black ones. We decided we wanted a harder dobie, so we got a Mexican in Springerville to make some red, which was much harder than the ones we made (they had more clay). His name was Ginger.

We got a mason—his name was Orson Bigelow—to help start the house. It was hard to get him to work steady. When he wouldn't work, we two would lay dobies. It was a very dry year, so we had to haul water to make the mortar.

We just kept working. We finally got the walls up. I had to mix the mud and see that Joe got it to lay the dobies. The walls were 18-inches.

When we got the lumber, we got a free-use permit from the Forest Service. We gave Uncle Ett half the lumber if he would have the logs cut and brought to the saw. When he got ready to saw the lumber, Joe and I went there and helped pull the lumber from the saw. William Lund (Grandfather Lund) brought it down with his four horses and two wagons.

We got the shingles from Uncle Henry Day. By December we had the rafters and the sheeting and part of the shingles on. We worked very hard.

On the 19th and 20th of December came a very hard rain. The house we rented wasn't very good. It leaked badly. The kitchen was so bad we just couldn't use it at all. The stove got full of water. We just had two rooms. I had a good heater in the front room. There I had to cook for four men while they were trying to get the shingles on. The old house got so bad we had to move out.

We had the chimney of the fireplace just through the roof of the new house.

My brother Will came from Holbrook with a load of freight. He stayed with us all night. That was on the 23rd of December 1908. He came and seen the way things were, and he said, "Your house is better than this house." So we loaded what few things we had in his wagon. He moved us in our home.

We never had all the shingles on. No floor, no doors, no windows. We spread boards around so we could put a bed up. We hung tarps and blankets up to the windows so it would be warm. The hearth in front of the fireplace was four foot below the floor joist, so I filled it up with rocks and dirt so it was level with the floor. That is where we cooked on the fireplace for a month.

While dad was busy trying to get the doors and windows in other parts of the house, I got busy and put the floor down in the bedroom. Sunday came, and I told Joe to go to Sunday and Priesthood meetings. He did. While he was gone, I got busy and set the stove up. It was a Charter Oak stove, just a small one. Then I moved the bed in, had dinner ready and things all straightened up. He was quite surprised when he came in.

In about a week, mother came down from Greer, and I went back with mother and stayed there a week. I just felt like I had to go home.

Mother brought me home and stayed all night. The next morning just at daylight, Ellis Lund came (my brother). He said little Mary was very sick—had been sick all night. We got breakfast, made some hot rocks, and wrapped mother and Ellis up good. She went home (of course it was a wagon and team). The folks got the doctor. He said it was scarlet fever. She was sick just a month and passed away. *[EDITOR'S NOTE: She was eight years old, Minnie's youngest sibling, and child number 11.]*

Of course, the folks were under quarantine—no one could go there.

If they did, they had to stay. Mary died March 3rd, 1909, at 5 p.m. The rest of the family had it: Maggie, Mabel, Ellis—Father was sick. They were surely having a time.

Molly Butler's little Renzo had the scarlet fever. Mary died at 5 p.m., Renzo died at 10 p.m., and Howard Hall had a little boy die that night too. Mother had to dress Mary and put her in a coffin. Molly had to do the same for Renzo. They put them in Daddy's wagon and brought them down here. They had to put them in their grave and had to put so much dirt over them. Then there were some men waiting to finish filling the grave. It was very sad.

Alta was our first child. She was born the 10th of April.

This is a sweet song Mary always liked:

"Little Mary's Song"

When the dewey light was fading
And the skies in beauty smiled
Came a whisper like an echo
From a pale and dying child:

"Mother, in that golden region,
with her pearly gates so fair,
Up among the singing angels,
is there room for Mary there?"

"Come, there is room.
Yes, there is room.
Yes, there is room
In that glorified angels' band."

"Raise me just a moment, mother.
You will forgive me when I say,
You were angry when you told me
I was always in your way.

"You were sorry in a moment:
I could read it on your brow.
You will not recall it mother.
Now you must never mind it now."

"Come, there is room.
Yes, there is room,
Room—
In that glorified angels' band."

Then she plumed her snowy pinions
Till she folded them to rest
On the welcome songs of rapture
On her loving Savior's breast.

APPENDIX F.

MINNIE: A FUNNY STORY

When we first moved in, this old house leaked so bad. It is where Gale Lund's house now stands. We thought we had to have a cow to milk, so we got one. Joe wanted to brand the calf, which was a good-sized calf. He didn't have a very long rope.

I asked him, "How will you catch the calf?"

He said, "You get on one side of the cow, I will get on the other, and I will catch the calf."

I did. And Joe got the calf.

You all know what a wild calf will do when you put a rope on it. He just jumped and balled and rung his tail. Where we caught the calf, there was an old tub setting. The rope got around the tub, and Joe fell back in the tub with his heels up, and the calf took him for a merry ride. He was calling as hard as he could: "For hell's sake, Minnie, stop him!"

When the calf got to the end of the lot, he made the turn, and that turned the tub and Joe over. His hat flew off while he was taking the ride. When he turned over, his face and head was full of dust. He got up rubbing his head and brushing and spitting.

APPENDIX G.

PATRIARCHAL BLESSING

A blessing given by Lorenzo Still, Stake Patriarch, upon the head of Joseph Harrison Pearce, son of James Pearce and Mary Jane Meeks, born Sept. 4th, 1873, at St. George Washington, Utah.

BROTHER JOSEPH, IN THE NAME of Jesus Christ of Nazareth, I place my hands upon your head and seal upon you a Patriarchal blessing.

Verily I say unto you, lift up your head and rejoice and be exceeding glad, for the Lord is well pleased with the desires and intent of your heart and will confer upon you a multitude of blessings.

Inasmuch as you will hearken to the whisperings of the Holy Spirit and become subject to the authority that God has placed upon the earth, you shall attain unto the gifts of eternal life. For I seal upon your head the blessings of Abraham, Isaac, and Jacob, for thou art an heir, being of Ephraim, to the blessings conferred upon Joseph who was sold into Egypt.

You shall be blessed with the good things of the earth and raise up a righteous posterity. And the keys of the Holy Priesthood in its fullness will be conferred upon you in due time. Great responsibilities will be required at your hands: to declare glad tidings, to preach the fullness of the gospel, to minister in the ordinances, and to become a Savior upon Mount Zion and do a great work in the redemption of your departed dead, to assist in the building of temples, to take part in the redemption of Zion, and to stand upon the earth when the wicked shall be overthrown and see a universal reign of peace and righteousness. It is your privilege to behold the Son of God when he shall come in power. None but the pure in heart will be able to abide his coming.

Your table shall be spread with plenty. The poor and the needy shall rise up and call you blessed.

I confer upon you the gifts of prophecy and of revelation. Cry in mighty faith unto the Lord in secret places, and you shall prevail, for it is your privilege to knock and receive, to seek and you shall find. And hidden treasure of knowledge shall be revealed unto you, and your words shall be loosened and your tongue shall become as the pen of a ready writer to declare good things unto the people to bless and reprove.

Therefore prepare thy heart, and no good gifts shall be withheld from you. And your guardian angel shall continue to watch over you, and you shall become a savior unto your Father's house. I seal these blessings upon your head, through your faithfulness and obedience, by the authority of the Holy Priesthood.

Snowflake Arizona Nov. 27, 1893

APPENDIX H.

LAST WILL AND TESTAMENT

I, Joseph H. Pearce, make my last will and testament. My mind is clear, and I make this will with the true spirit of fairness toward each member of my family and wife, Minnie Lund Pearce. While our son Ivan was here paying us a visit in August, 1954, he told me that he was prosperous and did not care to accept any part of the property and to give his legal share of the property to the other members of the family equally.

I now will Ivan $5.00 (five dollars). The two town lots in Eagar (Tr.#16 South West Quarter of Sec. 9. Tp. 8, Range 29 East), three acres more or less, I want divided equally among the eight children. The two houses on the lots, I wish to have them occupied by any and all of my family, but no one member shall own or claim the houses. Any of the children may live in them as they desire. The twenty (20) acres of farmland, Sec. 8 Tp. 8 Range 29 East, I want divided equally among the eight children. Alta may have the S.W. corner and Kent may have the S.E. corner. The water right shall be divided equally. The other members may select their own location. The Z Dart cattle, I desire them to be divided equally among the eight children. I now name Vinton as executor of the estate. I desire the cattle to be run until they become a big herd, and I desire them to be built up, and each member may have an interest in them, all eight children.

Should I die first, I desire Minnie to have and to own all of the property. I here wish to state that after Minnie passes on that should there be any money in a bank, I desire the money to be divided equally among the eight children. Should the cattle range be unfavorable in California and range not suitable, I would like to see the cattle returned to Arizona and built up to a big herd.

I do trust that you all may be wise stewards over what God has blessed you with—that you may be blessed with more property.

I desire my family to live together, work together, live in peace with one another. I trust that you may live the gospel. I desire you to become immediately identified in the wards and stakes of Zion. Do pay your tithing and all other church dues. Go do your temple work and do not delay—that must be done on earth that you may be sealed on earth and sealed in heaven, that you may have your wives and children on the other side. I have a strong testimony of the gospel. Had I lived my religion more faithfully I would have been a wealthy man.

I desire a short funeral, as I have accomplished little in life and little can be said of me. I wish my coffin to be made of the pine of the forest here, which I love so well. I desire my friends Clive Wiltbank and Bishop Wallace Ashcroft to make my coffin and to be paid well for their work. I do not want my body taken to the mortuary, as I have not lived in luxury and I do not desire it after I am dead. I desire my friend Wyatt Crosby to haul my body to the cemetery, and if Wyatt is not available, I wish Paris Ashcroft to haul my body in a pickup to the chapel and to the graveyard. I want Wyatt to use his pickup to haul this frail piece of flesh around. Don't haul this piece of withered flesh and bones around in a big hearse. I prefer the pickup.

Deposit this weakling of a body where you may feel.

I wish to have the song "Tis the Valley of Custer, and to Thee We Did Muster" at the graveside, and no more singing.

Had I kept the Word of Wisdom and taken good care of this old body, I would have lived a hundred years, but I have abused my body, have overworked it, have not taken care of it. So, my boys, listen to me and take care of your bodies, and your lives will be long in the land which God hath given you. I want you boys to live every day just like it was your last one, and be faithful and you shall prevail.

Please listen: I wish the cattle to be held together or run separately at times only. But I want them built up to a big herd and kept for the benefit of all of the family. Don't divide them up among each other. Hold them in one herd. They will make a living which will help the entire family. The fruit from the orchard may be used by all members as needed. Should you sell your share of the land, sell it to members of family. Should you sell your share of cattle, sell to members of family only.

My son Vinton, who is named executor of the estate, shall not be required to furnish bond in any sum or in any matter in handling the estate.

   S/ Joseph H. Pearce .
   Witness: S/ Wallace Ashcroft 12-26-56
   Witness: S/ J. Wallace Wilkins 12-26-56
   Witness: S/ Lynn Lockhart 12-26-56

Eagar, Arizona, December 26th, 1956

APPENDIX I.

LAST WORDS

Joe wrote this piece, which was found in his files after his death.

I GUESS THAT WHEN I leave this happy hunting ground that I will go to some Rustlers' park, as I have ridden many miles through such parks trying to keep down rustling. I have tried hard to drive the cattle rustlers and horse thieves from our good old territory. I was not a gunman, but I made the other fellow believe that I was—hence powder was saved by both of us.

I want no flowers at my funeral, but shall be happy to accept any bouquets while living. I want no long talks at my funeral. I have done little in life, hence is little to be said of me.

Don't anyone shed a tear, because I go to my happy hunting ground singing that endearing song, "My Last Roundup." Should I be promoted over there, I trust that it may be "Range Foreman," as I want my cattle to look after. And may God grant my wish.

I am not stingy, I just didn't have it. Had I made it, I would have made many poor families happy. I would also have made contributions to the Church and helped build monuments, instead of riding along through hilly country.

As I look back I am unable to find my tracks along trails or highways. Where have I been and what have I left behind me? Nothing but blank shells, filled with cheap promises and seldom fulfilled. Still, I have tried to pay my board bill, but I have had little credit. I have had no desire to beat the other fellow out of his income but have been satisfied to live along on scanty foods and walk through thorns and thistles. It was not my happy lot to own property, as dollars wore holes in my pockets and I just couldn't keep the holes sewed up.

I have worn out many pair of boots running away from trouble, and have worn the seat of many pants trying to settle trouble.

I now worry about the little things that I failed to do to help some poor fellow along in life, things I could have done had I only eyes to see and ears to hear. I have failed financially on account of my own follies. I could have died a wealthy man had I only used the least spark of sense. I have shoveled my dollars off to the other fellow and then pined in sorrow. If I had only ten years left to live, I would die a wealthy man.

— Joseph Harrison Pearce

APPENDIX J.

THE GENUINE ARTICLE

Below is one page from Joe's original manuscript.

..5..

their enemies. A solitary ranchman alone at his ranch, a sheep herder with his sheep, a miner off the beaten trails--these were often raided and sometimes killed and sometimes tortured before the killing, even as late as the eighties. Then the Indians would sneak back to the reservation and were hard to catch.

~~Before our first brush with them,~~ There was an Apache murder in ~~our~~ *part of the* country. I was about twelve years old at the time, Jim fourteen. Often we were alone with the sheep, or sometimes there was a Mex herder with us, as Father had several, and always a dog. ~~In times past~~ *Often* we had seen the Apache bucks in bunches of two and three and four. They ~~often~~ *sometimes* came to the ranch house and begged for things; they were ~~great~~ *the biggest in the world* beggars and looked harmless, but we knew they weren't harmless. Once in awhile we missed a horse or a sheep. If they got what they wanted they were peaceful enough, but if they were crossed some way there was blood in their eyes.

Nathan Robinson found that out. He had come on a band of them, fifteen or twenty, soon after a raid about six miles south of Taylor. They had slaughtered a beef, quartered it, and were roasting one of the hind quarters over a camp fire when he stumbled onto them--little brown men squatting on the ground as he came up and watching him with expressionless black eyes, but not moving.

Robinson guessed the beef had been stolen. He did a damn fool thing, pulled down off his horse and turned over the wet hide to look at the brand. Contrary to what is usually thought

This book was produced by
LOST BOYS INK.

www.jwashburn.com

Made in the USA
San Bernardino, CA
25 April 2018